RADICAL PASTORAL, 1381–1594

Radical Pastoral, 1381–1594

Appropriation and the Writing of Religious Controversy

MIKE RODMAN JONES
Girton College, Cambridge, UK

ASHGATE

Published by
Ashgate Publishing Limited
Wey Court East
Union Road
Farnham
Surrey, GU9 7PT
England

Ashgate Publishing Company
Suite 420
101 Cherry Street
Burlington
VT 05401-4405
USA

www.ashgate.com

British Library Cataloguing in Publication Data
Jones, Mike Rodman.
Radical pastoral, 1381–1594: appropriation and the writing of religious controversy.
1. Langland, William, 1330–1400? Piers the Plowman – Influence. 2. English literature – Middle English, 1100–1500 – History and criticism. 3. English literature – Early modern, 1500–1700 – History and criticism. 4. English literature – Protestant authors – History and criticism. 5. Religious literature, English – History and criticism. 6. Pastoral literature, English – History and criticism. 7. Reformation – England.
I. Title
820.9'3828'09024–dc22

Library of Congress Cataloging-in-Publication Data
Jones, Mike Rodman.
Radical pastoral, 1381–1594: appropriation and the writing of religious controversy / Mike Rodman Jones.
    p. cm.
Includes bibliographical references and index.
ISBN 978-0-7546-6694-3 (hardcover: alk. paper) 1. English literature – Middle English, 1100–1500 – History and criticism. 2. English literature – Middle English, 1100–1500 – History and criticism. 3. Langland, William, 1330?–1400? Piers Plowman. 4. Religion and literature – Great Britain – History. 5. Politics and literature – Great Britain – History. 6. Reformation – England. 7. Satire. I. Title.
PR257.J66 2010
820.9'3823–dc22
2010003929

ISBN 9780754666943 (hbk)
ISBN 9781409427698 (ebk)

Mixed Sources
Product group from well-managed forests and other controlled sources
www.fsc.org Cert no. SGS-COC-2482
© 1996 Forest Stewardship Council
FSC

Printed and bound in Great Britain by
TJ International Ltd, Padstow, Cornwall

Contents

List of Figures

Abbreviations

I use the spelling 'plowman' for the text *Piers Plowman* and the character 'Piers the Plowman'. I use the standard English spelling 'ploughman' elsewhere.

A&M J. Pratt, ed., *The Acts and Monuments of John Foxe*, 8 vols (London: Religious Tract Society, 1877)

EEBO Early English Books Online

RS *Rolls Series*

STC A. W. Pollard and G. R. Redgrave, compilers. Revised by W. A. Jackson and F. S. Ferguson, completed by Katherine F. Parker. *A Short-Title Catelogue of Books Printed in England, Scotland, and Ireland, and of English Books Printed Abroad, 1475–1640*, 2nd edn, 3 vols (London: The Bibliographical Society, 1976–1991).

YLS *Yearbook of Langland Studies*

Acknowledgements

This book emerged out of work originally done during a number of years at the University of York, under the supervision of Richard Rowland and Nick Havely. I could not have asked for better mentors: their intellectual input, encouragement and support were invaluable, and they continue to offer generous support both personal and academic. Thanks are due to the AHRC (and previously AHRB) for their financial support throughout my graduate study. Helen Barr and Isabel Davis have read numerous pieces of my writing and been acute, generous readers. I was also fortunate to have a number of friendly, enthusiastic and wise colleagues at the University of Leeds – Andrew Wawn, Alaric Hall and Alfred Hiatt in particular – who made a first step into professional academia (and much further development of this book) a great experience. More recently, Helen Cooper has been a very supportive presence during my time as a Leverhulme early career fellow at the Faculty of English in Cambridge.

Some debts go a little further back. I owe a great deal to Richard Rowland (again) and Sos Eltis. Their encouragement and support in Oxford at a very early stage in my academic career was invaluable. They had little beyond my naïve enthusiasm to go on, but offered amazing levels of personal and intellectual encouragement. Without it, anything I achieve academically would not be possible. Similarly, I owe my parents a huge amount. They have been unerringly supportive throughout my life, as far back as I can remember. My brother Daniel has witnessed the development of this book from instigation to completion with a supporting hand and numerous pints, all of which were appreciated, perhaps more than he knew at the time.

Finally, for so many reasons, this book is dedicated to Catherine Nall.

Preface

Notoriously, a figure named 'Piers Ploughman' was said to have made some appearances among the violence and turmoil of the 1381 revolt. A number of remarkable documents circulated amongst the rural insurgents who marched on London that summer, documents that utilized references to *Piers Plowman* in what seems to have been a kind of coded rallying cry for mass political rebellion. One, according to the chronicler Thomas Walsingham, was found 'in the tunic of a man who was to be hanged for his share in the disturbances'.[1]

Among the ominous prophetic passages – 'nowye is tyme', 'The Kynges sone of heuene schal paye for al' – Langland's iconic ploughman appears to have an explicit auxiliary role. The letter recorded by Walsingham commands its readers: 'stondeth togidre in Godes name, and biddeth Peres Ploughman go to his werk'. It goes on to echo other aspects of Langland's text with references to 'Hobbe the Robbere' and 'do wel and bettre'.[2] Similarly, a letter recorded by Henry Knighton urges its readers to 'doth wele and ay bettur and bettur', and promises that 'Hobbe robbyoure' will be 'chastysed' whilst 'Peres the Plowman my brother' will 'duelle at home and dyght us corne'.[3] In *The Dieulacres Chronicle*, 'Per Plowman' is so closely associated with the revolt as to be added to the list of names of its leaders.[4]

The precise nature of the letters' references to *Piers Plowman* is ambiguous, and there is no space here in which to add to the astute comments of other scholars, but this remarkable example of politicized appropriation is an exemplar for the kind of 'tradition' that this book explores.[5] As Steven Justice has written, whilst

---

[1]   R. B. Dobson, ed., *The Peasants' Revolt of 1381* (London, 1970), p. 381. Dobson collates the letters from various chronicles on pp. 379–83. The texts of the letters are taken from Thomas Walsingham, *Historia Anglicana*, ed. H. T. Riley (*RS* 1864), 2 vols, II. 33–4 and Henry Knighton, *Chronicon*, ed. J. R. Lumby (*RS* 1889–1895), 2 vols, II. 138–40.

[2]   Dobson, *Peasants' Revolt*, p. 381. The reference to 'Hobbe the Robbere' is a variant form of the 'Robert þe robbour' found in B.5.462 / A.5.235 / C6.315. The figure is called 'ruyflare' rather then 'robbere' in the C text.

[3]   Dobson, *Peasants' Revolt*, p. 382.

[4]   *Dieulacres Chronicle*, M. V. Clark and V. H. Galbraith, eds, *Bulletin of the John Rylands Library*, 14 (1930), 164–81, 164.

[5]   The most important recent discussions of the letters are: John Bowers, '*Piers Plowman* and the Police: Notes toward a History of the Wycliffite Langland', *YLS*, 6 (1992), 1–50; Anne Hudson, '*Piers Plowman* and the Peasants' Revolt: A Problem Revisited', *YLS*, 8 (1994), 85–106; Richard Firth Green, 'John Ball's Letters: Literary History and Historical Literature' in *Chaucer's England: Literature in Historical Context*, ed. Barbara Hanawalt

Piers Plowman might have been ideologically and aesthetically differentiated from these letters, it 'gave the rising a language and a style, an imaginative model of rural articulacy'.[6] As this book will show, it was not only to the political dissidents of Ricardian England that *Piers Plowman* bequeathed 'a language and a style', or indeed a way of imagining the politicized divides between country and city, simplicity and sophistication. John Ball's letters are the beginning of a tradition which I have termed 'radical pastoral', a tradition of polemical and satirical writing that depended on the efficacy of a language of rurality, and that was frequently characterized by a violently appropriative attitude to textuality and historicity which is anathema to modern scholarship.

These letters bring into focus ideas of appropriation, polemic and oppositional self-fashioning which recur throughout this study. This book's central focus lies not on the events of 1381 in itself, but on Reformation literature in England, and the way that this writing utilized pre-Reformation writing in generating a rich corpus of controversial literature. It deals with the body of writing that popularized reformist politics in the period 1530–1550, the reformist antiquarianism and literary culture of the mid-Tudor period, and finally the survival of radical pastoral writing into the Elizabethan period, in a dense network of texts surrounding the Marprelate controversy in the years 1588–1594.

The term 'pastoral' here demands some elaboration. It could be argued that the term should be differentiated from texts such as Bale's plays, Foxe's *Acts and Monuments*, or *Piers Plowman*. If classical poets such as Theocritus and Virgil can be said to have bequeathed a genre of pastoral, it is a literary mode that speaks of shepherds rather than ploughmen. Similarly, it is one that, dividing labour from the image of the countryside, produced an artful and elaborate image of unreality. Consequently, discussions of pastoral as a literary form regularly move directly from Virgil's *Eclogues* to Sidney's *Arcadia*, perhaps noting some 'transitional' writers such as Skelton and Barclay along the way.[7] Of course, the sixteenth century is full of a more straightforwardly canonical type of pastoral, and one that is not my central concern in this book. What might be described as the 'soft', Arcadian idylls of Sidney's *Arcadia* can also be seen in Marlowe's images of

---

(Minneapolis, 1992), pp. 176–200; Steven Justice, *Writing and Rebellion: England in 1381* (Berkeley, 1994). The letters are also discussed in *Signes and Sothe: Language in the Piers Plowman Tradition*, Helen Barr (Cambridge, 1994), pp. 10–12, and Justine Rydzeski, *Radical Nostalgia in the Age of Piers Plowman: Economics, Apocalypticism and Discontent* (New York, 1999), pp. 95–114.

[6]   Justice, *Writing and Rebellion*, p. 137.

[7]   Helen Cooper's *Pastoral: Mediaeval to Renaissance* (Cambridge, 1977) is worth singling out as an exception. As Cooper writes, 'Biblical parables, beast-fables, political criticism and panegyric have as rightful a place in the mode as pure poetry' (p. 3), although 'pure poetry' is an odd phrase in itself. For important considerations of pastoral as a genre, see Paul Alpers, *What is Pastoral?* (Chicago, 1996) and Annabel Patterson's classic *Pastoral and Ideology: Virgil to Valéry* (Oxford, 1988).

the 'shepherd-swains' that 'dance and sing', that could be parodied in Raleigh's counter-pastoral pastiche: 'flowers do fade, and wanton fields / To wayward winter reckoning yields' ('The Nymph's Reply', ll. 9–10). Shakespeare's version of the same pastoral strain is equally Arcadian: 'tongues in trees, books in the running brooks, / Sermons in stones, and good in everything' (*As You Like It*, 2.1.16–7). This is not to suggest, though, that these famed examples of sixteenth-century pastoral are somehow depoliticized: Shakespeare's Duke speaks in the language not only of pastoral but of a contested and sharply contemporary language of Protestant edification ('books … sermons') which Rosalind later takes up ('O most gentle pulpiter, what tedious homily of love have you wearied your parishioners withal' (3.2.152–3)); Sidney's *Arcadia* – as Blair Worden has shown – is far from free of ideological significance.[8] Indeed, one might argue that from its very origins in Theocritus and Virgil, pastoral has always been an inherently politicized genre.[9] But the nature of this pastoralism, and its porous border with satire – the evocations of the countryside in Horace's *Satires* spring to mind here – are formally very particular, often oblique and highly elaborate in their approach to contemporary history. While Spenser might take us as close to radical pastoral as any of these examples, the term 'religious politics' is not necessarily the first thing that springs to mind when dealing with the eclogue tradition and its surrounds.

Far more significant for my terminology of radical pastoral is a classic critical study which William Empson published in 1935. *Some Versions of Pastoral* contained discussions of a genre of twentieth-century novels which Empson termed 'proletarian literature'; Shakespeare's *Sonnets*; *Paradise Lost*; and ended with a discussion of Lewis Carroll's *Alice in Wonderland*. We hardly now need to offer an extended defence of a methodology which uses 'pastoral' as a term with which to productively describe literature which does not stand in an obviously Virgilian tradition. Writing of 'proletarian literature', Empson observed that the term was 'liable to false limitations', and I view the field of medieval and Tudor religious literature in a similar way: as not benefiting from our division of it into generic categories which might exclude or elide important parts of it.[10] It is striking also that we find Empson writing of a 'key text' for this study in his book on pastoral. In Empson's view, '*Piers Plowman* is the most direct case of the pastoral figure who turns slowly into Christ and ruler', one of a 'few examples which I am sorry to have let get crowded out'.[11] Empson's endearingly casual approach to his subject here hides the vitality of this most important text, and the reach of its religious and spiritual significance. But the rhetoric of rusticity and the polemical associations

---

[8]   See, in particular, Blair Worden, *The Sound of Virtue: Philip Sidney's Arcadia and Elizabethan Politics* (New Haven, 1996).

[9]   Annabel Patterson's discussion of Virgil's first eclogue in *Pastoral and Ideology* is now a classic example of Pastoral's ideological implications. On Theocritus see also J. B. Burton, *Theocritus' Urban Mimes: Mobility, Gender, Patronage* (Berkeley, 1995).

[10]   William Empson, *Some Versions of Pastoral* (London, 1935, repr. 1995), p. 11.

[11]   Empson, *Some Versions of Pastoral*, p. 74.

that accompany it, the language that threads its way through this book, from *Piers Plowman* to Lollard polemic, from early printed dialogue to the drama of John Bale and the literature of the post-Marprelate 1590s, is, I think, testament to the way that politicized forms of pastoral writing endured. Rather than asking just how 'minor' some of this writing is or even questioning whether we can call it such, it is perhaps more sensible to ask, as a contemporary writer of pastoral does, 'whether it is in the nature of the ghost of pastoral *ever* to be finally laid' (my emphasis).[12]

This book deals with a particular form of pastoral, one that proliferated in the writing of religious controversy between the Peasants' Revolt, when Lollardy seems to have first found its way into widespread discussion, and the final decade of the sixteenth century. This 'form' of pastoral is not 'formal' in the sense of a clearly defined literary genre, it is a language, a rhetoric, a set of associations centred on the differentiation of rusticity and the urban. I explore the way that this rhetoric was reconfigured by writers who consistently found politicized pastoral to be effective as the foundation of satirical and polemical writing, and as a way to shape religious identities and controversies in the Reformation period[13]

But the shift in focus from the pastoral of shepherds to that of ploughmen is also important. As scholars have noted, it was perhaps the 'shock' of Langland's 'chameleon hero', a figure at once agrarian labourer, *ur*-priest, and even Christ, that brought about a vital cultural phenomenon.[14] Whilst previous writing had tended to divide the shepherd and ploughman along biblical, typological, lines – stigmatizing Cain as the first labourer, blessing Abel as first shepherd and thus also first priest – Langland produced an imagery of potentially startling novelty.[15] Anticlericalism, and polemical anticlericalism at that, is, I think, the vital catalyst in the appropriations of Langland's imaginative initiative. Ploughmen become the focus of radical pastoral because Langland had drawn the authoritative and spiritualized elements of the cleric away from the shepherd and figured them as the defining characteristics of a member of the labouring laity. Lollard and Protestant alike were acutely aware of the polemical impact, and potential, of this shift. On the level of metaphor at least, it was a short step from aggrandizing the ploughman

[12]   J. M. Coetzee, 'Farm Novel and Plaasroman' in *White Writing: On the Culture of Letters in South Africa* (New Haven, 1988), pp. 63–81, 81.

[13]   Any book on such a topic owes a substantial debt to Raymond Williams' seminal book, *The Country and the City* (London, 1973). Although the relation of this thesis to Williams' work is often too broad to make explicit, its debt should be acknowledged from the beginning.

[14]   Elizabeth D. Kirk, 'Langland's Plowman and the Recreation of Fourteenth-Century Religious Metaphor', *YLS*, 2 (1988), 1–21, 2–11.

[15]   Elizabeth D. Kirk, 'Langland's Plowman', p. 9. On the Cain–Abel tradition, see also Paul Freedman, *Images of the Medieval Peasant* (Stanford, 1999), pp. 91–3; Jill Mann, *Chaucer and Medieval Estates Satire* (Cambridge, 1973), pp. 67–74.

to castigating those 'that scarce themselves know how to hold / A sheep-hook' (*Lycidas*, ll. 119–20).

The polemicized pastoralism that underpins the figure of the Reformation ploughman, and the figure itself, are central to this study. This book cannot be said to be restricted to a study of the reception of the text of Langland's *Piers Plowman*, but it is amongst its central interests. While other scholars have pursued this more narrowly delineated narrative, I view direct textual contact and evocation as only one amongst a number of ways in which texts and figures can have cultural afterlives, only one way in which the ploughman gathered and retained cultural, literary and rhetorical efficacy. I trace here not simply the reception of the text of *Piers Plowman* in terms of the literary modes and genres that I argue were its inheritance, or the editing of the text of *Piers Plowman*, but also the path of the rhetorical and polemical figure in a broader sense, and as Sarah Kelen has rightly argued, here 'the sixteenth-century reception of *Piers Plowman* (the poem) intersects with, but is not identical to, the reception of Piers Plowman (the character)'.[16] This book goes further than that, though. It traces both these things, but also focuses on the wider cultural trends, the pastoralism of controversial religious writing in the Reformation and before that made the ploughman figure such an iconic presence in early Protestant culture. Moreover, it follows the pastoralism, the character, and the text, into the 1590s: a period which has tended to be overlooked by scholars of *Piers Plowman* reception as they move from Crowley's editions in 1550 to the nineteenth-century editing and reception of the text.

A reader might also ask how this ploughman-centred pastoralism of Reformation literature is 'radical'. Most of the writing discussed in this book can hardly be said to be so in modern political terms. The social criticism of Langland or Crowley, the satirical moments of Tyndale or Nashe, the controversial self-fashionings of John Bale of Martin Marprelate: none of these strike the modern reader as standing at the avant-garde of socio-political thinking. Indeed, amongst the things commonly noted about much Reformation literature is, as John N. King has noted, its preservation of a 'synthesis of royalist politics and reformist art'.[17] This conjunction of religious reformism with social conservatism is present in many of the texts discussed in this book, but it is worth noting that the strictures of this portrait sometimes seem rather strained. Andy Wood argues that to call writers such as Robert Crowley 'conservative' 'is both to simplify and to dismiss their message', and sensibly asserts the importance of the 'tinge of radicalism to the commonwealth writers' rhetoric', and 'their contradictory, multifaceted nature'.[18] Crowley, for example, often seems to steer close enough to the socio-political wind to feel the need to make disclaimers such as the following:

---

[16] Sarah A. Kelen, *Langland's Early Modern Identities* (London, 2007), pp. 70–71.

[17] John N. King, *Reformation Literature: the Tudor Origins of the Protestant Tradition* (Princeton, 1982), p. 6.

[18] Andy Wood, *The 1549 Rebellions and the Making of Early Modern England* (Cambridge, 2007), pp. 33–5.

> Take me not here that I should go about by these words to persuade men to make all things common: for if you do, you mistake me. For I take God to witness I mean no such thing. But with all my heart I would wish that no man were suffered to eat, but such as would labour in their vocation and calling, according to the rule that Paul gave to the Thessalonians [2 Thess. 3]. But yet I would wish that the possessioners would consider who gave them their possessions, and how they ought to bestow them. And then (I doubt not) it should not need to have all things in common.[19]

The social conservatism of Crowley's Biblicism here strains against the stridency of his social criticism. Crowley's repeated (and therefore rather nervous-sounding) disclaimer about his own distance from a sort of early modern proto-socialism becomes rather strained when placed in such close proximity to intimations about Godly stewardship ('consider who gave them their possessions, and how they ought to bestow them'). This might not be Marx, but neither is it safely or unquestioningly 'conservative'. Authority here rests in scriptural and divine witness which can be synthesized with socially conservative imperatives, but which can also be seen to potentially escape from those same imperatives. What begins as a placatory renunciation of the idea of common property actually circles back on itself to suggest that 'to have all things in common' is precariously close to what an ideal commonwealth would be, even if 'it should not need to' be named in that language. This conflicted political aspect to medieval and Tudor social criticism is matched by the problems of religious controversy. The central controversy of the Reformation over biblical translation – and therefore the social breadth of access to this most central text – was inevitably haunted by the political language and imagery of democratization. This language, like Crowley's disclaimer, could be read as radical or conservative, as anti-institutional liberation, as dangerous social experiment, or the language used to mask a magisterial Protestantism's rhetorical opportunism.

'Radical pastoral', of course, also brings with it a nod towards Jonathan Dollimore's *Radical Tragedy* (1984). This hugely influential study is surely amongst the most important of late twentieth-century Renaissance scholarship. In Dollimore's vision of Shakespearian theatre there is, he writes, 'a substantial challenge; not a vision of political freedom so much as a subversive knowledge which interrogated prevailing beliefs, submitted them to a kind of intellectual vandalism; radical in the sense of going to the roots and even pulling them up'.[20] This book does not share the astonishing theoretical range and subtlety

---

[19]   Robert Crowley, *An Information and Petition against the Oppressors of the Poor Commons* (1548), in *The Select Works of Robert Crowley*, ed. J. M. Cowper (EETS e.s. 15, London, 1872), pp. 156–7.

[20]   Jonathan Dollimore, 'Introduction to the Second Edition' in *Radical Tragedy: Religion, Ideology and Power in the Drama of Shakespeare and his Contemporaries* (London, 1989), p. xxi.

of Dollimore's cultural materialism, but his etymological defence of his use of the term 'radical' is also apposite here. 'Radical' remains, I think, a vital and appropriate term. The word is used in two senses. Most importantly, it is used to signify the overtly politicized and polemical nature of much of the writing which is discussed here. But Dollimore's etymology is also revealing in itself. 'Radical' derives ultimately from the Latin 'radix', 'root' (Dollimore's 'going to the root'). As Raymond Williams points out, before the identification of the word with a particular type of political movement in the eighteenth century, the word was used 'to express an inherent and fundamental quality'.[21] But the political valence of the word was 'always latent'; its use to describe a genealogy of writing signals the fundamental nature of the controversies that occurred in the written word from the fourteenth to the sixteenth centuries, controversies that concerned the very nature – the very roots – of Christian life and the ideal form of a community in spiritual, social and political terms. Simultaneously, the word highlights the connotations of the agricultural language that dominated the writing of religious controversy. The agrarian figure of the ploughman is ubiquitous in early Protestant writing, and the spectre of the urban marketplace, of commercialism as a natural enemy of the ethical commonwealth is omnipresent across this period, from Langland's anti-urban satire, through Crowley's attacks on the exploitative nature of commercialism, to Marprelate's 'plain' laughter at the expense of the Elizabethan episcopacy.

Necessarily then this is also a book which crosses between the traditionally divided fields of medieval and early modern literary and cultural studies. The exploration of interconnections between these two fields has become far more prevalent over the last few years than at any point before. A number of 'key' studies have energized cross-chronological study of this kind. Work by scholars such as James Simpson, Jennifer Summit, David Wallace and Helen Cooper has served to make the idea of medievalists and early modernists conversing productively more plausible than it often has been.[22] But this study, while circumscribed with a vitally

---

[21] Raymond Williams, *Keywords: A Vocabulary of Culture and Society* (Glasgow, 1976), pp. 209–11, 209.

[22] See, in particular, James Simpson, *Reform and Cultural Revolution* (Oxford, 2002); Jennifer Summit, *Lost Property: The Woman Writer and English Literary History, 1380–1589* (Chicago, 2000); David Wallace, *Pre-modern Places: Calais to Surinam, Chaucer to Aphra Behn* (Oxford, 2004); Helen Cooper, *The English Romance in Time: Transforming Motifs from Geoffrey of Monmouth to Shakespeare* (Oxford, 2004). A number of other important studies cast their nets at least as wide as *c.* 1380 to the mid-Tudor period. See, for example, Wendy Scase, *Literature and Complaint in England, 1272–1553* (Oxford, 2007); Robert Meyer-Lee, *Poets and Power from Chaucer to Wyatt* (Cambridge, 2007); Alexandra Gillespie, *Print Culture and the Medieval Author: Chaucer, Lydgate and their Books, 1473–1557* (Oxford, 2006). For an engaging collection of essays assessing the 'medieval-Renaissance divide', and an excellent analytical survey of this new(ish) field, see Gordon McMullan and David Matthews, eds, *Reading the Medieval in Early Modern England* (Cambridge, 2007) and David Matthews, 'The Medieval Invasion of Early-Modern England', *New Medieval Literatures*, 10 (2008), 223–44.

'Med-Ren' chronology, runs along different, though related, lines to this spate of recent work by medievalists.

Few of the texts discussed in this book, barring the texts that begin and end it – Langland's *Piers Plowman* and Nashe's *Pierce Penniless* – have attracted a particularly large retinue of critical literature. To many literary scholars, much of the radical pastoral tradition is of a very restricted type of interest, examples of what Richard Firth Green, referring to John Ball's letters, calls 'a minor literary genre, variously categorised as estates satire, complaint literature, or the literature of popular protest'.[23] The attention that much of the Reformation literature discussed in this book has attracted, at least since John N. King's wonderful, ground-breaking *Reformation Literature* (1982), has come from medievalists.[24] The willingness of medievalists to look forward beyond 1500 is self-evidently a good thing, but it has often led to work which harbours a tendency towards a rather survey-like quality. Some of this is fine work, but it necessarily approaches Reformation writing looking for ideas of reception, tradition, continuity and evocation whose centre of gravity remains the medieval author, the originary point of a tradition. Rarely does such work focus on the writing of early English Protestantism in its own right, as the centre of its concerns. While I too consider medieval culture as an important – indeed vital – part of the cultural and literary heritage of English Protestant writing in the sixteenth century, this book is much more centrally focused on Reformation writing considered 'for its own sake'.

As David Wallace has written, medievalists have also frequently felt something akin to what he calls 'road rage' towards Renaissance and Reformation Studies: 'Such animus derives from recognition that the English Renaissance first creates English medieval studies (by fragmenting its textual culture and physical remains) and then ignores it: for the key motif of Renaissance is to proclaim the new and abjure the superannuation and darkness of the old; to move on and not look back'.[25] In recent studies by both medievalists and early modernists, early Protestant writing has tended to receive its fair share of hostility.

One of the most prominent scholars to energize work with a 'trans-Reformation' agenda – James Simpson – has now written a pair of studies which launch serious and sustained polemical attacks on the traditional divides between medieval and early modern cultures, and on the ethics of early Protestant culture.[26]

---

[23]   Richard Firth Green, 'John Ball's Letters', p. 180.

[24]   See King, *Reformation Literature*. Brian Cummings' excellent *The Literary Culture of the Reformation: Grammar and Grace* (Oxford, 2002) is worth singling out though. Recent 'survey' studies of Reformation writing by medievalists include the later chapters in John M. Bowers, *Chaucer and Langland: The Antagonistic Tradition* (Notre Dame, IN, 2007); and Sarah Kelen's *Langland's Early Modern Identities*.

[25]   David Wallace, 'Afterword' in *Reading the Medieval in Early Modern England*, McMullan and Matthews, pp. 220–27, 221.

[26]   These studies are the voluminous and immensely rich *Reform and Cultural Revolution*, and the rather less rich, and rather more hostile, *Burning to Read: English*

While this book shares this desire to work across canons of writing which often exist in mutual ignorance of one another, it does not share Simpson's extremely hostile view of Reformation writing and culture, which has led from the daring, exhilarating narrative of literary history between 1350 and 1547 as 'a narrative of diminishing liberties' to a wholesale attack on the theological ethics of early, and indeed twenty-first century, Protestantism.[27]

In a monumental and equally politicized – if less polemically-written – study, Greg Walker has described the early English Reformation as a period dominated by the shadow of Henrician tyranny, a period of mass cultural dysfunction in which the body politic, and the writing produced by its limbs, broke down in neurosis. Walker's study is inspiring, and chilling, but its narrative again posits the rise of the English Reformation as a cultural moment of blunt violence, institutional terror, and irrevocable loss.[28] Protestant culture in these accounts has an awful lot to answer for, as if the wave of revisionist religious history that characterized the 1980s and 1990s has suddenly caught up with literary studies all at once.[29] While indebted to these formidable studies, this book offers some analyses of Reformation writings which are a little less denunciatory and a little more appreciative of the complex differences between, and complications within, early Reformation literature.

In 1550, one of the many ploughman texts of the mid-century, *I Playn Piers*, launched an attack on 'legenda aurea, Roben Hoode, Beuys and Gower, & al baggage besyd'.[30] It was in many ways a highly conventional Protestant attack on what it saw as the survival of a literary and cultural tradition tainted with medieval Catholicism. There was, however, an opposing tradition of radical pastoral writing

---

Fundamentalism and it Reformation Opponents (Cambridge, MA, 2007).

[27] For an important counter to this thesis, see the review of Simpson's book by Thomas Betteridge, 'The Henrician Reformation and Mid-Tudor Culture', *Journal of Medieval and Early Modern Studies*, 35:1 (2005), pp. 91–109 and for Betteridge's view of the Edwardian reign as 'a period of real intellectual freedom', see his *Literature and Politics in the English Reformation* (Manchester, 2004), p. 113.

[28] Walker, *Writing under Tyranny: English Literature and the Henrician Reformation* (Oxford, 2007). The book builds on Walker's earlier scholarship such as *John Skelton and the Politics of the 1520s* (Cambridge, 1988) and *Plays of Persuasion: Drama and Politics at the Court of Henry VIII* (Cambridge, 1991). Walker, the editor of an anthology of medieval drama and some serious work on early editions of Chaucer, surely deserves to head the list of 'trans-Reformation' scholars I assembled above.

[29] I refer here to in particular to J. J. Scarisbrick, *The Reformation and the English People* (Oxford, 1984); Christopher Haigh, *The English Reformation Revised* (Cambridge, 1987); Eamon Duffy, *The Stripping of the Altars: Traditional Religion in England, 1400–1580* (New Haven, 1992). For an excellent account of recent Reformation historiography, see Peter Marshall and Alec Ryrie, 'Introduction: Protestantisms and their Beginnings' in *The Beginnings of English Protestantism*, eds Marshall and Ryrie (Cambridge, 2007), pp. 1–13.

[30] *I Playn Piers* (London: ?, 1550?), sig. E3v.

which deeply influenced, even shaped, the form and style of Protestant writing. Whilst this book moves, broadly speaking, forward chronologically, one of its purposes is to work retrospectively, to see how and why the ploughman we see in *Piers Plowman* became the figure of 'Playn Piers', the voice of Reformation literature and its attendant controversies.

In Chapter 1 I open by looking at mid-Tudor literature's cultural inheritance, and in particular the legacy of *Piers Plowman* in a particular sense. I argue that one of the most vital things that Tudor writers took from Langland's poem was a mode of anti-urban satire. I detail a key material example of this satire in Langland's poem, trace how proximate it is to the civic discourse of London legislation in the later Middle Ages, and then relate it to the prolific literature of social criticism produced by the 'commonwealthsmen' of the mid-Tudor period, most notable amongst them Robert Crowley, Langland's first editor in print.

The following two chapters situate this literary culture within forms of polemicized pastoralism in the early Reformation. Chapter 2 delineates the cultural horizons of early Protestant rhetoric, and locates Protestant pastoralism in a history of controversial self-fashioning, a history of self-representation and self-understanding in earlier religious writing, most importantly the controversial writing of Lollards and Mendicants in the fourteenth and fifteenth centuries.

Chapter 3 focuses on a particular example of this pastoralism, and traces the significance of the ploughman figure in early printed controversial literature between 1510 and 1550. I argue here for the complexity of the Henrician ploughman, and suggest ways in which the reformist controversy of the 1530s worked to polemicize the latent oppositional aspects of the figure, not just in terms of anticlericalism, but also in terms of Protestant antiquarianism and the literature of agrarian complaint. The chapter closes with an account of Crowley's editions of *Piers Plowman* which emphasizes how they should be considered as touched by, but ultimately differentiated from, this tradition of the polemical ploughman.

In the final chapter I follow this figure, and the text of *Piers Plowman*, into the years of the Marprelate controversy, in a group of texts bunched together in the years 1588–1594. Contrary to widespread narratives of the diminishing power of the ploughman figure in the Elizabethan period, I show how controversial writing during and after the Marprelate controversy, 1590s satire, and popular drama on the London stage all found new vitality and controversial capital in the figure of 'poor piers ploughman'.

Chapter 1

The Ploughman's Commonwealth

Thei richen þorugh regratrie and rentes hem biggen
With that the pouere peple sholde putte in hire wombe.

Piers Plowman (B3.83–4/C3.82–3)

Well, let thes forestallars
    repent them bytyme,
Lest the clarke of the market
    be with them ere pryme.
For he, when he cometh,
    wyll punysh them all,
That do any nedeful thynge
    ingrose or forestall.

Robert Crowley, *One and Thyrtye Epigrammes* (1550), ll. 965–72.

In an important introductory volume to Renaissance culture published at the turn of the millennium, William Langland's extravagantly complex and arresting medieval poem is accorded a short, but extremely significant, appearance. Patrick Collinson, the great scholar of the Elizabethan Puritan movement, writes that 'lurking in the arras [of Renaissance literature], as it were, was the living ghost of *Piers Plowman*'.[1] Amongst the vernacular Bible, *Book of Common Prayer* and Hugh Latimer's sermons, the name of *Piers Plowman* appears in a canon of texts that formed the foundations of a Protestant plain style that would influence English literary history at least until Milton's *Paradise Regained*, approximately 300 years after the text's influence sprang up in the coded letters of 1381. Collinson's statement owes a great deal to the ground-breaking scholarship of John N. King in his *Reformation Literature* (1982), a book that began, King recalls, 'in bewilderment when I encountered Robert Crowley's 1550 text of *Piers Plowman*', and continued as he 'became convinced … that Crowley's mid-Tudor edition was an immediate ancestor of Book One of Spenser's *Faerie Queene*'.[2] King's work may well have built upon the much older foundations of Helen C. White's *Social Criticism in Popular Religious Literature of the Sixteenth Century* (1944). White stated that 'the sixteenth-century reformers inherited a tradition of social-religious criticism from which they made their own selection, and which they carried on

---

[1] Patrick Collinson, 'English Reformations', in *A Companion to English Renaissance Literature and Culture*, ed. M. Hattaway (Blackwell, 2000), pp. 27–43, 33.

[2] King, *Reformation Literature*, p. xi.

to their own ends, often, in all probability, not entirely aware of what they were doing'.[3] White termed the appropriative merging of *Piers Plowman* with the political writings of John Wyclif 'The Piers Plowman Tradition', almost 50 years before medievalists came to use the term habitually, prompted by Helen Barr's foundational edition of some important fifteenth-century poems.[4]

That Langland's work gets any mention in a discussion of literary influence and canon formation is remarkable – Chaucer is habitually the originary figure of literary and cultural history that has been evoked from the fifteenth century onwards – but what is equally startling is the image the work seems to have.[5] Langland's ploughman appears in the sixteenth century as a shadowy, 'lurking' presence, a cultural phenomenon in the subconscious of Reformation writers only hazily aware of its workings, a 'living ghost' no less threatening than Marx's spectre hanging ominously over Europe in the middle of the nineteenth century. There is something spectral about Langland's poem: its presence is palpable and almost ubiquitous, yet frustratingly evasive. Whilst lurking in the imagination of the Reformation, *Piers Plowman* can also be seen loitering on the periphery of mainstream culture like a twentieth-century counter-culture icon. King awards *Piers Plowman* the title of 'underground classic'.[6] David Daniell, the great scholar of William Tyndale's biblical translations, amusingly writes about the idea of *Piers Plowman* or the Wycliffite Bible being printed by Caxton or De Worde as 'like trying to imagine the Library of Congress in the 1950s publishing a deluxe edition of the Communist Manifesto'.[7] This is the imagining of Langland's work in terms of the nineteenth- or twentieth-century gothic-revolutionary text: *Piers Plowman* written by Shelley or William Morris.[8]

This pervasive sense of ghostly influence is not, I think, to be dismissed. And yet there has been a reaction to this persistent suspicion amongst scholars of the early modern period that they are being haunted by William Langland. Oddly, it has come from medievalists. For a good few years, the trenchant good sense of Anne Hudson, without whom Wycliffite studies would not be the force they currently are, left the 'legacy' of *Piers Plowman* in serious doubt. In an influential

---

    [3]   Helen C. White, *Social Criticism in Popular Religious Literature of the Sixteenth Century* (New York, 1944), p. 2.

    [4]   Helen Barr, ed., *The Piers Plowman Tradition: a Critical Edition of Pierce the Ploughman's crede, Richard the redeless, Mum and the sothsegger and The crowned king* (London, 1993).

    [5]   For a recent revisionist survey of the interconnected Chaucerian and Langlandian traditions which ends, tantalizingly, in seventeenth-century America, see John M. Bowers, *Chaucer and Langland*.

    [6]   King, *Reformation Literature*, p. 27.

    [7]   David Daniell, *William Tyndale: A Biography* (New Haven, 1994), p. 101.

    [8]   Morris' *A Dreame of John Ball* is, perhaps, quite close to such an idea. See P. Hardwick, '"Biddeth Peres Ploughman Go to his werk": Appropriations of *Piers Plowman* in the Nineteenth and Twentieth Centuries', *Studies in Medievalism*, 12 (2002), 171–95.

essay, Hudson concluded that 'Regretfully, one must conclude that, at least after the immediate and usually Lollard imitations, *Piers Plowman* in the two and a half centuries after its composition was more honoured in the name than in the reading'.[9] In Hudson's account, despite the proliferation of usually Protestant 'ploughman texts' in the sixteenth century, so few demonstrated an obvious familiarity with the text of Langland's poem that the 'Piers Plowman Tradition' could well be seen as itself a thing of smoke and mirrors: everyone wrote about ploughmen, so we had assumed they had some contact with *Piers Plowman*. But when Hudson looked for the kind of verbal echoes and self-aware literary evocations we might expect from such a 'tradition', the ghost of *Piers Plowman* seemed to have vanished into thin air. As I argue in the Preface, to move beyond this impasse, it becomes necessary to view direct literary borrowing and textual contact as only *one way* in which texts have a cultural presence and a cultural impact (though, as Chapter 4 shows, 'real', close textual knowledge of *Piers Plowman*, of the kind that scholars tend to be more comfortable with, is clearly present even into the 1590s).

More recently, James Simpson's barn-storming reassessment of literary history in his *Reform and Cultural Revolution* (2002) again questioned quite what the ghost or legacy of *Piers Plowman* might have been for the sixteenth century. But here the question of the worth or value of sixteenth-century contact with Langland's ghostly text became one of theological rupture in a narrative of the Reformation as violent disruption of cultural continuity. In his chapter 'Edifying the Church', Simpson argues that '*Piers Plowman* both foresaw and forestalled the Reformation, by offering a reformation of its own in which grace is distributed in a wholly decentralised way'.[10] The overarching argument about theological centralization consequently requires a dismissal of the sixteenth-century encounters with *Piers Plowman* as 'a revival of sorts', but one 'incapable of deploying anything like the full force of the earlier poem'.[11] Rather than a portrait of readerly ignorance of the text of *Piers Plowman*, this is a picture of incapacity. Early Protestants might have got their revolutionary hands on Langland's poem, Simpson concedes, but their theological and political tyrannies prevented them from reading it *well*. Other recent work has sought to view the history of Langlandian reception in a less schematic and polemical fashion, and while Simpson's work in particular has energized scholarship on the 'medieval–Renaissance divide' in literary studies, this study assumes that Protestant writers were regularly affected by *Piers Plowman* in

---

[9]   Anne Hudson, 'Epilogue: The Legacy of *Piers Plowman*' in *A Companion to Piers Plowman*, ed. John A. Alford (Berkeley, 1988), pp. 251–66, 263.

[10]   Simpson, *Reform and Cultural Revolution*, pp. 328–9.

[11]   Simpson, *Reform and Cultural Revolution*, p. 330. Simpson's argument about the theological and ecclesiological thought of *Piers Plowman* is an expansion of an excellent discussion in his earlier *Piers Plowman: An Introduction to the B-Text* (London, 1990), esp. pp. 89–139, but now the previously labelled 'Augustinian' and 'semi-Pelagian' positions are re-named 'reformist' and 'revolutionary', medieval and modern, Catholic and Protestant.

a wide variety of ways, and that this contact was vital for the imaginative genesis of much early and mid-Tudor writing.[12]

But this conviction also needs some elucidation. As the role-call of previous scholarship above suggests, scholars working on both medieval and early modern literature and culture have long known, or at least 'felt', the presence of *Piers Plowman* in the writing of the sixteenth century. This presence is often described in the following terms: 'social criticism', 'prophecy', 'anticlericalism'. These terms remain useful tools for approaching both Langland's poem and much of the writing of the Reformation. But this chapter argues that amongst the most important things that *Piers Plowman* endowed to the sixteenth century was a particular imaginative preoccupation with the city – London in particular – and consequently a certain 'mode' of satire or polemic which was vital to mid-Tudor writing. This image of the city was overwhelmingly hostile – far more correlative with Horatian or Juvenalian images of the urban world than those of the *encomium civitatis* tradition which soon, meeting with the serious scholarly work of local history, produced John Stow's *Survey of London* (1598). This image of the urban world came with an imaginative preoccupation with London and an acute distrust of commercialism, and was part of a literary mode or sub-genre of 'anti-urban satire' which was the life-blood of mid-Tudor literature.

In this chapter I detail some key passages in Langland's poem itself, and show how vital, deep and artful was Langland's satirical preoccupation with the urban marketplace. Secondly, I argue that Langland's text at these moments bears a marked similarity to the language and mentality of civic, governmental legislation in the fourteenth and fifteenth centuries. There is in Langland's text and the period's civic legislation a developing image and associated language of community and common good which – while having its own specific contexts and rhetorical purposes – endowed something genuinely vital to the writing of mid-Tudor writers, particular the 'commonwealth-men', writers such as Langland's first print editor, Robert Crowley. This civic, anti-urban satire – emanating, of course, from the capital itself – was absolutely crucial to mid-Tudor writing.

For it is in the Edwardian period that the most prolific and vociferous heirs, readers and appropriators of Langland appear: in the form of a group of writers usually referred to as the 'commonwealth-men'.[13] Among this group, numbering

---

[12]   Important work has been done lately by a number of Langlandian scholars, for example: Kelen, *Langland's Early Modern Identities*, and a number of essays by R. Carter Hailey, Laurence Warner and Wendy Scase, collected in *YLS*, 21 (2007).

[13]   The term was first coined by R. H. Tawney, in *Religion and the Rise of Capitalism* (London, 1929), pp. 137–8. As Charlotte Davies has recently noted, the term has been strongly contested. G. R. Elton questioned both the existence of such a related group identity, and indeed the quality of their writing. He dismissed Crowley, Latimer and others as a dispersed group of insignificant writers connected only through the similarity of what even Davies calls their 'half-baked economic theories'. Davies attempts to rehabilitate the term through a concentration on a shared interest in antipapal writing. See Charlotte

Hugh Latimer, Thomas Becon, Henry Brinklow and William Forest, the most prolific was surely Robert Crowley, Langland's first textual editor in the era of print. Crowley's career as churchman, preacher, exile, publisher, polemicist and poet is strikingly eclectic, but it is worth noting that amongst the many controversies and occurrences of his life, Crowley was among everything else a man with an extraordinarily detailed knowledge of *Piers Plowman*, as the accumulative torrent of marginal comments and glosses in his editions of the poem demonstrates.[14] Around the middle of the sixteenth century, at the forefront of Edwardian reformism, was somebody who had both a keen interest and a peculiarly close knowledge of Langland's text.

A productive way to demonstrate this line of sympathy between the late fourteenth and mid-sixteenth century is through a concentrated discussion of one aspect of Langland's and the reformers' imaginative constructions of urban, and specifically London, culture. The term 'regratorie' used by Langland in the passage at the head of this chapter serves as a productive example. Occupying an ambiguous semantic space between demonstrable material practice and symbolic meaning, and between the institutional documents of civic government and those of literary productions, the 'regrator' appears as a persistent object of economic, social and spiritual anxiety between the reformist literature of the 1380s and that of the 1550s.

An analysis of Langland's use of the term in key passages of *Piers Plowman* demonstrates his awareness and manipulation of important connotations surrounding the language of commerce in the late fourteenth century, placing emphasis on the specific importance of the word when applied to the victualling trades. These trades, the 'Brewesters and baksters, bochiers and cokes' (B3.79/ C3.80), serve as a potent focal point for Langland's representations of the urban environment, bringing together connections between issues of charity, food, the deprivation of the poor, and the simultaneous foregrounding of conspicuous consumption and ostentatious wealth in the developing urban landscape of late fourteenth-century London. Langland's depictions of 'regrators' similarly show his awareness of the particular semantic associations of the term.

The 'tricks of the trade' with which Langland associates the term are a prolific part of the institutional language of civic government. The plethora of cases

---

Davies, *A Religion of the Word: The Defence of the Reformation in the Reign of Edward VI* (Manchester, 2002), p. 6, and G. R. Elton, 'Reform and the "Commonwealths-men" of Edward VI's Reign' in *The English Commonwealth, 1547–1640: Essays on Politics and Society Presented to Joel Hurstfield*, eds P. Clarke, A. Smith and N. Tyacke (Leicester, 1979), pp. 23–38. Betteridge also sees the Edwardian reign as a period which saw a genuine 'surge in interest in social reform and political theory', see *Literature and Politics in the English Reformation*, p. 90.

[14] For a concise account of Crowley's biography, see King, *Reformation Literature*, pp. 319–57. An exploration of Crowley's editions of *Piers Plowman* can be found in Chapter 3.

concerning 'regrating' in Leet books, civic courts and documents such as the *Liber Albus* demonstrate a persistent awareness about the problems of policing commercial life in late medieval urban culture. Moreover, a comparison between these documents shows how Langland conflates a number of different practices in the figures of 'Rose the Regrator' and her husband, 'Coveitise'. Whilst seemingly maintaining a simply denotative title of 'regrator' (a 'retailer'), both Langland and civic records harbour a pervasive suspicion of the connections between 'regrating' and commercial malpractice, in terms of the manipulation of goods and ultimately of defrauding the average buyer, frequently characterized as the needy poor.

Significantly, this discourse regarding commercial trade in the urban marketplace can be viewed as the product of a burgeoning construction of the civic 'common good', an urbanized form of the 'common profit' which so often accompanies Langland's figurations of the agricultural community. Whilst literary depictions of the medieval city, including Langland's, so frequently take recourse to the topoi of anonymity and moral disruption familiar from Horace's *Satires* or Jerome's *Epistles*, this discourse is the product of an opposing tradition of the celebrated city, and one in which the city is constructed as a community with shared values and aims.[15] Necessarily, the discourse of the urban 'common good' stigmatizes its opposite, what sixteenth-century writers frequently term 'commodity', the commercial self-interest which paradoxically both serves as an opposite to the 'common weale', and as the economic powerhouse of the successful city, providing the urban environment with its physical form, and much of its governmental class.

The sense of the urban marketplace as a chaotic moral disruption pervades sixteenth-century reformist writing, even as the imagined community was figured as predominantly urban. Indeed, the foregrounding of commercial deceit and the financial exploitation of the poor, as shown below, became a central part of a particular mid-century Protestant discourse. Langland's representations of the urban marketplace provided a rhetoric and imagery which the Edwardian reformers, centralized in London and frequently addressing their texts directly to the capital, took up and placed at the centre of their analysis of the state of the realm in both material and spiritual terms.

Finally, the reconfiguration of Langlandian topoi in a polemical Tudor context is strikingly revealed in one particular example, Robert Crowley's *Philargyrie of Greate Britayne* (1551). Crowley's text, published in the year following his editions of *Piers Plowman*, shows how Langlandian figures, in particular 'Hunger', were appropriated and reconfigured in the Protestant mid-century, serving a vital role in the imaginative genesis of Edwardian literary culture.

---

[15]   For contemporary literary examples of this tradition, see X. Brown, ed., *London 1066–1914: Literary Sources and Documents*, 2 vols (Mountfield, 1997), I. 47–79.

Langland's Anti-Urban Satire

While talking about Langland's editors, it is striking that one of the most important for twentieth and twenty-first century readers, students and scholars of the poem firmly believed that the apparent pastoralism of a poem like *Piers Plowman* disguised its real and deep-rooted imaginative preoccupation with London. In 1886, Walter W. Skeat wrote:

> It is clear, both from very numerous allusions and from the whole tone of the poem, that the place the poet knew best and most delighted to describe was the city of London. It cannot be too strongly impressed upon the reader (especially as the point has often been overlooked) that one great merit of the poem consists in its exhibition of *London* life and *London* opinions; and that to remember the *London* origin of, at any rate, the larger portion of the poem, is the true key to the right understanding of it.[16] (Emphases are Skeat's)

Other major scholars of *Piers Plowman* have concurred. A later editor of Langland's, Derek Pearsall, cited this passage of Skeat to launch his own compelling argument that 'London remains, in epitome, the problem that the poem does not solve', even as he wondered at 'how sharp and specific Langland can be when he is dealing with London malpractices and London government'.[17] More recently, C. David Benson's *Public Piers Plowman* (2004) similarly looked back to Skeat's sentiment in arguing that 'London practices are absolutely central to *Piers Plowman* ... urban life is used deliberately and eagerly by the poet to express his greatest hopes as well as his deepest fears'.[18] It is this imaginative preoccupation with London, the literary formation of the commercial marketplace as the moral challenge of Langland's age, that becomes such an important inspiration for sixteenth-century writers, and which we turn to now, by way of Langland's attack on those who

---

[16] Walter W. Skeat, ed., *The Vision of Will, regarding Piers Plowman*, 2 vols (London, 1886), II. 3.

[17] Derek Pearsall, 'Langland's London' in *Written Work: Langland, Labor, and Authorship*, eds Steven Justice and Kathryn Kerby-Fulton, (Philadelphia, 1997), pp. 185–207, 286, 288. Pearsall actually points out that Skeat 'exaggerates' for rhetorical effect, and argues that Langland's preoccupation with London goes side-by-side with the fact that Langland 'chooses agrarian models for his allegorical ideals of community' (p. 185). For another excellent essay on the poem's preoccupation with London, see Caroline M. Barron, 'William Langland: A London Poet' in *Chaucer's England: Literature in Historical Context*, ed. Barbara Hanawalt (Minnesota, 1992), pp. 91–109.

[18] C. David Benson, *Public Piers Plowman: Modern Scholarship and Late Medieval English Culture* (Philadelphia, 2004), p. 205. Benson, as the quotation makes clear, views *Piers Plowman* as a poem which finds some aspects of commercial and urban life redeemable. While Benson's analysis of the later passus of the poem in the light of civic legislation is intriguing, I find Pearsall's formulation more compelling.

'richen þorugh regratrie and rentes hem biggen / With that the pouere peple sholde putte in hire wombe'.

The *Middle English Dictionary* defines 'regratorie' as 'retail selling', 'usually at high prices obtained through forestalling the market'. To regrate, to forestall, is 'to buy up goods in advance of the market', denying close contact between producer and consumer.[19] As Crowley's lines, used as an epitaph to the chapter, suggest, this process has particular valence in the commercial exchange of 'needful things': sometimes of fuel or building materials, but habitually of food.[20] The term, as discussed below, encompasses a wide variety of commercial practices, covering issues not only of 'forestalling', but of food prices, the manipulation of goods, weights and measures and public health.

'Regratorie' first appears in *Piers Plowman* as part of Langland's extended depiction of the ubiquity and power of Lady Mede, the personification of financial corruption that dominates the first four passus of the text.[21] What is most apparent in this passage, at least to begin with, is the importance of Mede, of commercial transaction, in the prolific anticlerical satire of the text.[22] A 'confessour coped as a frere' (B3.35/C3.38) approaches Mede and proclaims 'I shal assoille þee myself for a seem of whete' (B3.40/C3.42). Absolution is being sold for material gain, the process of confession which should depend on genuine contrition for one's sins is being hijacked by financial self-interest in the form of 'wheat'. This is in many ways the hub of Langland's anticlerical anxieties, one that returns in the apocalyptic vision of the fall of the barn of unity in the closing passus. But the encounter is not limited to the issue of confession, but quickly becomes an issue regarding the process of endowment and the use of alms, centred significantly on the image of clerical – specifically mendicant – buildings.

Essentially, a commercial transaction takes place. The friar asks Mede to pay for the rebuilding and enhancement of the physical building which houses his order: 'Woldestow glaȝe þat gable and graue þere þy name, / Sykir sholde

---

[19]   Robert E. Lewis, Hans Kurath, Sherman A. Kuhn, John Reidy, eds, *The Middle English Dictionary*, 24 vols (Ann Arbor, 1952–2002), IX. 345–6.

[20]   For more detailed discussions of late medieval trade and economics see C. M. Barron, *London in the Later Middle Ages: People and Government* (Oxford, 2002), esp. pp. 45–63, 64–83, and R. H. Britnell, *The Commercialisation of English Society, 1000–1500* (Cambridge, 1993).

[21]   The most comprehensive survey of the origins and tradition of medieval venality satire that influenced the figure is still J. A. Yunck, *The Lineage of Lady Meed: The Development of Mediaeval Venality Satire* (Notre Dame, 1963). The key passage in *Piers Plowman* is B3.76–90.

[22]   For fuller discussions of the anticlericalism of *Piers Plowman* see especially Wendy Scase, *Piers Plowman and the New Anticlericalism* (Cambridge, 1989). On anti-fraternal satire more specifically, see P. R. Szittya, *The Antifraternal Tradition* (Princeton, 1986).

þi soule be hevene to haue' (B3.49–50).[23] In return, the mendicant takes it upon himself to offer salvation. Langland imagines a process in which the fate of a soul is quite literally determined by financial payment, by the action of paying the bill for a material building project. The sense of the process as commercial is consolidated by Mede's 'haggling' over her endowment, promising to fund repairs and adornment of the mendicant house only if the order will 'Haue mercy' on 'lordes þat lecherie haunten' (B3.59, 53/C3.63, 57). It is clear that this is above all a scene of commercial trade and exchange, in a marketplace that includes the spiritual commodity of heaven or hell as much as the material goods of bricks and mortar. The commercial negotiations seem to come to a satisfactory conclusion for everyone apart from Langland, who intrudes into his allegorical text with an authorial passage directly castigating 'gravyng', and those who have 'writen in wyndowes of hir wel dedes' (B3.64–5/C3.68–9).[24]

The obvious problem is one of pride; of the process of charitable alms-giving being tainted by self-interest. Yet the commercial nature of this transaction cannot be entirely controlled by the moralistic intercession, by its explication as an exemplary sermon on financial corruption. The sense that Langland's imagination is fixated on the marketplace seems to seep into the language of the polemical intrusion:

> For God knoweþ þi conscience and þi kynde wille,
> Thi *cost* and þi *coueitise* and who þe *catel* ouȝte. (B3.67–8/C3.71–2, my italics)

The moral and spiritual qualities of the individual Christian, addressed directly to the reader of the text in the second person, are themselves described in the language of the marketplace. The reader has a 'cost', a quasi-financial worth, gives money or goods ('catel') as alms, and must be aware of their 'true' ownership: only the 'coveitise' of the 'owner' can make the alms-giver think that they can measure

---

[23] The C text alters the Friar's promise of 'heuen' to: 'In masse and in mataynes for Mede we shal synge / Solempneliche and softlyche as for a suster of oure ordre' (C3.53–4).

[24] It is of course debatable whether the passage is 'authorial' as such. The first-person narrator is obviously 'Long Will' throughout the poem, who must be seen as a malleable textual persona rather than a simplistic authorial presence; indeed much of the self-reflexive comedy of the text demands it. However, a number of things suggest a momentary authorial intrusion here: the passage has no identifiable speaker between Mede's direct speeches at 3.63 'I am suster of youre house', and 3.91 'For my love, quod that lady'; the direct polemical address of the passage ('Forthi I lere yow lordes'), and the fact that the first-person narrator, rather than being 'inside' the textual world of personifications, as he is when we see him kneeling before Holy Church at the start of passus 2, seems to be commenting on the action from an omniscient moral position. For a fine discussion of mercantile sponsorship of such 'gravyng', see Sarah Stanbury, 'The Vivacity of Images: St. Katherine, Knighton's Lollards, and the Breaking of Idols' in *Images, Idolatry, and Iconoclasm in Late Medieval England: Textuality and the Visual Image*, eds J. Dimmick, J. Simpson and N. Zeeman (Oxford, 2002), pp. 131–50.

the spiritual benefit they receive in return for parting with money. In a striking forerunner of Crowley's image of a vengeful God appearing as 'a Clarke of the market', something to which we will return later, Langland's sense of spiritual value, though obviously differentiated from the self-interested commerce between Mede and the friar, is wrought with the language and economic structures of the marketplace.[25]

Significantly, though, Langland's intrusion into the allegorical world of Mede, Conscience and Favel suddenly swerves abruptly into what seems like rather disjointed material.[26] From the issue of the ethics of alms-giving, the reader is suddenly directed to 'Maires and maceres', the figures of civic government whose duty it is 'To punysshe on pillories' those who 'richen þoruȝ regratrie', harming the poor who 'parcelmele buggen' (B3.76–83/C3.77–81). What seems to be a sudden change of theme is, however, a complex continuity of the previous material. It is a continuity that rests on an implicit set of connections between 'regratrie' and commercialism in a broader sense and significantly between, on the one hand, the material buildings that are the palpable product of commercial success, and on the other, the deprivation of the urban poor. The presence of commercial bargaining between Mede and the mendicant orders is narrowed in scope and focused on the material actions of the urban market – 'regrating', selling 'somdel ayeins reson' (B3.92),[27] as Mede puts it; the exchange of money required for charging of 'rentes' (B3.83/C3.82) and the buying of 'burgages', 'tenements' (B3.86/C3.85). The

---

[25]   This imaginative construction of divine judgement of the human soul as a moment of quasi-financial reckoning is in fact emphasized by the increasingly regular citation of '*Redde quod debes*' ('pay your debts') towards the latter part of the poem (for example, B19.186, 194, 261). The short quotation is taken from Matthew 18:28, a parable emphasizing the value of essentially forgiving 'debts' or sins against oneself in return for similar forgiveness from God. Langland seems to have appropriated the text in a slightly different sense, in line with his preoccupation with the decay of contrition, laying emphasis on the imperative to be repentant for your own sins, rather than on forgiving others. The ubiquity and importance of financial language in Langland's thinking about spirituality and salvation is discussed in an important essay by James Simpson; 'Spirituality and Economics in Passus 1–7 of the B Text', *YLS*, 1 (1987), 83–103.

[26]   Editors of *Piers Plowman* have noted the suddenness of the transition. A. V. C. Schmidt regards it as 'abrupt'; A. V. C. Schmidt, ed., *Piers Plowman: A Parallel-Text Edition of the A, B, C, and Z Versions* (London, 1995), p. 418, notes 77–86, and J. A. W. Bennett as 'not clearly related'; *Piers Plowman: The Prologue and Passus I–VII of the B-Text* (Oxford, 1972), p. 136. Andrew Galloway, in the wonderful recent *Penn Commentary* likewise comments on the 'stylistic shock' of the transition. See Galloway, *The Penn Commentary on Piers Plowman*, vol. 1 (Philadelphia, 2006), p. 299. On the passage as a whole, see pp. 298–305. C. David Benson describes the moment in similar terms: 'After the account of Meed's corrupt dealing with friars, a speaking voice, which may or may not be identified with the author, abruptly and with no clear transition addresses mayors', see Benson, *Public Piers Plowman*, pp. 231–2.

[27]   The C text has 'selle aȝeyne þe lawe' (C3.120).

commercialism that threatens the integrity of ecclesiastical activities is sharpened at the point of its most obvious and most material exemplification, in the secular business transactions of the urban market.

Notably, the images of buildings, the physical structures that shape and control the space of the urban environment, are the connecting link between the allegorical world of ecclesiastical commercialism and the material world of secular finance. The mendicant house that Mede promises to endow is not a simple chapel but a building with windows that 'wole stonden vs ful hye' (B3.48/C3.51): that will cost the order a great deal of money. After Mede has applied the desired improvements, not only will the church be 'covered' or roofed, but painted ('whiten'), 'glazed' and decorated with 'portraye' (B3.60–63/C3.64–6). The mendicants seem to be looking forward to something more in the vein of the Vatican City than the caves and forests of Francis' La Verna. Similarly, the commercial aspiration and enrichment of the secular merchant envisioned through 'regratrie' culminates in the building of extravagant structures. As Langland puts it, if merchants 'toke þei on trewely, þei tymbred nouȝt so heiȝe' (B3.85/C3.84). If they gained their money more honestly they would not be able to afford to construct such imposing and elaborate houses for themselves. Again, the change from ecclesiastical to secular images of commercialism is marked by a more concrete vocabulary. Whilst the mendicants have their house 'a-werchynge' (B3.48/C3.51), the merchants are 'timbering', in an image that substitutes the material used for building with the process of building itself. The mendicants are gracefully corrupt; the 'regrator' is earthier, winning his wealth through less dignified means of persuasion, and expressing it in ways that are more transparently self-aggrandizing. The commercial self-interest that creates the wealth necessary to construct ostentatious, luxurious buildings is, however, the same.

Moreover, Langland makes an important connection between the expression of wealth and the process of moneymaking as necessarily contributing to the deprivation of the poor. The money that allows the mendicants and regraters to 'timber so high' is gained through the manipulation of food and 'rents', the overcharging for basic requirements 'þat þe pouere peple sholde putte in hire wombe' (B3.84/C3.83). The images of needy stomachs and towering urban housing are deliberately chosen to stress the massive differentiation of status and comfort implied between them. The issue of alms-giving that preceded the appearance of regratrie in the text has not disappeared, but whilst before it was a matter of attempting to separate pride from charity, in the world of the urban market it has become a matter of open exploitation and financial predation.[28]

---

[28]   R. H. Britnell's characterization is quite accurate: 'He [Langland] saw tradesmen … living by craft and cunning. The growth of occupational specialisation away from the simplicity of rural life implied the decay of Christian standards of behaviour'; Britnell, *The Commercialisation of English Society*, p. 172. The connections between the 'craft and cunning' of commercialism and the moral decay of social community made by the text are even more close, and damning, than Britnell suggests.

Charity and financial transaction are still connected, but a crime of the misuse of charity has become a crime of active harming of the poor, 'poisoning' the people to pay for the 'high timbers'. The connections, though powerfully expressed in *Piers Plowman*, were not necessarily original. Earlier in the century the Dominican preacher John Bromyard launched an attack on 'false merchants … who deceived Christ's members … committed theft … by their deceits'.[29] Two centuries earlier, one of the shining lights of monastic reform produced a scorching attack on the conspicuous consumption of the wealthy, an attack that could easily be shifted from the traditionally well-off nobility to the newly affluent merchant:

> The naked cry out; the starving cry out. 'What good to us, toiling miserably in hunger and cold … are all your many changes of raiment spread abroad on your perches, or folded in your portmanteaus? It is our stuff that you are squandering; it is from us that you have cruelly stolen what you expend so inanely'.[30]

When Langland first displayed the merchants, those who 'chosen chaffare' as their vocation in his opening vision of society, and notes ambiguously how 'it semeþ to oure siȝt that swiche men þryueþ' (B.prol.31–2/C.prol.33–4), he could expect his reader to realize that a torrent of fairly brutal criticism was on its way. The very term 'regrator' was already intrinsically bound up with the fate of the poor, and the spiritual fate of those who neglected a duty of care for them.

Indeed, the passage, 'disjointed' though it has seemed to modern editors, was something that Langland chose to elucidate at greater length in the C text (C3.86–114). The added passage continues from the condemnation of merchants who 'tymbred … heigh' and develops Langland's attack into a wider lament for the 'Many sondry sorwes' that have fallen 'in citees … ofte' (C3.90). These 'sorwes' are described as the calamities of 'fuyr' and 'flood' caused by 'fals peple' who 'bygyleth' and 'greueth' the poor (C3.91). The archetypal fallen cities of Sodom and Gomorrah are suggestively hinted at in Langland's assertion that the divine punishment for such moral degradation is the visitation of divine wrath – 'God on hem sendeth / Feuer or fouler euel other fuyr on here houses (C3.95–6) – a wrath that consumes both perpetrator and victim: 'thenne falleth ther fuyr on fals men houses, / And goode mennes for here gultes gloweth on fuyr aftur' (C3.102–3). The indiscriminate effects of fire lead Langland to what seems to be a particular example, strikingly prescient of the great seventeenth-century fire of London, of such divine vengeance for profiteering, involving a 'breware' whose candle caused 'alle þe rewe' (C3.104, 107) to burn down.[31] Langland moves from the

---

[29]   Cited in G. R. Owst, *Literature and Pulpit: A Neglected Chapter in the History of English Letters and of the English People* (Oxford, 1961), p. 300.

[30]   The quotation is from Bernard of Clairvaux's sermons, cited along with Bromyard, in Owst, *Literature and Pulpit*, pp. 300, 304.

[31]   Indeed, the text seems to take a particularly antipathetic stance towards the brewing trade. A brewer reappears towards the end of the poem, castigating Conscience with the

horrific image of 'burgages ybrent and bodies þerynne' (C3.105) back to the cause of such destruction: 'vsurers oþer regraters' who mayors have 'yfranchised' for their 'marchandise' (C3.114, 110). Whilst historians have seen the early fifteenth-century *Liber Albus* as a testimony to conservative anxiety over civic government after the controversy and violence of the Brembre–Northampton years, it seems likely that Langland's 1380s revision of his satire against mayors and regraters was developed in response to just the same milieu.[32]

This portrayal of the regraters and the connotations that surround them is elaborated in a later passage, describing 'Coveitise' and his wife, 'Rose the Regrator' (B5.186–227/C6.196–235). The passage is part of the sequence of 'confessions' of the deadly sins, and introduces 'Coveitise' in a striking sequence of descriptions. He appears 'bitelbrowed and baberlipped, wiþ two blered eiȝen' (B5.188/C6.198), and 'as a bondeman of his bacon his berd was bidraueled' (B5.191).[33] The image of covetousness is one of grotesque physicality, an example of the Rabelaisian corporality that regularly haunts literary depictions of both the urban market and the labouring classes.[34] Here again, the connections between the urban body and the over-consumption of food is apparent, the 'over plentee' that sinks biblical cities into hell reappears. But here the associations are not simply with the consumption of food, but with the buying and selling of it, the 'regrating' with which the victualling trades are so regularly connected. Coveitise is explicitly a merchant, confessing how he 'wente to þe feyre / Wiþ many manere

---

words: 'y wol nat be yruled, / By Iesu! For al ȝoure iangelyng, aftur *Spiritus Iusticie* / Ne aftur Consience, bi Crist! while y can sulle / Bothe dregges and draf and drawe at on hole / Thikke ale or thynne ale; and þat is my kynde' (B19.400–404 / C21.399–403).

[32]   See, for example, Helen Carrel, 'Food, Drink and Public Order in the London *Liber Albus*', *Urban History*, 33:2 (2006), 176–94. Carrel in fact compares the language of the *Liber Albus* with that of *Piers Plowman* in a way that is correlative with my analysis below. Unfortunately, she does not explore the C text additions on civic government and regraters.

[33]   The C text alters the image somewhat. Whilst the B text imagines Coveitise's beard 'bidraueled', 'covered' in bacon 'as a bondman', the C text has 'as a bondemannes bacoun his berd was yshaue' (C6.201). The image is altered by the different verb to focus not on the grease covering the beard, but on the way the beard is cut: hacked unevenly 'like a bondman's bacon'. See Derek Pearsall's gloss in *Piers Plowman – the C-Text* (Exeter, 1978), p. 118, note 201.

[34]   A network of associations existed around the ideas of overconsumption, food markets, and the aural chaos of the market place in poems analogous with *Piers Plowman*. See, for example, the fifteenth-century poem *London Lickpenny*, whose depictions of the urban marketplace are evocative of those at the close of the *Piers Plowman* prologue. The poem is available in *Medieval English Political Writings*, ed. James Dean (Kalamazoo, MI, 1996). The earlier *Wynnere and Wastoure* (*c.* 1351) also depicts Cheap – the part of London we associate with the rotund, Rabelasian shape of Falstaff in Shakespeare's *1 Henry IV* – as synonymous with 'wasting' and 'pies', see Warren Ginsberg, ed., *Wynnere and Wastoure and The Parlement of the Thre Ages* (Kalamazoo, MI, 1992), esp. ll. 474–95.

marchaundise' (B5.201–2/C6.211–12). His confession, rather than being limited to the already problematic practices of 'regratorie' in terms of raising prices by pre-buying large quantities of goods, is a virtual 'conduct book' of commercial deceit. Most significantly, Langland's figures conflate a number of 'tricks of the trade', all of which also surrounded the practice of 'regrating' in the documents of civic government in the period.

Firstly, Coveitise's 'trade' is one of manipulating the apparent weight of food to maximize profit: 'Wikkedly to weye was my firste lesson' (B5.200/C6.210). The manipulation of weights and measures in the trading of food is something whose condemnation can be traced back a long way, and traced forward a long time after the turn of the fourteenth century. The Old Testament commands 'thou shalt have a perfect and just weight, a perfect and just measure' (Deuteronomy 25:15), but as is apparent from the documents of civic courts discussed below, the ethics of trade had changed little between ancient Hebraic society and Langland's contemporary marketplace, and similar imperatives would be used in the mid-sixteenth century. The deliberate manipulation of weights and measures to produce substandard products and maximize profits for the commercial middleman was still in high fashion. Even more appropriate for Coveitise's attachment to the victualling trades is his second activity. He confesses that: 'Ne hadde þe grace of gyle ygo amonges my ware, / It hadde ben vnsold þis seuen yer, so me God helpe!' (B5.203–4/C6.213–14). In a suggestive pun on an expected compounding of 'grace' and 'God', Coveitise tells us that what he was selling was, barring the agency of deception, unsellable. Only through the ethereal, quasi-spiritual presence of 'the grace of guile' amongst his goods could they have possibly been sold. In the context of the regrating of victuals, this is a far more dangerous practice, putting at risk the health, as well as the purse, of the exploited buyer.

Coveitise then relates his move into the draping trade, the learning of his 'Donet', a perverted image of the learning of basic grammar, which he had begun with learning 'a leef ouþer tweyne' (B5.199/C6.209) about commercial malpractice. Amongst the 'riche rayes' being pulled and 'peyned' to yield a higher yield of sellable material, we meet Coveitise's wife: 'Rose þe Regrater' (B5.222/C6.232). Importantly, she is not named at the moment of her appearance in the text. She is simply referred to as 'My wif' (B5.211/C6.221), identified as a cloth worker, and described as manipulating wool so that 'The pound þat she paied by peised a quarter moore' (B5.213/C6.223). Like Coveitise's education in mis-weighing, his wife's trade lies not in the practice of 'England's prime industrial activity', but in the manipulation of it for personal economic gain.[35] But the identification of Coveitise and his wife with the drapers is brief. The next lines describes them working together as a team of regrating 'brewsters', back in the victualling trades: 'I bouȝte hire barly – she brew it to selle' (B5.215/C6.225). The quick switch between different trades serves to suggest the sheer ubiquity of commercial malpractice: whilst 'bakers, brewsters, cokes' might be particularly prone to the

---

[35]   Barron, *London in the Later Middle Ages*, p. 65.

deceptions of regratorie, all trades seem as wrought with deceit and self-interest as each other. As Thomas Brunton, Bishop of Rochester lamented: 'In every craft so much trickery is employed ... that each man strives to deceive his neighbour'.[36] Again, what is described is the victualling equivalent of selling low-quality cloth. Cheap, low-quality beer ('Peny ale') and expensive, luxury product ('puddyng ale') are 'poured togideres' (B5.216/C6.226), the product being presumably sold at the higher price.

Likewise, the profiteering and deception is practised at the cost of the 'labourers' and 'lowe folk' (B5.217/C6.227). This is not likeably ingenious scamming of wealthy and ignorant customers in the manner of Jonsonian comedy, but the deliberate victimization of those with precious little money to spend in the first place.[37] In terms of the symbolic proximity that Langland constantly draws between spiritual integrity and 'lowliness', from the first introduction of Piers to the vision of an impoverished figure entering Jerusalem on Palm Sunday barefoot and 'semblable ... somdeel to Piers þe Plowman' (B18.10/C20.8), the regraters might as well be defrauding Christ.

This deeply unsympathetic representation of the commercial trades is rounded off by the text's carefully planned focus of the term 'regrator' itself. As noted above, 'Rose' is not named when she first appears in the text (B5.211/C6.221). Instead what the reader receives is the accumulative build-up of deceit after deceit, scam after scam, as Coveitise and his wife seem to skip from one trade to another. The delayed naming of Rose is rhetorically very effective. By the time she is identified as 'regrator', as 'holden hukkerye' (B5.222–3/C6.232–3), we have seen not simply the selling of food 'somdel ayeins reson', but a cornucopia of greed, exploitation and malpractice. Consequently, the terms themselves lose any clearly defined sense as either simple descriptive names of 'retail traders', as Schmidt's somewhat bland gloss has it, or as the definition of a particular commercial trick. The vocabulary associates an array of deceptions, manipulations and exploitative tricks with the premeditated deprivation of the poor in a way that far outreaches the eloquent self-aggrandizement of the mendicant friars. The text produces an effect through which the word 'regrator' suddenly seems as if it should be virtually spat out in disgust.

---

[36]   Cited in Owst, *Literature and Pulpit*, p. 353.

[37]   A line of continuity could perhaps be drawn between the alchemical activity of Chaucer's 'Canon's Yeoman's Tale' and Jonson's *The Alchemist*. Apart from the subject matter, both could be argued to depict their swindling protagonists with a certain relish at their intelligence and outrageousness. Langland's depictions of commercial deception clearly strive to avoid such a sympathetic response. What is striking about Langland's descriptions of mercantile corruption is their emphasis on the poor as victims of commercial malpractice. As Jill Mann has argued, it is this concentration on the victim which is curiously lacking from Chaucer's satire, where emotive references to victims are 'conspicuous by their absence'; see Mann, *Chaucer and Medieval Estates Satire*, pp. 100–101.

C. David Benson has argued that passages such as those discussed above are full of 'echoes of city ordinances' – a point to which I turn now – but he also argues that 'despite its exposures of market frauds, *Piers* finds little that is simple or unredeemable in such public commerce'.[38] 'Unredeemable' is something of a slippery word here, especially as it appears during a passage which self-consciously depends upon evocations of the Sacrament of Penance. In such a context, we wouldn't expect Langland to want to make *anything* absolutely 'unredeemable'. What seems more palpable to me, though, is that polemical hostility towards commercial exchange that blurs economic deception with images of the exploitation of the urban poor. This, after all, is the vital literary and cultural mode that Langland's poem shared with civic discourse, and which it bequeathed to the writing of the Reformation.

'The community may be served without regrators': Regraters and Civic Government

Langland's digression on regratrie is made significantly in the context of the duties of civic government. Those responsible for policing the commercial self-interest of the traders are 'Maires and maceres', who hold a vital judicial position 'bitwene / The kyng and the commune to kepe the lawes' (B3.76–7).[39] But whilst the heads of civic government should 'punysshe' them 'on pillories', Langland imagines the mayors taking Judas-like bribes to avoid their duty: 'pieces of siluer, / Rynges or oþer richesse, þe regratiers to mayntene' (B3.89–90).[40] The context of the discussion demonstrates the high level of social realism that exists within Langland's occasionally surreal poem. The deep suspicion with which Langland looks on the victualling trades was similar to the gaze of civic authorities. As R. H. Britnell puts it:

> Upholding justice in urban life implied the regulation of craft activities. Town officers assumed that individual crafts would conspire against the public interest. To bring the various crafts into harmony with each other, and thereby to promote the health of the whole body of a community, was accordingly one of the tasks of government.[41]

---

[38]   Benson, *Public Piers Plowman*, pp. 232, 227.

[39]   The C text has 'ȝut Mede the mayr myldeliche heo bysouhte - / Bothe schyreues and seriauntes and suche as kepeth lawes' (C3.77–8). The satirical target of the following lines is unchanged.

[40]   Again, the C text is altered slightly, and reads: 'and oþer priue ȝeftes, / And haue reuthe on this regraters þat han riche handes' (C3.117–18). C. David Benson discusses the historical 'Cornhill pillory', and its relation to commercial fraud, in *Public Piers Plowman*, pp. 228–45, esp. 231–3.

[41]   Britnell, *The Commercialisation of Society*, p. 173. Caroline Barron similarly writes: 'to ensure an adequate supply of reasonably priced goods (especially food)' was one

The regrater had an important and prolific place in the language of official documentation of civic government. As cities attempted to adjudicate between the power of different social groups, crafts, trades and parties, some groups necessarily appear in court records for transgressing against 'the health of the whole body of the community'. Regraters, especially of foodstuffs, were more likely to be regular, and more literal culprits. At the same time, the increasing financial wealth that was the product of increasingly diversified commercial ventures was what cities depended upon for their power and prestige, and the scores of traders, wholesalers and regraters provided the bulk of the city's governmental class.[42] Whilst the image of the harmonious community driven by a desire for the common good was propounded, the reality of the urban market that produced the money and opportunity that provided such an attraction for immigrants to the city depended inherently on competition, on a network of competing interests.

Paul Strohm's excellent work on civic politics, particularly as they pertain to the writer Thomas Usk, has helped bring the culture of 1380s London to the attention of many medievalists. But while the Brembre–Northampton controversy of the 1380s can be argued to be one of the sharpest points in the history of the politics of trade, food and political control in the city; the problems of economic politics were a constant presence.[43] The competitive presence of 'strange' traders would contribute to the violence of 'evil May Day' in 1517, in which Thomas More played, according to Shakespeare's, Munday's et al.'s play, a heroic role in quelling the unrest. The threat of rioting over the price of food would still influence the reception of Shakespeare's *Julius Caesar* in the late 1590s and of *Coriolanus* in the following decade, and the financial pressures of urban life on the poor would at no time be as anxiously discussed as they were in the Edwardian mid-century.

But the conflicts of the late fourteenth century were even more pressing in the early fifteenth century, when the memory of the Brembre–Northampton controversy was still fresh. The *Liber Albus* (1419), compiled under the eponymous mayoralty of Richard Whittington, the most enduringly famous of the self-made men who dominated London politics, is filled with precautions against the repetition of such

---

of the central roles of civic government; Barron, *London in the Later Middle Ages*, p. 48.

[42] See Barron, 'London 1300–1540' in *The Cambridge Urban History of England*, ed. D. Palliser (Cambridge, 2000), p. 399; and F. R. H. Du Boulay, *The England of Piers Plowman: William Langland and his Vision of the Fourteenth Century* (Cambridge, 1991), p. 62.

[43] For more detailed accounts of the Brembre-Northampton controversy, see R. Bird, *The Turbulent London of Richard II* (London, 1949); Pamela Nightingale, 'Capitalists, Crafts and Constitutional Change in Late Fourteenth-Century London', *Past and Present*, 124 (1989), 3–35; and Paul Strohm, 'Politics and Poetics: Usk and Chaucer in the 1380s' in *Literary Practise and Social Change in Britain, 1380–1530*, ed. Lee Patterson (Berkeley, 1990), pp. 83–112. For a revisionist perspective questioning the often punitive assumptions of scholars working on Usk, see Isabel Davis, *Writing Masculinity in the Later Middle Ages* (Cambridge, 2007), chapter 2.

an upheaval. The text lays down 'precautions against tumults at the election of the mayor' by preventing the 'vast multitude' of partisan activists that had terrified Usk from gathering at the Guildhall for elections.[44] Moreover, following Northampton's campaign against the massive political power of the victualling guilds, the text proclaims that 'Neither Mayor, Sheriff, nor Alderman' (and just about anyone with an official position in the city government, even down to the 'vadlets' – 'valets' – of prison officers at Newgate) 'shall henceforth, either themselves or by others, brew for sale, keep an oven, or let carts for hire; nor shall they be regrators of any provisions, or hucksters of ale, or in partnership with such'.[45] The penalty for refusing to take this particular oath was being stripped of office without hope of return. The 'regrator' reappears, again closely associated with the victualling trades, but after the controversies of the 1380s, worryingly close to the officers of civic government: close enough for an institutional attempt at separating the office of government from the trade of 'regrating'. The connection, however, obviously weighed heavily on the minds of government. Another proclamation demands that no sheriff 'take a fine from bakers or from Brewsters', as 'some persons do say that the assize of bread and of ale is not so well kept, through the taking of fines'.[46] Langland's corrupt mayors, taking bribes to 'the regraters … mayntene' (B3.90) are a nagging presence in the writing of civic government, and as Langland used the term 'regratorie' as a symbolic, pejorative word which encompassed all kinds of activities, the broad anxiety about commerce, honesty, trade and the poor continued in the streams of fifteenth-century legislation regarding trade in London.

The group of commercial ploys with which Langland surrounded the term 'regratorie', as we have seen, are more numerous than the dictionary definition of 'forestalling'. The issues of over-pricing, of manipulating weights and measures, and of selling substandard produce, all reappear in civic legislation in the fourteenth and fifteenth centuries. The connection between regratorie and selling 'ayiens reson' is one that commanded attention not only in localized civic records, but in parliamentary statutes. The group of fourteenth-century statutes usually referred to as the 'Statute of Labourers' contained a chapter dedicated to the subject of food prices. The statute commands that 'Butchers, fishmongers, regrators, hostellers, brewers, bakers, pultors' should 'be bound to sell the same victual for a reasonable price … so that the same sellers have moderate gains, and not excessive'.[47] Langland's comment that regraters sell 'against reason' echoes the language of the institutional document which uses the term 'reasonable prices' repeatedly in opposition to the 'excessive' profiteering that was perceived to be happening in the plague years. The complaints are repeated in the more localized documents of the capital. In 1345 a proclamation was made at the Leaden Hall to

---

44   H. T. Riley, ed. and trans., *Liber Albus: The White Book of The City of London* (London, 1861), p. 17.

45   Riley, *Liber Albus*, p. 41.

46   Riley, *Liber Albus*, p. 235.

47   *Statutes of the Realm*, I. 308.

the effect that regraters of poultry were avoiding the officially defined places and times of trade and were selling their goods 'at extortionate prices ... to the great loss and grievance of the citizens'.[48] In 1363 a proclamation made by the then mayor, Stephen Cavendish, regarding 'the prices of victuals' laid down exact prices for the sale of everything from a hen (4d) to 'the best suckling pig, for 8d'. All food was to be sold 'at a reasonable price, according to its value'.[49] Again, in 1371, as the Peers, Lords and Commons were 'summoned to the parliament of our lord the king, for the common profit of the land', the regraters of London were told that people should 'not be subjected to outrageous demands for the price of victuals', 'that all other victuals in the city shall be sold at a reasonable price'.[50] Again and again, the word 'reasonable' echoes around, presumably receiving very little response from the regraters who might have seen the assembly of wealthy men and women arriving in their streets as a magnificent opportunity to make some money.

'Unreasonable' prices were not the only aspect of Langland's representation of regratorie that reflects wider contemporary concern. Coveitise's training in learning how 'wikkedly to weye' would have kept him in good company in London's regrating community, who were being incessantly caught and punished for abusing the correct 'assize', the correct form and acceptable specification for food sold in the capital, especially bread. In 1316, Godfrey le Rede was tried for selling bread insufficient in weight: 'the penny loaf of light bread of the said Godfrey weighed 15s. and was wanting of its right weight to the amount of 8s'. After denying that he either made or sold the bread, a number of witnesses identified Godfrey as the joint owner of a bakehouse in which such underweight loaves were produced. Like the punishments laid down for mixing the work of regrating and government after 1419, the punishment for a baker making, or anyone selling, food 'weighed wickedly' was not slight. The 'punishment of the hurdle' awaited: a form of secular public penance in which the offending culprit was drawn on a hurdle around the main streets of the city.[51] It is noted that 'he is now so punished for the first time', presumably because it was tacitly expected that it would not be the last time.

The *Liber Albus* includes a categorized scale of punishment for those bakers who produce underweight bread, beginning with the 'hurdle', moving onto the hurdle followed by the pillory, and a final hurdle and the forswearing of the trade of baker if the same individual offended a third time.[52] The harshness of the penalties, and the fact that they were obviously repeated over and over again, suggest both that the matter of correctly weighing food was one that civic government had a continued interest in policing, and that it was a problem that simply could not be

---

[48] H. T. Riley, ed. and trans., *Memorials of London and London Life in the Thirteenth, Fourteenth and Fifteenth Centuries* (London, 1868), p. 220.

[49] Riley, *Memorials*, pp. 312–13.

[50] Riley, *Memorials*, pp. 347–8.

[51] Riley, *Memorials*, p. 119.

[52] Riley, *Liber Albus*, p. 232.

solved. That 'wikked weighing' is the first skill that Langland's Coveitise learns in his striking commercial education is perhaps not entirely accidental.[53]

Finally, the issue of public health is one that repeatedly appears in cases against victuallers and regraters. The image of Langland's regraters 'poisoning' the people 'pryveliche and ofte' (B3.82) is again remarkably prescient. The *Coventry Leet Book* records a proclamation made in 1521 demanding that 'no fyscher of town ner of contrey by no maner of fysche on Thursday over-night by way of regrating' on account of the risk to public health of the sale of 'stynkyng fysche' on the day when the entire population of the city would need to buy it.[54] In London in 1311, a baker was arrested for selling 'putrid bread', because 'the persons eating that bread would be poisoned and choked'.[55] Five years later a regrater and baker were both punished for selling bread that was 'found to be of bad dough within and good dough without'.[56] Clearly the 'grace of guile' resided in the streets of London as well as in the imagination of its poets. In fact, the activities of regraters were seen primarily as a threat to the welfare of other citizens. Whilst the most powerful members of the civic administration might have been victuallers at particular moments, the language of institutional documents constantly shapes these commercial figures as directly assaulting the 'public good', 'the people' and 'the poor', in a way that assumes that commercial self-interest necessarily collides with the natural state of common benefit that exists in the city. Their 'falsity redounds much to the deception of the people', says a London document of 1316. The government of Coventry in 1474 punishes regraters because they 'gretely hurte ... the pore comons'. Overall, the government of any city should ideally be organized 'so the community may be served without regrators'.[57]

Whilst the close contact between civic government and the regraters of victuals in the 1380s and the early fifteenth century seems to suggest that regraters were to be found amongst the highest echelons of urban society, Langland's Coveitise, his beard covered in bacon grease, and appearing 'as a bondeman', may reflect contemporary attitudes towards the trade. Despite the intersection between the victualling trades and the high politics of the Ricardian era, regratorie seems to have had particular connotations in terms of both class and gender. The *Liber Albus*, in its attempt to legislate a divide between governmental officials and regraters, reiterates its command that the two vocations are not to be combined with the words: 'it is forbidden that the Mayor, Sheriffs, Aldermen, or their clerks ... shall trade in any other thing to which a low estimate is attached ... of no manner of

---

53 See also Carrel, 'Food, Drink and Public Order', pp. 188–9.

54 M. D. Harris, ed., *The Coventry Leet Book*, 4 vols in 2 (EETS o.s. 134, 135, vol. 1; 138, 146, vol. 2. London, 1907–1913), I. 25.

55 Riley, *Memorials*, p. 90.

56 Riley, *Memorials*, p. 120.

57 Riley, *Memorials*, p. 120; Harris, *Coventry Leet Book*, I. 401; Riley, *Liber Albus*, p. 239.

victuals or other things shall they be regrators'.[58] The 'brewesters and baksters, bochiers and cokes' that Langland sees 'richen thorugh regratorie' are meant to be of a lower social class than the governmental officials who police their activities. Similarly, 'Rose the regrater' seems to reflect the high proportion of women who earned money as regraters revealed by civic legislation. 'Regratress' is as common a word as 'regrator', and the brewing trade, especially, seems to be commanded by 'brewsters' rather than brewers. For example, legislation regarding the measures of beer and wine, the measures and qualities that Langland's Rose manipulates, sometimes exclusively uses the female pronoun 'she': 'If anyone shall be found selling by a measure not sealed, she shall be amerced … the second time, she shall be amerced … the third time, she shall be amerced'.[59] The 'common forestallers' were 'smaller traders, many of them women, who made a living by buying up small consignments of poultry, rabbits or other foodstuffs on their way to market and retailing them at a profit in the town market'. The regraters were frequently identified not with commercial power but with 'poorer families' working in 'a degrading occupation'.[60] Within the same period, the regrater appears as both an example of the exploitative power of the victualling trades, and as an image of the least 'respectable' member of a city's population.

The figure of the regrater therefore holds a paradoxical place in both *Piers Plowman* and the discourse of civic government. In a manner similar to that which Paul Freedman has demonstrated in representations of the medieval peasant, the regrater has the very worst of both rhetorical worlds. In terms of worldly status the regrater is belittled as 'common', smeared with grease 'as a bondeman' (B5.191) in the familiar imagery of grotesquery associated with the agricultural labourer, now transferred to the small-scale selling of bread, meat, beer and fish.[61] At the same time, their commercial activities resulted in them being characterized as the grasping victimizer of the 'genuine' poor. The 'poor' works as a vague and idealized category into which all the alternative associations of the medieval peasant, the quasi-biblical simplicity, the peasant as deservingly Christian recipient of alms, were shifted. The regraters, denied access to the world of civic government in which their wealthier fellows thrived, were simultaneously denied access to the world of symbolic integrity and ready charity in which the citizens who bought their (admittedly rather suspicious) goods resided.

The discourse of civic government, then, was wrought with the political entanglements between victuallers, regraters and the trades 'of low estimate' that were most regularly associated with them. Yet, at the same time, this discourse constructed itself as a kind of neutral and disinterested arbiter, a paternal carer of 'the people' variously defined as the 'community', the 'poor commons', or 'the

---

[58] Riley, *Liber Albus*, pp. 237–8.

[59] Riley, *Liber Albus*, pp. 232–3.

[60] Britnell, *Commercialisation*, p. 165.

[61] For a discussion of 'Rabelaisian' representations of the medieval peasant see Freedman, *Images*, esp. pp. 140–57.

citizens'. This category, especially when defined as 'the poor', was only partially an empirical description of those individuals who lived in material poverty.[62] More significantly, it was a malleable rhetorical construction, working here as a projection of a 'public sphere', an idea of the civic 'common good' which was defined in opposition to the commercial interests of particular parties.[63] This conception of the public sphere, apparent in both Langland's *Piers Plowman* and the discourse of medieval civic government, was increasingly important in the sixteenth century. After a long history it was appropriated and reconfigured in the new synthesis of economic complaint, urban satire and religious polemic that stood at the centre of the literature of the Reformation.

Commonwealth and Commodity, Commercialism and Complaint

If scholars of Renaissance English literature think of the mid-Tudor period it is probably fair to say that Richard Tottell's *Songs and Sonnets* (1557), the verse miscellany that first brought Wyatt and Surrey to the attention of a wide audience in print, is one of the few things that comes to mind. But on the heels of 'Tottell's Miscellany' might also come the term 'Commonwealth-men' – the sobriquet used by R. H. Tawney to describe a group of writers in the 1540s and 1550s who could be described as almost proto-socialist figures, who were given the name by their political enemies for 'their advocacy of social reconstruction', 'the group of which Latimer was the prophet and Hales the man of action naturally incurred the charge of stirring up class-hatred, which is normally brought against all who call attention to its causes'.[64] Later historians, particularly G. R. Elton, had particular problems with Tawney's formulation, but this 'group', if indeed it was one, did after all

---

[62]   Such an apparently simple descriptive use was itself somewhat complicated by the realities of economic life for many. The 'urban poor' were not only the truly indigent, but could also include house-holding families who seemed financially independent in times of commercial health. Sudden movements in particular markets and especially in the price of food could throw many people not traditionally categorized as 'poor' into dependence on private or civic charity, or into serious debt; see C. R. Friedrichs, *The Early Modern City, 1450–1750* (London, 1995), p. 215.

[63]   The development of 'common profit' as a major presence in fifteenth-century literary culture is suggested by D. Lawton, 'Dullness in the Fifteenth-Century', *English Literary History*, 54 (1987), 761–90, and earlier by A. Middleton, 'The Idea of Public Poetry in the Reign of Richard II', *Speculum*, 53 (1978), 94–114. This broad literary tradition is surely important in the development of late medieval literary culture, but is perhaps defined almost too broadly. The idea of 'common good', and indeed of the 'public sphere' described above, seems more closely interlinked with economic issues and the institutional discourse of urban government than the authorial position described by Lawton and Middleton. Moreover, especially after the Reformation, it takes on the highly polemical form of Protestant ideas of 'Godly communities', as well as the secular civic community.

[64]   Tawney, *Religion and the Rise of Capitalism*, p. 137.

include men involved with supporting and even implementing a contentious and even dangerous reformist initiative in 1548–1549 – the Royal Enclosure Commission.[65] It is also frequently used to describe one of the most prolific writers of verse fiction in the mid-century: Robert Crowley. It is therefore not a huge surprise to see Crowley's interest being raised by the particularly economic preoccupations of *Piers Plowman* (see Figure 1.1).

In his editions of *Piers Plowman*, next to Langland's passage on regratorie – 'Thei richen þorugh regratrie and rentes hem biggen / With that the pouere peple sholde putte in hire wombe' – Robert Crowley printed the marginal comment 'What harm yll vitaillers do & what abuseis in regrating' (sig. D1r).[66] Crowley's marginal additions, as I argue in Chapter 3, are often of a less polemical nature than they are of a utilitarian one, providing brief notes regarding the figures and narrative of Langland's text in an effort to produce a readable version of a vernacular literary-cultural classic.[67] However, any paratextual guidance for the reader, however seemingly innocuous and free of intrusive appropriative intent, is often necessarily interpretative. The editor's decision to annotate particular passages at the expense of others assumes a judgement about the comparative significance and importance of different parts of the text; a judgement that always tacitly supports the editor's reaction to the text, a reaction formed by the particular interests and priorities of the person in control of presenting the text to an unseen, un-consulted reader.

For example, 'The image of couetise' (sig. F4v) seems to simply inform the reader of what is happening in the text at the appropriate point, which is indeed an 'image' or written portrait of the figure 'Coveitise'. But the very existence of an annotation demonstrates the importance of Crowley's involvement with the specifically economic preoccupations of Langland's anti-urban satire. Likewise, Crowley's comment on regrating blurs the narrow line between practical reference guide and interpretative guidance. It signifies a deeply felt sympathy on Crowley's part with *Piers Plowman*'s depictions of commercialism, exploitation and impoverishment in the urban marketplace. It is this construction, in reconfigured

---

[65] The commission is discussed in Andy Wood's excellent *The 1549 Rebellions and the Making of Early Modern England*, pp. 38–9. Wood also discusses the commonwealth writers, including Crowley, and argues, counter to Elton, that 'Although it is difficult to establish a direct causal link between this literary genre and Edwardian policy, the similarities between the two in both form and language are unmistakable. In this context it seems perverse to deny a link between the commonwealth writers and Protector Somerset's social policies: the one laid the intellectual ground for the other' (p. 38). See also Betteridge, *Literature and Politics in the English Reformation*, p. 90.

[66] Robert Crowley, ed., *The Vision of Piers Plowman* (London, 1550).

[67] See also R. Carter Hailey, '"Geuyng light to the Reader": Robert Crowley's Editions of *Piers Plowman* (1550)', *Publications of the Bibliographic Society of America*, 95:4 (2001), 483–502; Larry Scanlon, 'Langland, Apocalypse and the Early Modern Editor' in *Reading the Medieval in Early Modern England*, eds Gordon McMullan and David Matthews (Cambridge, 2007), pp. 51–73.

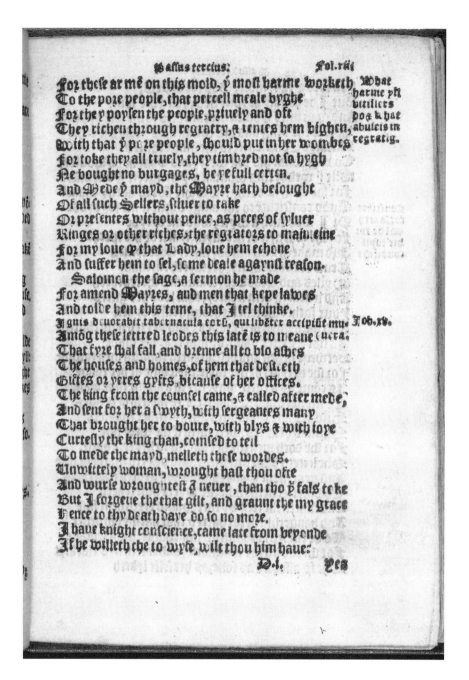

Figure 1.1   Robert Crowley, ed., *The Vision of Piers Plowman* (London: Robert Crowley, 1550), sig. D1r. © The British Library Board.

form, that pervades sixteenth-century polemical writing. Protestant polemics display a particular synthesis of doctrinal and economic complaint that is heavily influenced by *Piers Plowman*. Whilst the ploughman texts discussed in Chapter 3 concentrate on the predominantly rural problems of enclosure, the engrossment of farming, and the distribution of land following the dissolution of the monasteries, the texts under consideration here foregrounded images of commercial exploitation and deceit in the urban marketplace as a central part of reformist discourse. Commonwealth writers, of course, had access to other formulations of the city – the polemical address of the Old Testament prophetic books and Petrarch's anti-Avignon, 'Babylonian' *Canzoniere* both come to mind – but *Piers Plowman* provided an equally important, and more economically specific, model. Langlandian topoi of the urban landscape provided a rhetoric and imagery which the Protestant reformers, especially in the Edwardian period, took up and reconfigured as a distinctively Protestant analysis of the state of the realm.

In 1546, barely a year before the death of Henry VIII, an anonymous text appeared in print called *The Supplication of the Pore Commons*. A potential buyer of the text was tempted doubly by not one, but two such works: 'whereunto is added the Supplication of Beggers'.[68] The volume may, possibly, have been produced with the help of Crowley.[69] The printer connected the contemporary text with the founding father of its genre which had appeared nearly two decades before, producing the outlines of a polemical tradition in one volume.[70] Simon Fish's *Supplication of the Beggers* (1529) was, barring *Rede me and be not wroth* (1528), the first discernibly Protestant text printed in English, and served as an archetype for the polemical reformist tradition of writing that followed it, including the group of ploughman polemics discussed in Chapter 3. As I argue in Chapter 2, the form of polemical pastoralism that characterized early Protestant self-fashioning made 'beggars', 'poor men' and 'ploughmen' analogous, and powerful, figures of Protestant self-understanding and self-representation.

Whilst some of the major polemical points raised by these supplication texts were directed towards anticlericalism and doctrinal reformation, they were

---

[68] *The Supplication of the Pore Commons* (1546), all quotations are from the readily available text in *Four Supplications, 1529–1553*, eds F. J. Furnivall and J. Meadows Cowper (EETS e.s. 13, London, 1871), pp. 60–92, apart from this title page comment. The EETS volume unfortunately omits it, effacing the fact that the later text was deliberately printed as a 'compilation' of supplication texts.

[69] See King, *Reformation Literature*, pp. 473–7, 475. There is little definite evidence for Crowley's involvement. Nevertheless, Crowley was surely well-read in the polemical material of the 1540s. One of his later printed works in verse, *The Opening of the Wordes of the Prophet Joell* (1567), *STC* 6089 actually claims on the title page to have been written in 1546, and the first text which identifies itself as by Crowley is *The Confutation of the Mishapen Aunswer to the Ballade, called the Abuse of the blessed sacrament* (1548), *STC* 6082.

[70] On the importance of Fish's text for the complaint tradition, see Wendy Scase, *Literature and Complaint in England*, pp. 149–56, esp. 151.

frequently, as in this case, addressed directly to the king. The *Supplication* ends with a daringly imperative passage addressed to the aged monarch: 'Remember that you shal not leave this kyngdome to a straunger ... empty your study to leave hym a commune weale to governe, and not an island of brut beastes ... loke after the crowne of this realme after your daies' (pp. 81–2). Two things are striking about the stance taken towards the text's recipient here. One could be said to be the sheer bravery of it: reminding a man like Henry VIII that he was not only mortal, but was at risk of reducing the land to a state of 'brute beasts', was perhaps rather courageous. However, the impulse to advise and educate contemporary government can be linked to the long tradition of 'Speculum Principum' texts which stretched from the pseudo-Aristotelian *Secretum Secretorum*, through such texts as Gower's *Confessio Amantis* (*c*. 1390–1392) and Hoccleve's *Regiment of Princes* (*c*. 1411), and into the sixteenth century, affecting such texts as Erasmus' *Institutio Principis Christiani* (1516) and the opening books of Spenser's *Faerie Queene* (1590–1596).[71]

The addressing of reformist advice directly to a member of the ruling elite cannot be said to be an entirely new phenomenon, but it is one which was newly invigorated by the intersection of the 'civic' humanism that dominated Thomas More's *Utopia*, and the political consciousness of the 'new religion'. What is important for our purposes is the central concern for the state, and the writer's role in this state. It is the 'kingdom', the 'realme', the 'common weale' that concerns the polemicist. The writer draws a line between the state of the country as it is, or is likely to become in the image of the 'brute beastes', but constantly draws attention to what the country should be, an idealized political community. Likewise, the writer speaks not as one of the people who are currently bestialized through lack of good government, and not in the official capacity of an adviser to the monarch. Instead he creates for himself a space 'in between' the people and king, much in the way that Langland sees mayors 'between king and people'. As Thomas Betteridge has argued, it is this stance which defines the Tudor public sphere; the 'strong' public capable of influencing and debating religious politics.[72]

Not only was the Edwardian reformer living in a city whose physical form was to some extent shaped by the medieval city, he was also living with economic problems that were all too familiar to a reader of *Piers Plowman*.[73] Moreover, the familiar problems appeared even worse when it was considered that a Reformation

---

[71]   For a detailed account of this tradition, see Judith Ferster, *Fictions of Advice: The Literature and Politics of Counsel in Late Medieval England* (Philadelphia, 1996). Similarly, the address shapes the text as a version of the judicial supplication genre described by Wendy Scase in *Literature and Complaint.*

[72]   See Thomas Betteridge, *Tudor Histories of the English Reformations, 1530–1583* (Aldershot, 1999), esp. p. 30.

[73]   On the 'historic' nature of London's topography, see for example Peter Borsay, 'Early Modern Urban Landscapes, 1540–1800' in *The English Urban Landscape*, ed. P. Waller (Oxford, 2000), pp. 99–124: 'The Tudor citizen lived in an essentially medieval

effected in the previous generation, promising the spiritual rejuvenation of Christian society, seemed to have had no effect on the economic individualism which threatened to erode the foundations of the 'godly commonwealth'. 'With a reformation in religion should come a reformation in morals' was the watchword of Edwardian writing.[74] But in economic terms, the years when the Reformation seemed to have come to fruition were also years of a now notorious set of circumstances. Between 1544 and 1551, prices in London rose by a staggering 89 per cent, and the rate of inflation, driven on by the government's repeated debasements of the coinage, ran at about 21 per cent per year between 1549 and 1551. Harvests failed terribly in 1550 and, in the following year, the price of flour doubled. Necessarily, the assize and quality of food, especially that food the poorer citizens of London depended on, deteriorated drastically.[75] To make things worse, the population of the city itself was finally beginning to rise towards pre-1348 levels, and the expansion in population meant more pressure on the economic structures which civic government had done so much work to protect. As Caroline Barron puts it:

> Much of civic regulation was aimed at excluding the middleman and bringing the producer into direct contact with the consumer. In the medieval period, when London was comparatively small, this was a reasonable goal, but as the city quadrupled in size in the sixteenth century the role of the middleman developed to meet the logistical problems of getting the supplies into the city, and this, inevitably, contributed to the rise in prices.[76]

The Langlandian figures of economic self-interest and commercial guile, those who 'richen thorugh regratorie' at the expense of the poor, who sell 'somdel ayeins reson', would not be waved aside as being signs of a quaint 'antiquity' in such a context. They would become highly relevant, pressing models on which to base new observations, made sharper by the fact that the intervening doctrinal upheaval

---

town; and in some respects and in some places, the same could still be argued for his Georgian successor' (p. 99).

[74] Susan Brigden, *London and the Reformation* (Oxford, 1989), p. 471.

[75] Brigden, *London and the Reformation*, p. 476. Significantly, it is the 'halfpenny loaf', the type of bread which so often appears in the medieval court record as the subject of commercial deception, which Brigden singles out as being particularly altered by the economic situation.

[76] Barron, *London in the Later Middle Ages*, p. 58. Another factor in the perception of growing economic abuses is to be found in the civic legislation itself, which 'could not distinguish between monopoly and scarcity as the reason for high prices'. A situation of dearth and high prices was likely to result in the sharpening of scrutiny towards mercantile practices, whether they were a direct cause of the problems or not; see Britnell, *Commercialisation*, p. 174.

had not had the least effect on the culture of 'commodity' that threatened the Christian character of society.

Crowley's marginal annotation about 'abuses in regrating' in his editions of *Piers Plowman* was the tip of a mountainous polemical iceberg. 'Regrators', 'forestallers', the commercial middlemen who drove prices higher when the average buyer could afford less and less, were a constant target for Crowley's invectives about the state of England. *One and Thirty Epigrams* (1550), a text which is ostensibly encyclopaedic, treating a vast range of issues alphabetically, in fact returns to economic issues more often than the one entry on 'Forestallers' suggests. For example, a whole section is dedicated to a character named 'the Colier of Croydon'.[77] In a notably fictional figure, Crowley focuses on the tradesman from the perspective of his prices: 'A lode that of late yeres / for a royall was solde, / wyll coste now xvi. S' (20.501–3). The increase in prices of 'nedeful things', here fuel, is linked with an analysis of social mobility. The seller of coal has become so wealthy that he has literally jumped classes, reaching the status, financially at least, of a member of the nobility. Crowley narrates that 'For his riches thys Colier / might haue bene a knight' (20.485–6). In a kind of 'aside', Crowley underlines the importance of traditional estate categories by inverting the two figures, asserting the importance of separation between knight and Collier; though he had the financial status of a knight, the Collier had no interest in 'knyghtyng', and likewise, Crowley notes, we would prefer it if 'all our knightes / dyd minde colinge no more' (20.489–90). From an observation about the unsettling wealth of a traditionally poorly paid profession, Crowley turns the figures into an image of societal status easily traversed with the passport of wealth. Colliers are rich enough to be knights, and knights aware enough of the financial benefits of selling coal to view it as a potentially acceptable vocation.

Differences between vocations and the cultures that traditionally accompany them are suddenly and dramatically effaced with the power of money. In the past, Crowley notes, 'pore Coliers' sold their goods 'At a reasonable price' (20.493, 495). Massive price increases are analysed as the product of a dangerous and novel social aspiration. In his simultaneous concern about rising prices and social mobility, Crowley reiterates a civic anxiety about the same issue which surfaced in the mid-fourteenth century. The figure of the Collier gives fictional life to the two main tenets of the *Statutes of Labourers*: that, as Crowley repeats incessantly, every worker should stay in his 'vocation', and that the price of essential goods should be 'reasonable'. The failure of these policies is manifest in the 'Colier of Croydon', a figure who 'men thyncke … is cosen / to the Colyar of Hell' (20.511–12). The merchant selling overpriced coal in London is analogous to a bizarre figure who keeps the fires of hell burning.

---

[77]   All references to Crowley's texts apart from *Philargyrie of Greate Britain* are from *The Select Works of Robert Crowley*, ed. J. M. Cowper (EETS e.s. 15, London, 1872), by page and line number.

The 'Colier of Croydon' is itself a reworking of the collier who appears in Crowley's *The Voyce of the Last Trumpet* (1549), in a passage named 'The merchant's lesson'. All those who 'bie and sell' are commanded to ply their trade for the 'commonwealth': 'to maintaine the publike state', 'To profit thy countrey' (86.1027, 1029). Commercialism must serve the 'common profit', not the reverse, and the common profit required commercial interests to bow before the imperative to be charitable. When selling 'thynges profitable', Crowley advises, to avoid divine judgement, the merchant must 'Let pore men haue them at thine handes / Upon a price reasonable' (86.1034–6).

The threat of divine judgement haunts Crowley's regraters, culminating in the remarkable passage cited at the head of this chapter. In *Epigrams*, Crowley dedicates a section to 'forestallers', concentrating at first on the strict definition of the term in the commerce of wool and grain. 'Some saye', Crowley notes, 'the woule / is bought ere it do growe, / And the corne long before / it come to the mowe' (33.941–4). In such a situation, there can be no contact between producer and consumer, the commercial interests of the middleman dictates the availability and price of anything being traded. Crowley sweeps through the commercial trades, noting the financial self-interest and detrimental effects of people trading in everything from wool and corn to farms and clerical benefices, but returns always, as Langland had done, to the trade in 'needful things', and the effect of rising prices on the poor. After the long list of goods, buildings and positions being exchanged, Crowley centres on the image of a generational divide in the prices paid in terms of rent, of a father who 'payde a peny, / and a capon or twayne' to his son, who 'muste paye ten pownde'. The rise in prices of things which are not luxuries, which make up the necessary, habitual financial life of the average citizen, says Crowley, 'passeth my brayne' (34.961–4).

This is, as with Langland, much more than a nostalgic gripe about the rising cost of living: it is the condemnation of a commercialism that transgresses basic Christian duties. Unless the 'forestallers', the rent-racking, over-charging regraters 'repent them bytyme', the 'clarke of the market' promises to appear and 'punysh them all' (34.966, 970). In a striking image, Crowley imagines the moment of judgement, the end and culmination of history, as the arrival of a kind of civic official to adjudicate over the commercial practices of the marketplace. The threat comes with the identification of a previous moment in God's intervention in economic politics: 'when he went laste awaye, / He sent vs his seruaunt, / And thus dyd he saye' (34.974–6). What the servant said was a metrical, rhymed version of 1 Corinthians 10:24 ('Let no man seek his own, but every man another's wealth'): 'Se that emong you / None seke his owne gayne, / But profyte ech other / With trauayle and payne' (34.977–80). Crowley clearly read the Pauline epistles, as well as *Piers Plowman*, with an eye to the relevance of texts for the reform of economic, as well as spiritual, ethics.

Crowley was not alone in his concentration on the threats of commercialism to the newly reformed commonwealth. Henry Brinklow similarly condemned the 'ratyng of vytellys, which is most grevious euyn to the poore sort', and like

Langland linked 'regratorie' to 'rentes' in his analysis of the economics of the 1540s:

> In London and other placys ther be many offended with the great price of vitells, but fewe men consider the grownd and original occasion therof; that it is only by enhancing of rentys, fynes, &ce., that maketh all things dere, which is an urgent damage to the commonwelth.[78]

Commercial 'coveitise' was seen to have a 'trickle-down' effect: the greed of one merchant led to the greed of another, until the commonwealth risked collapse. As Thomas Becon put it, 'whyle they study for their owne priuate commodite, the common weale is lyke to decay'.[79] Brinklow bunched together the villains of agrarian complaint, the 'inclosers … grossers up of fermys' with the 'extorcyonars' (48–9) who commanded the urban marketplace charging 'unreasonable' prices for basic food and fuel. Crowley's vision of the collier in *The Voyce of the Last Trumpet* made a similar point: the collier's defence of his high prices came from the assertion that he in turn was paying over the odds from other merchants who kept the whole trade 'in fere' (88.1092). Similarly, William Forest complained that 'In tyme of plenty the riche too upp mucker / Corne, Grayne, or Chefre hopinge upon dearth'.[80] The effect was felt much further down the social scale when food prices were so high that 'scarce the pooreman can bye a morsall' (l. 378). Again, the demand came for commerce to be driven less for 'pryuate wealthe' and more for the good of the community, and the marketplace controlled by the imperative to Charity. The vocation of a regrater was 'too helpe the poore for a reasonable pryce' (l. 105), not to force the poor into further penury.

Whilst the more radical calls for the reform of the clergy were, of course, a mainstay of Edwardian polemic, it was the issue of economic ethics, of food prices, 'covertise', charity and the dangers of regratorie, that formed a central part of these texts. Whether, as Elton put it, their economic analysis was 'half-baked'

---

[78]   J. Meadows Cowper, ed., *Henry Brinklow's Complaint of Roderyck Mors* (EETS e.s. 22, London, 1874), pp. 13, 19. Brinklow was actually a Henrician writer, and the *Complaint* first printed in 1542, necessarily abroad, at Strasbourg, with the imprint 'savoye: per Fransicum de Turona (probably Wolfgang Kopfel), *STC* 3759.5. Its significance and popularity in the Edwardian years is witnessed by its reprinting, in London, twice in 1548 (*STC* 3760–1), although it again had a false imprint: 'at Geneve in Savoye by Myghell boys'. The printers were most likely Anthony Scoloker and William Seres.

[79]   Thomas Becon, *The Jewel of Joy*, extract in *England in the Reign of King Henry the Eighth*, ed. S. J. Herrtage (EETS e.s. 32, London, 1871–1878), pp. lxxvi lxxvii, lxxvi.

[80]   Sir William Forest, *A Pleasaunt Poesye of Princelie Practise* (1548), an extract of which is in *England in the Reign of King Henry the Eighth*, ed. Herrtage, pp. lxxix–xcix, lines 92–3. Forest's text is extant only in British Library MS Royal 17. D. 3, a manuscript dedicated to Protector Somerset in 1548. Line references are to the extract in Herrtage's volume.

or not is to some extent beside the point.[81] The commonwealth-men focused a great deal of Edwardian Protestant discourse around precisely the problems of economic ethics which Langland had found so arresting. Their grim descriptions of urban poverty and economic exploitation are the sixteenth-century offspring of Langland's anti-urban satire.

As Langland had placed his narrator 'in Cornehull' (C5.2), the commonwealth-men centred themselves on an attack on London itself, in comparison to an idealized godly commonwealth which harboured deep sympathies with the stability and integrity that shaped Langland's ideology of rurality. Time and time again, the reformers addressed their polemics not simply to the king, but directly to the capital. Brinklow's *Lamentation of a Christen Agaynst the Cytye of London* (1545) rounded on 'these inordinate riche styfnecked cytezens' and asked 'oh lorde God, how is it possible for this cytie to expulse vice and seke after vertue'.[82] Hugh Latimer directed his now famous 'sermon of the plough' to the 'ryche citizens of London', the preacher's command being 'Repente O London'.[83] Crowley repeatedly referred his texts directly to the capital, calling for the moral reform of a place he characterized somewhat brutally as 'An hell with out order / I may it well call / where everye man is for hum selfe / And no mane for all'. To Crowley, the reformation of the nation was the reformation of the capital, which could be described, with a Langlandian turn of phrase, as: 'a citye in name, but in dede, / It is a packe of people that seke after meede'.[84] As Lawrence Manley has written, the prevalence of London as the centre of address for these mid-century polemics:

> bears witness to the power of the marketplace to extend its reach from London to the remotest corners of the realm, and to reconstellate the countryside and its population around the new magnetism of the capital.[85]

As the power and importance of London rose, so also did its population, and the attendant problems of supplying necessary goods at 'reasonable' prices, and in economic circumstances as dire as those in the mid-sixteenth century, the topoi of commercial complaint inherited from a medieval tradition would necessarily

---

[81] Elton, 'Reform and the "Commonwealths-men" of Edward VI's Reign', p. 37. For a counter to Elton's view, see Betteridge, *Literature and Politics in the English Reformation*, p. 90.

[82] The *Lamentation* is printed in *Henry Brinklow's Complaint of Roderyck Mors*, ed. Meadows Cowper, pp. 79–120, 79–80.

[83] John Chandos, ed., *In God's Name: Examples of Preaching in England from the Act of Supremacy to the Act of Uniformity, 1534–1662* (London, 1971), pp. 12–15, 12. See also R. L. Kelly's essay 'Hugh Latimer as Piers Plowman', *Studies in English Literature*, 17 (1977), 13–26.

[84] Crowley, *Epigrams* in *The Select Works of Robert Crowley*, pp. 9–11.

[85] L. Manley, *Literature and Culture in Early Modern London* (Cambridge, 1995), p. 100.

become sharper and more pressing. London in Edwardian reformist discourse becomes a more foregrounded and particularized version of Langland's vision of the urban world. The problems of deceit, commercialism and the deprivation of the poor were no longer issues solely of civic government or of an imagined Christian community based around allegorical visions of the 'barn of unity'. The figures of the extortionate regrating were now the dark shadows of a more centralized nation, for which the capital itself had become symbolic, a city which 'stood for' the moral and spiritual condition of the commonwealth as a whole.

This symbolic aspect of the city in the Edwardian imagination led to an outpouring of images correlating the contemporary city of London with the fallen cities of biblical history and prophecy. 'Gospellers' as they were, writers such as Crowley and Brinklow quickly saw the polemical potential for using biblical analogies to make their reformist points. Crowley's image of the city as 'hell' was swiftly identified with biblical types, and the polemical writer with Old Testament voices such as 'Ionas to the Niniuits' and 'Daniel to the Babilonians' (159). Latimer similarly appropriated the Jeremiad form and the biblical city topos to shout from the pulpit: 'oh London London, repente repente, for I thynke God is more displeased with London than ever he was with the city of Nebo'.[86] But the most striking aspect of these sixteenth-century polemics is the proximity of their concerns and their imaginative constructions of the urban world and its significance to those found in *Piers Plowman*. The Langlandian mode of anti-urban satire had been taken up and reconfigured in a highly controversial literary culture – one which placed the sixteenth-century equivalent of 'Rose of the Regrater' and her husband 'Coveitise' at the centre of their calls for moral and doctrinal reformation.

The importance of *Piers Plowman* in the formation of the Edwardian literary imagination can be seen in action in what is now Robert Crowley's best known work: *Philargyrie of Greate Britayne* (1551). Crowley's text was published in the year after his multiple editions of *Piers Plowman*, and is clearly indebted to the close knowledge of Langland's text that Crowley accumulated in the process of annotating, setting and publishing the three imprints in the previous months. The status of *Philargyrie* as 'Crowley's masterpiece' has recently been reinforced, albeit briefly, by James Simpson's assessment of the text as 'moving and intelligent', and it is certainly high time that the reputation of a writer John King viewed as 'the most significant poet between Surrey and Gascoigne' was reassessed.[87] However, what is important here is to explore the indebtedness of *Philargyrie* to *Piers Plowman*, especially considering the proximity between the

---

[86]   Chandos, *In God's Name*, p. 13.

[87]   John N. King, ed., 'Philargyrie of Greate Britayne by Robert Crowley', *English Literary Renaissance*, 10 (1980), 46–75, 51. References to the text are to King's edition provided in this article, as Cowper's *Select Works* oddly does not include it. See also King, *Reformation Literature*, pp. 319–57, 320, and Simpson, *Reform and Cultural Revolution*, p. 382. Crowley's text unfortunately receives no sustained treatment in Simpson's work. The text is similarly highly rated by Betteridge as 'an exemplary mid-Tudor history of the

two texts in Crowley's career, as it seems very likely that Crowley was working on his editions of Langland's text until within a few months of writing, or at least publishing, his own reformist 'fable'.

The indebtedness of *Philargyrie* to *Piers Plowman* is repeatedly noted by the foremost scholar of Crowley's work: John N. King. He notes that 'Crowley modelled it and his related series of verse satires on *Piers Plowman*', and that Crowley's writing is influenced by what he calls the 'prophetic estates satire' of Langland's text.[88] This is surely an acute observation, but the specific aspects of Langland's text which are most influential are perhaps different to those that King suggests. He writes that 'The history of the gold-eating giant Philargyrie runs parallel to that of Lady Meed, the figure Langland employs to personify avarice and bribery'.[89] The Langlandian archetype of Lady Meed is indeed a vital one, but the concentration on Meed unfortunately veils the importance of other pressing correspondences between the texts which suggest that other figures from *Piers Plowman* also have a formative role in Crowley's satire. It is in fact Langland's 'Hunger' that seems to have grasped Crowley's imagination in the creation of Philargyrie. In the emphasis on the figure's insatiable greed, and the image of greed as gastronomic excess, as the act of over-eating, Crowley constructs 'careful Covetise', 'the rote of al mischife', by associating it with an economic anxiety about food. Moreover, in the images of casual and extreme violence that characterize Crowley's figure, Langland's Hunger is again echoed. But Crowley, in line with the writings of the commonwealth-men more generally, reconfigures the significance of Langland's text. When Hunger appears in *Piers Plowman*, it is in the context of the discourse about rural labour in a time of massively depleted population following the Black Death. Crowley's version, however, turns the figure into a characteristically Edwardian indictment of urban economic corruption.

The frontispiece of Crowley's text shows a figure wearing what seems to be the clothing of an Edwardian nobleman, using a bible to sweep coins into a sack. Under the illustration is a vernacular, rhymed version of 1 Timothy 6:10, 'The rote of al mischief that ever dyd spring / Is careful Couetise, & gredy Gathering' (p. 46).

The 'deadly sin' that is destroying the possibilities for reformation in 1551 is the husband of 'Rose the Regrator': 'Coveitise'. But whilst the giant Philargyrie roams the country, it is the explicitly urban figures of his lieutenants 'Hypocrisy' and 'Philaut' who supply him with a swiftly deteriorating source of money.

The preface to *Philargyrie* demonstrates how strong the correspondences between Crowley's editions of *Piers Plowman* and his own work are. The early Protestants were notoriously cagey about the ethics of writing fiction, but Crowley makes a case for his own writing in terms that are strikingly congruent with the

---

process of reformation'; Betteridge, *Tudor Histories of the English Reformations*, p. 1. See also his discussion in *Literature and Politics in the English Reformation*, pp. 110–12.

[88]   King, 'Philargyrie', p. 47; *Reformation Literature*, p. 340.

[89]   King, ed., 'Philargyrie', p. 50.

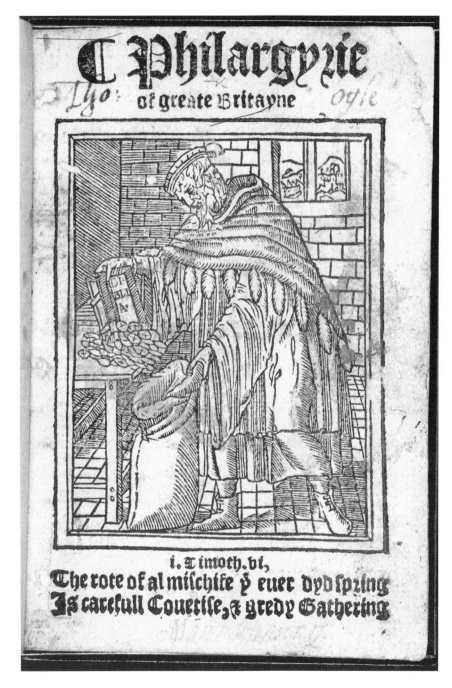

Figure 1.2   Title page of Robert Crowley, *The Philargyrie of greate Britayne*
(London: Robert Crowley, 1551). © The British Library Board.

'version' of Langland's poetics that he constructed in the prefaces to his editions of *Piers Plowman*.

'If', Crowley states, poets can write, 'feyneying of fables greate Vices to blame / And if they be blamelesse although they do hytt ... / Then maye I by right (me thyncke) do the same' (ll. 1–5). The self-justification is wrought with doubts and qualifications magnified by the repeated 'ifs', the bracketed 'opinion', and the separated categorization of 'poets' from Crowley himself as a writer. But the confession that he has 'feyned and written a lye' (l. 8) is ultimately justified not by Crowley's nervous rhetoric, but by the fact that his 'fable' is actually not a 'fable', but a reality. Crowley almost wishes, he says, that his 'lye' was more 'lowde' than it was, as the reality is that 'thys Gigant greate Philargyrie / Is present in greate Brytayne even euery where' (ll. 10–11). Crowley allows himself to write fictional narrative verse because it is, he asserts, only pretending to be pretence, it is mimetic but has been forced into an assertion of complete realism. This rather uncomfortable contortion is exactly what was used to justify and defend the publication of *Piers Plowman* the year before.

Langland, Crowley had stated, inspired by the same divine enlightenment that set Wycliffe apart from his contemporaries, 'in reportynge certayne visions and dreames, that he fayned hymselfe to haue dreamed, doth most Christianly enstructe the weake, and sharplye rebuke the obstinate blynde' (sig. *2r). The dream vision genre, what could be viewed as the aspect of Langland's text that forms it as 'lye' rather than 'truth', is actually itself a 'fayned' thing, in the sense that the sole purpose of the text, at least in Crowley's eyes, is essentially didactic, in the same way that a guide to Christian life could be categorized as didactic. Langland's purpose is always the 'amendement of mysses', not the 'wondres' that seem to be promised by a visionary literary structure (sig. *3v). It is the reality of moral corruption, of social sin, which justifies and prescribes the only acceptable form of literature. When Crowley makes reference to 'poetes' who 'In feyening of Fables greate Vices ... blame', William Langland (or Robert Langland, as Crowley knew him) must have been foremost in his mind. The Edwardian reformer's foray into literary fable was justified by the exemplary predecessor that he had edited so recently.

At the centre of Crowley's text lies the giant 'Philargyrie', a figure who, though surely influenced by the financial connotations of Lady Meed, is characterized most obviously not by a financially seductive enticement, but by insatiable and violent greed. He is seen taking control of the government of Britain with tyrannical authority, proclaiming: 'I am your God / And have the rod / Of honger in my fyste / Wherefore take hede / Ye do me fede / Wyth gold that is the finest' (ll. 245–50). Philargyrie is an insatiable devourer of the 'common wealth', both personifying the threat of hunger, of dearth, and producing it through his unremitting consumption. Later his servant, Hypocrisy, sends him more gold than 'thousandis ten / Of brutish men / Coulde bare', yet Philgaryrie 'eate up / At one sup / And yet was not content' (ll. 596–601). Endlessly, the giant consumes 'Goblettes', 'ryngis', 'tablettis' and gold: 'So faste he eate / Than he gan swete … / And yet he was not ful' (ll. 683–94).

This is, I think, deeply influenced by Langland's 'Hunger' (B6.171–330/ C8.167–353). Hunger is the coercive and extremely problematic answer to the quandary of labour in Piers' half acre.[90] Summoned to control the 'Bretoner' and 'wasters' who threaten to thwart Piers' community of labour, Hunger appears literally with 'the rod of hunger' in his fist, instantly terrifying recalcitrant labourers back to work. But after an ostentatiously ascetic sermon to Piers about gastronomic temperance, Hunger refuses to leave until 'I haue dyned bi þis day and ydronke boþe' (B6.278/C8.302). At the key moment at which Piers seems to be endorsing his advice to force asceticism on the rural labourer as 'profitable wordes' (B6.274),[91] Hunger counteracts this advice by contradicting his own sermon, demanding food from a ploughman who has 'no peny', and very little food to share. Like the gold that needs to be constantly harvested to service Philargyrie's hunger, Langland's hunger is brought 'pescoddes', 'benes', 'baken apples', 'Chibolles', 'chervelles', 'ripe chiries', and yet still 'Al Hunger eet in haste and axed after moore' (B6.291–5/C8.316–19). Hunger is, to Piers' apparent surprise, absolutely insatiable, and soon the 'povere folke for fere fedden Hunger yerne': anxiously, desperately trying to fend off the insatiable greed of hunger with anything they can find. The movement from dearth to plenty is marked simply by a change in the quality, rather than the quantity of produce. When the harvest comes, Hunger is fed 'new corne … good ale … þe best' (B6.298–300/ C8.321–4).[92] The apparent comedy of the people attempting to poison Hunger with 'grene poret and pesen' in times of dearth, and sending him to sleep with 'good ale' in times of plenty hides a frightening, cyclical pattern that alternates between plenty and poverty. Hunger will not sleep forever; rather than a grace period, the overindulgence of 'wastours' on luxury foods will actively cause the shortages that will see hunger return – 'For Hunger hiderward hasteþ hym faste' – and the people will soon return to a state in which 'Hunger', like Philargyrie, 'was hir maister' (B6.317, 320/C8.340, 343).

The violence of Hunger is something else that clearly left a mark on Crowley's creation. Philargyrie is figured repeatedly in a state of violent rage, as when he is described as 'Al ragynge than / This God beganne / On them his wrath to wreake / He layed about / Emonge the route / Tyl none of them colde speake' (ll. 605–10). His rage does not end until he had 'Lyke one halfe madde / Slayne all that companye' (ll. 612–13). Later he is described attacking the poor 'with strokes

---

[90] For varying discussions of the figure Hunger in *Piers Plowman*, see R. E. Kaske, 'The Character Hunger in *Piers Plowman*' *Medieval English Studies Presented to George Kane*, ed. E. D. Kennedy et al. (Woodbridge, 1988), pp. 187–97, and Margaret Kim, 'Hunger, Need, and the Politics of Poverty in *Piers Plowman*', *YLS*, 16 (2002), 131–68.

[91] The C text has 'thow poyntest neyh þe treuthe' (C8.297) for the B texts 'profitable wordes'.

[92] C has 'dentiesliche' (C8.323) for 'þe best' (B6.299).

sore / He smote the pore / And then they gan to crye' (ll. 1331–3). This unhinged violence is directly related to that of Langland's Hunger, who enters the poem in a violent rage, grabbing a labourer 'by þe mawe', assaulting him 'þat al watrede hise eiȝen', 'buffetting' another 'about þe chekes / That he loked lik a lanterne al his lif after' (B6.174–7/C8.171–4). In fact, the violence is so sudden and extreme that 'He bette hem so boþe, he brast hire guttes / Ne hadde Piers wiþ a pese loof preyed him bileve' (B6.178–9/C8.175–6). This is the sharp end of Hunger, and of the dearth that accompanies him. It is brought about, Langland suggests, by the triumph of economic self-interest, in this case the demands of labourers for higher wages and better quality food, over the perceived interests of the community as a whole. Crowley clearly saw the significance of Langland's text. Whether Crowley worked in terms of consciously mimicking a source or not, Hunger was clearly vital to the imaginative genesis of Philargyrie.

However, Crowley reconfigured the hints and images he collected from *Piers Plowman* and refigured them in a significantly new form. Where Langland's Hunger was part of a predominantly rural discourse, Crowley's Philargyrie transposes him into the ideology of urbanism that proliferates in Edwardian reformist writing. Hunger's activity in *Piers Plowman* prompts the return of labourers to work, but it is strikingly agricultural work. The terrified workers 'flowen into bernes / And flapten on wiþ flailes', or 'wenten as werkmen wiþ spades and wiþ shovels, / And doluen and dikeden to dryue awey Hunger' (B6.183–4, 189–90/C8.179–80, 186–7). When Crowley refigures the approach of his insatiable figure, it is no longer in the fields, ditches and barns where Langland's characters laboured, but in the quasi-biblical fallen city of 'Nodnoll', a city constructed from the foundations upwards by Philargyrie and Hypocrisy: 'Then builded he / A greate Citie / Nodnoll he dyd it name / It was all one / Wyth Babylon / If it were not the same' (ll. 509–14). This Babylonian city, both mythical and actual – 'Nodnoll' being 'London' spelt backwards – is where the action of Crowley's text always takes place, it is the world of the text. It is where Hypocrisy goes to gain gold for Philargyrie (e.g. l. 590), it is where 'Philaute' manipulates the people into a bizarre, petty version of reform in which they will still be preyed upon by Philargyrie, simply swapping Hypocrisy for 'self-love' in Crowley's bitter parable of a compromised reformation. Instead of a rural world of agricultural labour, Crowley figures the city as the centre of consumption, a kind of black hole at the centre of the state which seems to endlessly take in wealth and sustenance to supply an insatiable and demonic greed. Just as Langland's labourers required a 'pardon' from 'Truth' to stave off the apocalyptic fate of greed and growing covertise, the city of *Philargyrie* can only be saved by the intercession of 'Truth', prompting the ethical intervention of the reforming king. But whilst 'Truth' interceded to save the recalcitrant agricultural labourer from Hunger, 'Truth' in Edwardian culture was required to prompt the reformation of a newly configured community. The 'barn of unity', the 'half-acre', had developed into a nation state dominated by its capital city, even as it cleaved to the imaginative figurations of anti-urban satire provided by Langland's *Piers Plowman*.

Chapter 2

Polemical Pastoralism:
The Reformation and Before

In whose [Edward III's] tyme it pleased God to open the eyes of many to se hys truth, geuing them boldenes of herte, to open their mouthes and crye oute agaynste the worckes of darckenes, as did John Wicklefe, who also in those dayes translated the holye Bible into the Englishe tonge, and this writer who in reportynge certaine visions and dreames … doeth moste christianlye enstruct the weake, and sharply rebuke the obstinate blynde. (sig. *2r)[1]

the fervent zeal of those Christian days seemed much superior to these our days and times; as manifestly may appear in their sitting up all night in reading and hearing; also by their expenses and charges in buying of books in English … some gave a load of hay for a few chapters of St. James, or of St. Paul in English … To see their travails, their earnest seekings, their burning zeal, their readings, their watchings, their sweet assemblies, their love and concord, their Godly living, their faithful demeaning with the faithful, may make us now, in these our days of free profession, to blush for shame.[2]

The two quotations above come from Robert Crowley's preface to his editions of *Piers Plowman* (1550) – a text which I have argued in the last chapter to be a vital source of literary-polemical inspiration for mid-Tudor Protestant writing – and John Foxe's *Acts and Monuments* (first edition 1563) – arguably the most influential of all Protestant texts beside the English Bible. They are both characterized by a certain shared rhetoric and certain shared ideas, most importantly about the nature of England's pre-Reformation history and the relationship between that past and the mid-Tudor present. They are nostalgic, highly emotive, and polemical; they both assume the presence of a narrative of religious history filled with resistance, struggle and persecution, in which 'boldenes of herte', 'earnest seekings' and, perhaps most vitally, 'readings' are actions of heroic struggle against 'worckes of darckenes' in Crowley's case, and what seems to be rural poverty in Foxe's. These are images of reading which can not help but move readers, for they are about the act of reading as something oppositional, democratizing and liberating. The book itself here – whether a copy of *Piers Plowman* or a few chapters of Paul or

---

[1]   Robert Crowley, ed., *The Vision of Piers Plowman*.

[2]   *A&M*, IV. 218.

James bought in exchange for agricultural produce – is itself a symbol of religious liberation and moral courage.

This chapter argues that this similarity in Crowley's and Foxe's writing here is not coincidental, and that the Protestant interest in *Piers Plowman* that I outlined in the previous chapter didn't come out of nowhere. Much excellent recent work on early Protestantism has dwelt at length on Protestant historiography, in particular the idea of the 'search for precedent'.[3] But I am concerned here with a different, though related, phenomenon. What I find most important in these quotations is not necessarily the idea of history 'behind' the rhetoric, but the rhetoric itself. For it seems to me that *Piers Plowman* was a natural point of interest for a religious culture which from its earliest textual appearance in England figured itself in those texts in a particular way. Early English Protestants represented themselves, and perhaps even understood themselves, in terms of a powerful form of polemical pastoralism.

The efficacy of this pastoralism is perhaps most tangible in contemporary attempts to resist it. It is striking that at the beginning of the 1530s, we find Thomas Elyot famously attempting to drive a scholarly, humanist and etymological wedge between two things: the 'commonwealth' and commoners. In the opening of his *Boke Named the Gouernour* (1531) Elyot attempted to deconstruct the linguistic and social synthesis that existed in the word 'commonweal'. '[T]he communaltie', he wrote, 'signifieth only the multitude, wherin be contained the base and vulgare inhabitants not auanced to any honour or dignite'. What was 'common', argued Elyot, was not mutual to all parts of a political body, but restricted to one class-defined part of it. Drawing on comparisons with Latin, Elyot continued, 'And consequently there may appere lyke diuersitie to be in englisshe between a publike weale and a commune weale, as shulde be in Latin between *Res publica* and *Res plebeia*'.

Greg Walker's monumental *Writing under Tyranny* (2005) has characterized Elyot as, like John Heywood and Thomas More, a conservative writer attempting to offer alternative counsel in a decade of increasingly unadvisable tyrannical government. Elyot's attempts to differentiate the '*res publica*' from the '*res plebeia*' here seem to tally rather well with Walker's thesis, for Elyot's point is not simply philological, but political. He shifts from linguistic issues to wider historical, even cosmological, ideas about 'order' and 'degree', to the extent that he sounds like a sketchbook version of Shakespeare's Ulysses: 'Take but degree away, untune that string, / And hark what discord follows' (*Troilus and Cressida*, I.3.109–10). We might not imbue Elyot here with Machiavellian political manoeuvring that hides behind Ulysses' musical imagery, but both the sentiment and the language

---

[3]   See in particular Alec Ryrie, 'The Problem of Legitimacy and Precedent in English Protestantism, 1539–47' in *Protestant History and Identity*, ed. Bruce Gordon, 2 vols (Aldershot, 1996), I. pp. 78–92; Sarah Kelen, 'Plowing the Past: "Piers Protestant" and the Authority of Medieval Literary History', *YLS*, 13 (1999), 101–36, and her recent *Langland's Early Modern Identities*, pp. 8, 12, 43–76.

are virtually identical: 'the potter and the tynker, only perfecte in theyr crafte, shall littell do in the ministration of iustice. A ploughman or carter shall make but a feble answere to an ambassador. Also a wayur or fuller shulde be an unmete capitaine of an armie, or in any other office of a gouernour'.[4] Elyot's and Ulysses' language, and the imagery and arguments they forward, are fundamentally anti-pastoralist, and they are the opposite to Protestant modes of self-fashioning. Despite sensible political attempts to differentiate Protestantism from popular movements – Tyndale's *Obedience of a Christian Man* (1528) springs to mind here – reformist writing was absolutely full of ploughmen who make far from feble answers to ambassadors.

This form of polemical pastoralism is, of course, highly rhetorical. Much of the revisionist work done by historians on the nature of the English Reformation has made it clear that a great deal of earlier historiography harboured a deeply partisan strain of Foxean triumphalism.[5] We should, of course, be wary of the rhetorical power of Protestant self-fashioning. But we should also be wary of assuming that Foxean triumphalism existed during the early Reformation period. As Thomas Betteridge has put it, it is vital to recognize 'the uncertain and fragile nature of Protestantism as a social identity in the period 1520–1570'.[6] Just as recent studies of Lollardy have highlighted the need to think about the movement in less restrictive terms than the theological catch-alls that the records of ecclesiastical courts assume, it is necessary to recognize that the very word 'Protestant' might not automatically denote a matching set of theological beliefs and form of self-image.[7] In a culture in which heretics were still referred to as 'Lollards' and texts such as Fish's *Supplication of Beggers* were theologically indistinguishable from Wycliffite views, one must, as Betteridge writes, 'ask, what is Protestantism in this text? How does this text construct its writer as a Protestant author?'.[8]

---

[4]　Thomas Elyot, *The Boke Named The Governour* (London, 1907), I. 1, pp. 1–7. The passage is used by Raymond Williams to exemplify the differences between the words 'commonwealth' and 'common', see Williams, *Keywords: A Vocabulary of Culture and Society* (London, 1976), p. 71.

[5]　For an excellent digest of the historiography, see Peter Marshall and Alec Ryrie, 'Introduction: Protestantisms and their Beginnings' in Marshall and Ryrie, *The Beginnings of English Protestantism*, pp. 1–13.

[6]　Betteridge, *Tudor Histories of the English Reformations*, p. 18.

[7]　The most important 'revisionist' studies of Lollardy are Havens et al., eds, *Lollardy and Its Influence in Late Medieval England* (Woodbridge, 2003), and the recent Andrew Cole, *Literature and Heresy in the Age of Chaucer* (Cambridge, 2008).

[8]　Betteridge, *Tudor Histories*, p. 17. The theological content of Fish's text is assessed in Anne Hudson, *The Premature Reformation* (Oxford, 1988), p. 501. A wider analysis of Fish's text is given below. As numerous scholars have noted, the term 'Protestant' continued to refer specifically to German dissent, particularly the princes and free cities who dissented against the Diet of Spires (1529), 'protesting' against its opposition to reform, for much of the sixteenth century. The word was not used as a term for English heretics until the Marian years, and even then co-existed with the word 'Lollard'. See Daniell, ed., *The Obedience*

This chapter seeks to delineate some of these dynamics of Protestant self-fashioning, to see how central polemical pastoralism was to early English Protestant identity. Polemical pastoralism of this sort contains, of course, a number of paradoxes. One is not to assume that all early Protestants were from comparatively poor or agrarian social backgrounds (often quite the opposite). But this Protestant pastoralism was powerful for a number of reasons. To construct oneself in texts as a community of marked simplicity in both material and intellectual terms obviously had biblical connotations, but it also evoked important, highly emotive ideas about the democratization and liberation of the Bible itself in this period. Protestant self-fashioning worked by appropriating an iconic image of a spiritualized laity; early Protestant writers persistently, in some way, imagined themselves as ploughmen.

This chapter also shifts backwards historically. For Foxe's emotive memorialization of Wycliffites in 'the fervent zeal of those Christian days', and Crowley's contextualization of *Piers Plowman* lead us back into two striking phenomenon that have, I think, an important impact on the way we view early Protestant writing. Firstly, while there are all kinds of historical reasons to doubt the continuity drawn here between Lollards and reformers, the way that Foxe and Crowley memorialized Wycliffites was so very close to the way that Wycliffites fashioned themselves. Both *corpora* of writings have an important, and hard to avoid, investment in similar forms of polemical pastoralism, and for similar reasons. Secondly, I return to the Reformation by way of a digression on the polemical altercations between Lollards and mendicants. The extremely hostile relationship between the friars and Wycliffites in the period from 1381 onwards is striking because the rhetorical constructions of religious identity we find in their writings are again so similar. Lollards and mendicants can be seen to quite literally wrestle over ownership of emotive ideas of 'simplicity'. This shared investment in forms of pastoralism and religious identity may, I suggest, be amongst the reasons why we might finally turn to John Bale – like a number of early Protestant polemicists a convert from the mendicant orders – to find an exemplary case of Protestant self-fashioning.

---

of a Christian Man (London, 2000), p. xiv and MacCulloch, *Tudor Church Militant: Edward VI and the Protestant Reformation* (London, 1999), p. 144. 'Lollard' is the word generally used for 'heretic' in dominant conservative discourse about heresy well into the years of Lutheran influence. See, for example, Skelton's 'your Lollardy lernyng teched', 'Replycacion', l. 209, probably written at a similar time to More's *Dialogue Concerning Heresies* (1528–1529) as part of an institutionally backed attempt to discredit Lutheranism. Just as Hoccleve mentioned Wycliffe in the same breath as Arianism, Lutheranism was frequently referred to as 'Lollardy'.

Protestant Self-Fashioning and Polemical Pastoral

Simon Fish's *Supplication of the Beggers* (1529), it has been said, was 'the most influential of all early English Protestant tracts', in fact, 'nothing since the New Testament had appealed so strongly to the popular imagination'.[9] It was a key text in the group of works that proliferated around the end of the 1520s, including William Roy's *Rede Me and Be Not Wroth* (1528), More's *Dialogue Concerning Heresies* (1528) and Skelton's 'Replycacion aginst certain Scolars recently Abjured' (*c.* 1528). This moment, the milieu of the Reformation Parliament, was one of massive and bitter controversy which attracted stunned responses from continental visitors who bore witness to the extent and acuteness of anticlerical feeling at the time.[10] If the written war of words had seemed dominated by the institutional reaction to a German reformer in Henry's *Assertio Septum Sacramentum* (1521) and More's *Responsio ad Lutheram* (1523), by 1528 it had exploded in English. Fish's text would drag Thomas More, in particular, into his voluminous altercation with Tyndale, whose 1526 Worms New Testament, and the official reaction to it, most likely triggered the tidal wave of vernacular controversy.[11]

Fish's text was addressed directly to Henry VIII ('to the king oure souereygne lorde'); despite the wide readership of the text, the monarch himself was the 'reader' for whom it was written, the ideal recipient.[12] The point of Fish's emphasis on the 'beggars' is a carefully aimed attack on the clergy which uses the idea of clerical oppression of the poor to make its argument. Fish begins with the image of the 'sore people, nedy, impotent, blinde, lame, and sike, that live only by almesse' and the observation that 'theyre nombre is daily so sore encreased' (p. 1). The cause of this rising population of beggars, says Fish, is another type of beggar, one that 'in the tymes of youre noble predecessours passed, craftily crept ynto this your realme', 'an other sort ... of strong, puissaunt, and counterfeit holy and ydell, beggers and vacabondes' (p. 1). The genuine beggars are utterly destitute and totally defenceless. The other 'sort' of beggars are by contrast 'strong' and

---

[9]   W. A. Clebsch, *England's Earliest Protestants, 1520–1535* (New Haven, 1964), pp. 240, 242. On the impact of the text see also Walker, *Writing under Tyranny*, p. 47, and Stephen Greenblatt, *Hamlet in Purgatory* (Princeton, 2001), pp. 10–14, 28–33, 133–8.

[10]   See Walker, *Writing under Tyranny*, p. 38; Brigden, *London and the Reformation*, p. 172.

[11]   Fish's text was overtly referenced as the 'father figure' of Protestant controversial texts in the *Proper Dialogue* (1530) and the later *Supplication of the Pore Commons* (1546), and is still, perhaps, being referred to, albeit with a somewhat different purpose, in Nashe's *Pierce Penniless, His Supplication to the Devil* (1592).

[12]   Simon Fish, *A Supplication for the Beggers*, ed. F. J. Furnivall (EETS e.s. 13, London, 1871), p. 1. The story of Anne Boleyn's and Henry's reading of the text may well be Foxean folklore, but there is some evidence of an interest in reformism in court circles. Whether this was faddism or serious commitment to the cause of the Reformation is open to debate.

'puissaunt', and are, of course, the clergy. In fact, these 'strong' beggars '(setting all laboure a side) have begged so importunately that they have gotten ynto theyre hondes more then the therd part of all youre Realme' (p. 2). Fish, like the *Lollard Disendowment Bill* (1410) had done before him, attempts a kind of economic audit, laying out exact figures for the average parish income, mendicant incomes, and household expenditures on clerical payments.[13]

This is the centre of Fish's strategy; the text is directed to Henry not, perhaps, because of an underlying centralization of power, but because the success of his anticlerical project depends upon the crown's desire for increased income. As James Simpson has noted, writers of such polemics 'were acutely aware of the secular attractions of their programmes for ecclesiastical disendowment'.[14] The *Supplication*, if it did not actually influence the governmental policy of the following decade, was prophetic of the mass scramble for wealth and land which followed the Dissolution. At the very least, it was the product of a culture in which the idea of wholesale clerical disendowment by the monarchy was possible, and financially enticing. We might well argue that Fish's text is proof that monarchical greed was a key dynamic of religious reform, but the purpose of Fish's championing of 'real' beggars was slightly more complex. He strictly divided government taxes, which Fish said, had been 'so sloughtfully, ye, painfully leuid' (p. 3) from the 'greuous and peynfull exactions' of the clergy from which, significantly, 'the people of your nobill predecessours, the kinges of the auncient Britons, euer stode fre' (p. 3). Again, if the government taxes Fish was referring to were part of the Amicable Grant (1525), the modern reader is likely to think that they were 'painfully leuid' because they were themselves painfully high. But the simultaneous attack on 'painful' clerical taxes and the foregrounding of the 'ancient freedom' of Britain's monarchs and people are there for a rhetorical purpose.

The essential polemical strategy was to transfer the category of governmental 'tyranny' away from any association with the monarch and place it in the lap of the clerical class. The 'rule, power, lordishippe, auctoritie, obedience, and dignitie' which the clergy had managed to move 'from your grace unto them' must be taken back (pp. 4–5). Henry becomes a perfect governmental foil for the archetypal tyranny of the clergy. The power of the 'beggars' was their ability to come between the clergy and the monarchy, as a plea for protection and the common good of the realm. There is in Fish's text an idea of the 'people' which fissured religious discourse throughout the period. Whereas Protestant texts like Fish's promised an ideal 'strong' public in the form of a needy beggar or an agricultural labourer, a figure who would repay the king's fulfilment of his protective duties with unflinching loyalty, religious conservatives continued to depict the lower classes

---

[13]   See Hudson, *Premature Reformation*, p. 501: 'Fish's text was entirely couched in Lollard terms. Its appeal to Henry VIII is exactly that of Nicholas Hereford in 1382, of the Lollard Disendowment Bill, and of numerous less formal tracts'; also Clebsch, *England's Earliest Protestants*, p. 244.

[14]   Simpson, *Reform and Cultural Revolution*, p. 337.

as a bomb waiting to go off. All it would take was a hefty dose of heterodox reading and the stability of the country would buckle under the weight of civil disorder and sedition.

It is this nightmare of lower-class heresy which preys on Thomas More's mind so often. In the *Apology* (1533), for example, More describes the potential effects of a relaxation of antiheresy laws producing a proliferation of people such as 'a tynker or a tyler which could (as some there can) rede englysshe, and beynge instructed and taught by some olde cunnyng weuer in Wycliffe Wyckette, & Tindals bookes, and Frythes, & frere Barnes' would begin 'lurkyng about and teachynge hys gospel in corners'.[15] This is Elyot's view of the *res plebeia*, but now tangled with anxiety and hostility about social mobility. The figure of the 'old cunning weaver' who is so threatening to More is the same figure that Protestants like Fish championed, imagining themselves as, at base, just those sort of people. Moreover, whilst More threatened ensuing chaos, Fish promised a faithful and active people, rescued from the clutches of the clergy by a godly monarch and eternally grateful for it. Given the general trend in the sixteenth century towards the centraliztion of care for the 'real beggars' and an increased severity in penalties for vagrancy and begging, it might seem bizarrely unwise for Fish to have bound heterodoxy and poverty together.[16] But playing on the long history of figurations of idealized 'simplicity', Fish made an attempt to manipulate the idea of governmental care for the 'common good' which was wrought with the imagery of class difference. The positive connotations of the beggar's neediness were used to manipulate the idea of the government's protective responsibility towards its people, and Fish in return made the precarious promise that the fall of Catholicism would produce better citizens and a better state, even as Protestantism was constantly being characterized in some quarters as an oppositional and antiestablishment movement.[17]

---

[15] J. B. Trapp, ed., *The Complete Works of St. Thomas More*, 15 vols (New Haven, 1963–1997), IX (1979), pp. 163–4. For the connection between civil disorder and heresy in More's thought, see Trapp's introduction, p. xx. Taking into consideration his witnessing of the rabidly xenophobic rioting of 'Evil May Day' in 1517, More's fear and loathing of civil disorder amongst the artisanal classes is perhaps understandable. He had good reason to be suspicious of what a nationalistic 'vox populi' could produce.

[16] Bronislaw Geremek, *Poverty: A History*, trans. A. Kolakowska (Oxford, 1994), esp. pp. 120–41 ('Reformation and Repression: the 1520s'), 123. Also Michel Mollat, *The Poor in the Middle Ages: An Essay in Social History*, trans. A. Goldhammer (New Haven, 1986) who terms the process 'from charity to policing of the poor', pp. 251–93, 251.

[17] Wendy Scase has recently argued that Fish's text 'clearly appropriates the strategies and arguments of earlier complaints … In ventriloquising the voice of the poor who are oppressed by their masters, Fish revives the tradition of using personal plaint', Scase, *Literature and Complaint in England*, p. 152. What Scase does not emphasize here is that Fish's ventriloquizing of the poor is not simply conventional – this type of pastoralism had a profound emotive efficacy for early Protestants in terms of religious identity and self-fashioning.

Simplicity in intellectual terms was also vitally important to the self-understanding of a culture that, like Lollardy, placed a huge significance on the vernacular text of scripture at its centre. In many ways the most important episode in the English Reformation, at least in textual terms, was not the official responses of Church and state to *Exurge Domine*, the papal bull which excommunicated Luther in 1520, but the printing of William Tyndale's translation of the New Testament.[18] Montaigne's assertion that 'nostre contestation est verbale', that the Reformation was a battle over words, was nowhere more apparent than in the work of one of English Protestantism's greatest scholars.[19]

Simplicity was, in a way, one of the key terms associated with the calls for 'sola scriptura'. If salvation was to depend on the reading of scripture alone, a reminder of the baffling ambiguities and interpretative difficulties of the Bible was not going to win many converts. Consequently, it was simplicity which was to be most associated with a man who not only excelled in the traditional humanist studies of Latin and Greek, but who taught himself Hebrew. Foxe's *Acts and Monuments* figures Tyndale in the same way it does the Lollards, as guileless and 'simple'. His betrayal by Henry Philips is an exercise in exploitation and violence. Tyndale was captured, writes Foxe, 'for in the wily subtleties of this world he was simple and inexpert'.[20] As James Simpson has noted, the point of Foxe's narrative is that 'Tyndale was a simple, entirely readable man, just as he produced a simple, entirely readable text'.[21] Protestantism was determined that the ideal Christian life was to be an exact and 'pure' re-writing of the divinely-ordered text, a copy of which they now had to hand.[22] Even if in practice this idea was constantly compromised, the idea of the 'plain', 'simple' text remained a central hallmark of Protestant discourse.[23]

---

[18]   The importance of Tyndale's translation, which, though not advertised, formed the basis of the Matthew, Great, and King James translations, is explored in Daniell, *Tyndale: A Biography*.

[19]   Cited in Brian Cummings, *The Literary Culture of the Reformation*, p. 15.

[20]   *A&M*, V. 123. Foxe's description somewhat flies in the face of the evidence in Tyndale's letters that he was 'wily' enough to ask his fellow reformers to follow the party line when it was politically important to show a united front. For example, in a letter to Frith, Tyndale warns him 'Of the presence of Christ's body in the sacrament meddle as little as you can, that there appear no division amongst us. Barnes will be hot against you'; G. E. Duffield, ed., *The Work of William Tyndale* (London, 1964), p. 394.

[21]   Simpson, *Reform and Cultural Revolution*, p. 458. The point is reiterated in Simpson's highly polemical and rather unsympathetic *Burning to Read*, p. 109.

[22]   As John Morgan notes in a study of later Protestantism, the occasionally overwhelming anti-intellectualism of the Puritans could never quite be absolute; the imperative to interpret the scriptures required a recognition that human reason and reading could yield 'concrete evidence from God' from the biblical text. See J. Morgan, *Godly Learning: Puritan Attitudes Towards Reason, Learning and Education, 1560–1640* (Cambridge, 1986), p. 49.

[23]   The fact that Bibles became increasingly supported by interpretative and polemical glosses as the Protestantism that shaped them became more radicalized has been readily

Indeed, the call for a plain text of vernacular scripture came with familiar attacks on the sophistication of Latin academics. Tyndale launched a sequence of vicious attacks on scholastic practice, condemning 'the smoke of their bottomless pit ... juggling with the text, expounding it in such a sense as is impossible to gather'.[24] The only thing that can clear the air is an unmediated English text, 'for as long as they may keep that down, they will so darken the right way with the mist of their sophistry ... that, though thou feel in thine heart, and art sure, how that all is false that they say, yet couldst thou not solve their subtle riddles'. Tyndale's writing is a veritable cornucopia of terms for intellectual deception; the clergy 'darken', 'tangle', 'delude', 'amaze' the sense of scripture for the people 'when it hath but one simple, literal sense, whose light the owls cannot abide'.[25] The luminary metaphors that emanate from these passages are part of a rhetoric that synthesizes the call for a 'clear' vernacular scripture with an image of Latinate scholasticism as a culture of deliberate intellectual obfuscation.

Tyndale's *Obedience of a Christian Man* (1528), written as a defence of Protestantism against the associations of heterodoxy with civil disorder witnessed in Germany, was also a polemical response to the condemnation, criticism and destruction that had characterized the English state's reaction to his New Testament.[26] Tyndale repeats his attacks on the 'sophistry' of the clergy, who he images 'disputing and brawling' with one another whilst proclaiming that 'A man must first be well seen in Aristotle ere he can understand the scripture'.[27] Borrowing Erasmus' coinage of '*philautia*', 'self love', and playing on its proximity to '*philosophia*', 'the love of knowledge, Tyndale bombards the reader with a chaotic example of the 'worldly wisdom' of the over-intellectualized clergy:[28]

> First they nosel them in sophistry and in *benefundatum* ... and whether *species fundata in chimera* be *vera species*. And whether this proposition be true *non ens est aliquid*. Whether *ens* be *equivocum* or *univocum*. *Ens* is a voice only say some. *Ens in univocum* saith another and descendeth into *ens creatum* and into *ens increatum per modos intrinsecos*. (p. 23)

The 'good foundation' is obviously ironic considering what ensues, which is a baffling compilation of scholastic terms about existent and non-existent things,

---

noted by scholars; see for example Evelyn B. Tribble, *Margins and Marginality: The Printed Page in Early Modern England* (Virginia, 1993), pp. 55–6.

[24]   Duffield, ed., *The Work of Tyndale*, p. 32.

[25]   Duffield, ed., *The Work of Tyndale*, p. 31.

[26]   See Daniell, *William Tyndale*, pp. 150–71.

[27]   Tyndale, *The Obedience of a Christian Man*, pp. 19–22.

[28]   See *Obedience*, p. 208, note 152. The reference is to Erasmus' *Praise of Folly* (1509), which wasn't actually available in English until Thomas Chaloner's translation in 1549. Tyndale transposes Erasmus' Latinate satire into a polemical English context. See also the use of the figure in Crowley's *Philargyrie*, chapter 1.

created and ambiguous voices, the sense of which is deliberately 'darkened': as Daniell concisely puts it, 'Tyndale expects his reader to give up' (p. 209, note 181). Ridiculing scholastic Latin is hardly unusual for someone with an investment in humanism and its disdain for medieval philosophy: Erasmus and the Franciscan Rabelais merrily do the same. But what is vital about Tyndale's comedic writing is that it is in English, being used as polemical evidence to support a biblical text in English. The parodic use of Latin in English writing has crystallized into a central aspect of the discourse that supports vernacular scripture. While this study does not share his sharply hostile stance towards early Protestantism, James Simpson's point that simplicity might be less a part of Protestant 'textual practice' and more a 'weapon in its self-advertisement' is surely an acute one.[29]

Although Latin remained the kudos language of intellectual debate, even amongst later radical Protestants such as John Milton, whilst the future of an available English Bible was at stake, Latin was used as a synonym for Catholic deviousness and obfuscation.[30] Despite the continued influence and vitality of Latin, we must consider Protestant discourse about scriptural translation, such as that in Tyndale's writing, as a hugely influential phenomenon. When the author of *Pyers Plowman's Exhortation* (1550) wrote of his text as a 'bold enterprise ... in rude language', and another writer called himself 'I Plain Piers which cannot Flatter', they were both echoing Tyndale's writing and Protestant pastoralism more generally, and aiding the development of the 'Plain-speaking Englishman', the self-fashioned identity that was to mark literary history for years to come. Shakespeare's 'Kent' would not speak the way he does if it wasn't for Tyndale.[31]

Indeed, Tyndale's contemporary John Bale had already used both Tyndale's text, and this vital polemical tactic in his plays. Bale overtly takes on the construction of the simple vernacular and the satirical idea of Latin as a deceptive,

---

[29]   Simpson, *Burning to Read*, p. 110.

[30]   Tyndale's commitment to writing in the vernacular was, in fact, extremely unusual: 'To be a scholar and not to write in Latin was odd to the point of standing condemned; both John Wyclif and Reginald Pecock had suffered in this way. All university work and most printed books were in Latin'; Daniell, *William Tyndale*, p. 45. John Bale's recognition of the importance of Latin as an international language is, however, worth noting here. In many ways, the status of Latin for Protestants varied strikingly depending on the nature and genre of their writing. In some cases it could be used to spread Protestantism across Europe, but in many instances (like those described above), the language itself was imagined to exist in a virtually synonymous relationship with Rome, Catholicism and medieval scholasticism. See Cathy Shrank, 'John Bale and Reconfiguring the "Medieval" in Reformation England', in McMullan and Matthews, *Reading the Medieval in Early Modern England*, pp. 179 92, 192.

[31]   Christopher Hill suggests that Kent was a place of notorious 'heretical reputation' throughout the sixteenth and seventeenth centuries; see Hill, 'From Lollards to Levellers' in *Religion and Rural Rebellion*, ed. J. Bak and G. Benecke (Manchester, 1984), pp. 86–103, 87–8. It seems possible that Kent's name alone might have played on connotations of 'plain-speaking' resistance to authority.

pernicious language demonstrated in Tyndale's *Obedience*.[32] In a striking moment in *King Johan*, the figures 'Usurpid Powre' and 'Privat Welth' enter the stage singing in Latin, in a raucous parody of the Vespers for the Dead. Apparently singing the Vulgate Psalm 136:1–4, the figures sing: '*Super flumina Babylonis suspendimus organa nostra / Quomodo cantabimus canticum bonum in terra aliena*', 'we have hung our harps over the rivers of Babylon, How shall we sing a good song in a foreign land?' (ll. 764–5). Bale's attack on Latin comes from its blatant manipulation. The Psalm text has '*domini*' for '*bonum*', giving the sense 'song of the lord'. The vice-like figures have altered the text to be a lament for their inability to sing a 'good' song in England, a country which is not receptive, Bale suggests, to 'usurped power' and 'private wealth'. The text is littered with similar moments. 'Sedition', for example, utters a parodic blessing with the words '*Dominus: In nomine domini pape, amen*' (l. 1149), substituting the name of 'pope' for the name of God. The purpose of these passages, as Thomas Betteridge has pointed out, is that they show 'the language of papistry as inherently antithetical to the production of coherent, stable meaning'.[33] If the 'plain ploughman' made sense, the Latinate Catholic priest made nonsense.

Fish, Tyndale and Bale all demonstrate here the pervasive investment in polemical pastoralism in early English Protestant texts. Simplicity of style and simplicity in material terms are both key parts of these writings. The key thing that underpins these ideas of beggarly, simple reformers is of course access to scripture. Revisionist accounts of early Protestantism now abound, from historians emphasizing the 'top-down', 'elitist', imposition of Lutheranism on England's population, to literary critics preoccupied by the 'tyranny' that accompanied its first political successes and the modern legacy of the 'dark, energizing paradoxes of Protestant modernity'.[34] This new cynicism about the early English Reformation might have a number of sound points to make, but its dismissal of Protestant rhetoric and polemic as being 'just' rhetoric, as being somehow deliberately disingenuous and even destructive, fails to acknowledge the importance of this self-fashioning as something not always manipulative and untrustworthy, but something that had real emotive significance. Protestant pastoralism rested finally on the idea of the democratization of the word. Contrary to Elyot's and More's counsels about the terrors of disorder and the risks of literate artisans getting their hands on the Bible, Protestant writing intimated – in a way which still has powerful emotive resonance

---

[32]   Indeed the connections between Tyndale's text, Fish's *Supplication*, and Bale's drama are very close indeed. Bale's sources for the concept of King John as a proto-Protestant martyr were Fish and Tyndale; see Peter Happé, ed., *The Complete Plays of John Bale*, 2 vols (Cambridge, 1985), I. 14. All references to Bale's plays are to this edition.

[33]   Betteridge, *Tudor Histories*, p. 76.

[34]   Simpson, *Burning to Read*, p. 2. I refer here in particular to Walker's excellent *Writing under Tyranny*, and pioneering work by historians Eamon Duffy, Christopher Haigh and J. J. Scarisbrick. For references see Marshall and Ryrie, *The Beginnings of English Protestantism*, p. 3.

– that the 'communaltie', the beggars, the simple, the ploughmen, could be trusted to read a vernacular Bible.

Wycliffite Writing and Polemic Pastoralism

The efficacy of Protestant pastoralism, then, circulated around the idea of widespread access to the Bible. The anticlericalism of Fish's *Supplication for the Beggers* aimed at clerical disendowment fitted into a wider Protestant self-fashioning which foregrounded the separation of interests between the laity and clergy as different estates or classes. It is this potent form of controversial rhetoric and self-understanding that makes Protestant writing resonate so closely with the writing of Lollard polemic – the writing of those that Foxe and Crowley remembered in 'the fervent zeal of those Christian days'.

To some extent, recent historical scholarship is 'rightly becoming more alert to the bridges and connections between late medieval and early reformist mentalities'.[35] Yet in terms of the connection between late medieval heterodox culture and Protestantism, there remains an enduring lack of critical consensus. From James Gairdner's voluminous *Lollardy and the Reformation in England* (1908–1913) through A. G. Dickens' *Lollards and Protestants in the Diocese of York, 1509–1558* (1959), to Anne Hudson's and Margaret Aston's work, there remain deep divisions of opinion regarding the scope and nature of the relationship.[36] The most recent 'post-revisionist' work perhaps suggests that whilst Lollardy was surely not the central causal factor of the English Reformation, it was still 'a tributary stream of English Protestant development'.[37] Scholars have rightly looked also at the traffic of heterodox books as an important point of intersection between Lollards and Protestants, arguing that 'Lollards played some part in the distribution of illegal

---

[35]   Peter Marshall, *Religious Identities in Henry VIII's England* (Aldershot, 2006), p. 6.

[36]   It is perhaps significant, however, that the scholars who deny any connection between the Wycliffites and the Reformation all systematically limit the 'significance' of Lollardy generally. Gairdner, Scarisbrick and, most recently, Richard Rex all view the number and influence of Lollards as an 'optical illusion'; see esp. Rex, *The Lollards* (London, 2002), p. 88. There is also a tradition of scholarship which suggests that the 'significance' of the later Lollards might have remained considerable well into the seventeenth century. Christopher Hill has made a tentative suggestion that the sudden outpouring of radical pamphlets after the breakdown in censorship in the 1640s may have been the product of a continuity between fifteenth- and seventeenth-century non-conformity disguised from historical enquiry by the heavy hand of state censorship; see Hill, 'From Lollards to Levellers', pp. 86–7. Derek Plumb's work suggests a similarly enduring influence. See D. Plumb, 'The Social and Economic Status of the Later Lollards', and 'A Gathered Church? Lollards and their Society' both in *The World of Rural Dissenters, 1520–1725*, ed. M. Spufford (Cambridge, 1995), pp. 103–31 and 132–63.

[37]   Marshall and Ryrie, *The Beginnings of English Protestantism*, p. 9.

printed literature', including 'Tyndale's groundbreaking translations'[38] and that, as Alec Ryrie puts it, there was a demonstrable 'social relationship between the established Lollard book-trading networks and the nascent evangelical ones, and such relationships could be a conduit for more than Bibles'.[39]

But in terms of the ways in which religious identity is constructed in the polemic of Lollard and Protestant writings, this connection is far more palpable. Protestants and Lollards shared a way of writing about themselves and against their enemies – the same strain of virulently polemical pastoralism. Indeed, the way in which Lollards were presented by Protestant writers was not simply an act of historical legitimization, a violent appropriation of the past in the way we might think, for example, of the proto-Protestant Chaucer as a radical departure from our own image of the 'truth' about medieval culture. The manner in which John Foxe, for example, remembered the Lollards was, perhaps, close to the way the Lollards would have liked to have been remembered. 'Simplicity' here is a faithful recreation of the Lollards' own sense of self, and simultaneously doubles as both a precursor and an ideal for Tudor Protestantism. The persistent refrain of Foxe's descriptions is of the 'poor simple' Wycliffites and their persecution. In describing Bishop Longland's prosecution of Lollardy around London in the early 1520s, Foxe raises the image of the ecclesiastical authorities to an almost satanic height. Longland 'serpent-like ... constrained the simple poor men to accuse and impeach one another', writes Foxe.[40] Again, Foxe asserts, 'there was no learned man with them to ground them in their doctrine, yet they, conferring and communing together among themselves, did convert one another, the Lord's hand working with them marvellously'.[41]

The censorship measures of Arundel's *De Haeretico Comburendo* (1401) and *Constitutions* (1408–1409), and the persecution of Lollard leaders like Williard White in Norwich or John Hacker in St. Stephen Coleman Street, London,[42] had

---

[38] Nicholas Tyacke, *Aspects of English Protestantism c. 1530–1700* (Manchester, 2001), p. 44.

[39] Alec Ryrie, *The Gospel and Henry VIII: Evangelicals in the Early English Reformation* (Cambridge, 2003), pp. 233–4.

[40] *A&M*, IV. 218–19.

[41] *A&M*, IV. 241.

[42] The fifteenth-century statutes effectively banned the writing and use of English scriptural texts and lay discussion of ecclesiastical or theological issues. Bizarrely, considering the Church's sporadic enthusiasm for enforcing the statutes, they seem to have done little to prevent the ownership of Wycliffite Bibles proliferating. The issue, as it was in the 1543 statute, which attempted to regulate access to scripture even after the publication of the Matthew and Great Bibles, seems to have been class. Ownership of such texts was permissible for the gentry and higher clergy, but extremely risky for labourers or artisans. On the statutes see Margaret Aston, *Lollards and Reformers* (London, 1984), pp. 41–3; Hudson, *Premature Reformation*, p. 406 and, more widely, Simpson, *Reform and Cultural Revolution*, pp. 334–6; on White, see Aston, *Lollards and Reformers*, pp. 71–99.

in many ways led to a 'leaderless' movement who depended on books 'such as which they could find in corners'.[43] The image of the lurking heretical artisan that haunts More's writing is used by Foxe to suggest a moving, impassioned desire to read. The image of 'simple' laymen reading in corners is a portrait of terror to More, but a picture of spiritual inspiration for Foxe. Foxe returns to the image of material and intellectual simplicity repeatedly, describing the Lollards 'of which few or none were learned, being simple labourers and artificers; but as it pleased the Lord to work in them knowledge and understanding, by reading a few English books, such as they could get in corners'.[44] The Lollards, as they themselves were fond of writing, did not have the advantage (or disability) of formal education, in Foxe's narrative, ever.

Foxe's image of the Lollard has been so successful, in one sense, because of the amount of emotional investment he had in it, because the self-fashioning of Protestants was so similar. Writers of the Protestant 'Ploughman texts' such as *I Plain Piers* were fond of recalling the 'innocent blood' that was spilt by the wolf-like clergy.[45] Brinklow's parodic attack on the clergy's policy of 'Death, death, even for trifles', in 1542, was laden with memories of an aspect of the pre-Protestant age which had re-emerged with a vengeance.[46] John Bale remembered growing up in Norwich, a place which, like London's 'Lollard's Tower', had the Wycliffites' name written into its local geography, in the form of the 'Lollards' Pit', the centre of the 1428–1431 antiheresy campaign. Norwich, he says, 'was diversely oft plagued for the slaughter of innocents', and was duly punished by a massive fire in Easter week, 1506, after an incident Bale recalls seeing, in which he 'beheld it in effect most wonderful, being then but a lad of xi. Years of age ... their blind bishop and clergy, by their full consent, had brent a younge man there, after the most tyrannouse manner (I think) that ever was seane, only for hauynge the lordes prayer in English'.[47]

Whether we take Foxe's idea of the historical continuity between Lollardy and Protestantism at face value or not, the significant point here is to recognize the way in which the image of the poor Lollard, and the high pitch of emotion associated with it, *worked* for Foxe and his readers. The 'simple', 'poor' self-fashioning of the Wycliffites was reiterated in a new context and, joined with the figure of the agricultural labourer, became an icon of the ideal of Protestant identity. In times

---

[43]   *A&M*, IV. 240–41. This was something of a stock phrase to refer to the shady, or necessarily circumspect, nature of underground heretical activity. More uses it in his *Apology* (1533).

[44]   *A&M*, IV. 240.

[45]   *I Playn Piers*, sig. B1v.

[46]   J. Meadows Cowper, ed., *Henry Brinklow's Complaint of Roderyck Mors*, pp. 30–31.

[47]   *A Treatise Made by John Lambert unto King Henry the viii* (Wesel, 1548?), sig. A3v; Bale's 'To the reader' is sig. A2r–A5r.

of perceived moral laxity, the Lollard was a heated reminder of spiritual origins, a reminder of what it was, ultimately, to be a Protestant.[48]

But, strikingly, it is apparent that as the demand for direct contact with the text of the Bible increased, as Lollards and Protestants both placed more and more emphasis on the power of the written word, there was a simultaneous heightening of consciousness regarding the need to regulate and police the nature and scope of textuality, education and intellectual sophistication as sources of spiritual enlightenment.[49] Whilst Lollards centred their activities and communities on lay reading and education, the writing of Wycliffite controversy frequently harboured an almost primitivistic preferencing of uneducated, intuitive simplicity which sometimes threatened to rule out education and literacy as a worthwhile pursuit altogether.[50]

Wycliffite writing is littered with hostile comments towards university learning and intellectual sophistication. If clerics 'traveilen faste in aristole [*sic*] and newe sophymes to be clepyd maistres', says one text, they are to be recognized and condemned as 'ypocritis' and 'pharisees'.[51] Another contrasts the study of 'Holy

---

[48]   Latimer's highly rhetorical 'Sermon of the Plough' works, it seems to me, in exactly the same way, particularly at the moment: 'I fear me some be rather mock gospellers than faithful ploughmen', Chandos, *In God's Name*, p. 14.

[49]   Eamon Duffy and Richard Rex have both raised serious doubts regarding the wider significance of Lollardy to medieval culture. In the polemical introduction to his *The Stripping of the Altars*, Duffy remarks 'To judge by the amount of interest that has been shown in them, the English religious landscape of the late Middle Ages was peopled largely by Lollards, witches, and leisured, aristocratic ladies', p. 2; Rex follows suit, asserting that 'none of this [evidence] suffices to justify the significance which has been ascribed to the Lollards'; Rex, *The Lollards*, p. 143. One of the remarkable things that scholarship on the Wycliffites has foregrounded, and which runs counter to these assertions, is the astonishing proliferation of the Wycliffite Bible in the period. No fewer than 235 copies are extant, making it one of the most copied, most owned, vernacular works before the advent of print; see Anne Hudson, *Lollards and Their Books* (London, 1985), p. 183. Regardless of whether the owners of these books can be said to be 'Wycliffite', or even sympathetic towards the Lollards' other concerns, the sheer weight of this number demands the recognition of the widespread demand for vernacular scripture at a time when, in certain circumstances, such books were tantamount to a written confession of heresy; see Aston, *Lollards and Reformers*, p. 97 and Rex, *The Lollards*, p. 102.

[50]   On the Lollards' 'conventicles', so prescient of the Puritan gatherings of the later sixteenth century, see especially Aston, *Lollards and Reformers*, pp. 101–33, 198–9 and Shanan McSheffrey, *Gender and Heresy: Women and Men in Lollard Communities, 1410–1530* (Philadelphia, 1995), esp. pp. 22–46, on the Coventry Lollards prosecuted in 1511–1512. The buying, reading and discussion of vernacular scriptural texts was the central way in which Lollard communities functioned, and certainly the central means through which they were identified and prosecuted by the ecclesiastical authorities; see Aston's discussion of the statute *De Haeretico Comburendo* in *Lollards and Reformers*, p. 41.

[51]   F. D. Matthew, ed., *The English Works of Wyclif Hitherto Unprinted* (London, 1880, EETS o.s. 74), p. 6. All references to texts in this volume are given as simply *Matthew*

writt' with the 'veyne sophistrie & astronomye & … popis decretalis & fables & cronyclis' (*Matthew*, p. 225). Yet another condemns the clergy for having 'many grete bokis & costy of mannes lawe & studien hem faste. But fewe curates hau þe bible' (*Matthew*, p. 145). Just as the clergy are figured as refusing 'true' learning and replacing it with sophistry and pointless intellectual sophistication, they are regularly attacked for 'hoarding' scriptural codices, letting the word of God rot whilst they refuse to share its text with the Lollard 'poore priests' who remain to teach the people: 'þei han manie bokes, and namely of holy writt…& suffren þes noble bokes wexe rotten in here libraries' (*Matthew*, p. 128), states one writer. Another attacks monastic houses because 'þei drawen … noble bokis of holy writt … in-to here owene cloisters, þat ben as castellis or paleicis of kynges & emperouis, & suffer hem be closed þere & waxe rotyn' (*Matthew*, p. 221). Not mincing many words, the Lollards looked at ivory towers and saw whited sepulchres.

The apparent paradox of the Lollards' rampant hostility to university learning and simultaneous emphasis on unusual levels of lay education and literacy has been repeatedly noted by scholars. Anne Hudson, for example, has described the connection between heresy and literacy as the central 'parodox of Lollardy', the most striking feature of a persistently anti-intellectual movement.[52] A culture which increasingly placed massive emphasis on the spiritual authority of a text, ultimately of one single text, inevitably witnessed a heightened need to regulate the truth value of textuality in general. The sense of the 'simple' text so often associated solely with the era of print is palpably present in the world of Langland and the Lollards. This sense of textual authority was necessarily always embattled, always defined by a kind of negative outline of 'simple truth' in comparison with perceived textual complexity and proliferation, just as the 'simple integrity' of the

---

and page number. It is highly unlikely that the texts in this volume are in fact from the pen of Wyclif himself; see Hudson, *The Premature Reformation*, p. 9 and *Lollards and Their Books*, p. 10. Hudson also argues that many of the texts assumed to be written by John Purvey are anonymous tracts; see *Lollards and Their Books*, pp. 85–110. All of Matthew's *English Works* are anonymous, and are likely to be a product of the movement of Lollardy itself from a university context in the 1370s to a wider vernacular culture over the course of the fifteenth century. See Hudson, *Lollards and Their Books*, pp. 1–6 and Aston, *Lollards and Reformers*, p. 189.

[52]   Anne Hudson, 'Laicus Litteratus: the Paradox of Lollardy' in *Heresy and Literacy, 1000–1530*, eds Peter Biller and Anne Hudson (Cambridge, 1994), pp. 222–36, 228. Aston also discusses this paradox in the chapter 'Lollardy and Literacy' in *Lollards and Reformers*, pp. 193–217, noting particularly the fact that the origin of Wycliffite theology, if not the self-fashioning that came to be associated with it, lay specifically in Merton College, Oxford (p. 198). A more recent discussion by Fiona Somerset concludes that there was a constant tension in Lollardy between their high valuation of learning and an anti-rational affectivity correlative with orthodox spiritual instruction, one that is suggested by curious evidence such as the presence of copies of Richard Rolle's works in Wycliffite manuscripts; Fiona Somerset, 'Wycliffite Spirituality' in *Text and Controversy from Wyclif to Bale*, eds H. Barr and A. Hutchison (Turnhout, 2005), pp. 375–86.

reformist ploughman is defined in opposition to the perceived chaotic business of the urban landscape or the Latinate sophistication of the clergy.

Moreover, as Fiona Somerset has suggested, the Lollards harboured a deeply ascetic impulse to move away from the written text altogether, into a kind of affective, unmediated vatic conception of knowledge and language. *The Lanterne of Lighte* is an exemplary Wycliffite text in terms of this kind of polemical, ascetic thinking about language and intellectuality.[53] The work's author is clearly highly educated, as the text is packed with a huge number of scriptural and patristic texts in Latin, each one of them diligently translated into English. The high degree of literacy demonstrated by the text is, as Anne Hudson puts in, testament to the 'continued memory of Lollardy's university origins'.[54] Yet the text begins, after a densely scriptural prologue, with an arresting 'petition':

> Faile we not God þanne in good lyuyng & he mai not faile to giue vs suche wisdam as is needful to vs & also to stere yne oure neighbour ... for þe apostlis of Crist & oþir seintis weren not graduat men in scolis but þe Holi Goost sodenli enspirid hem & maden hem plenteuous of heuenli lore & þei þat hau traueilid in deedli lettirs mekid hem silf as simple ydiotis ... And so seiþ Seint Austin ... *surgunt indoctie celum rapiunt & nos cum doctrinis nostris in infernum dimergimur.* þat is to seie ... vntaught men risen & cachen heuene & we wiþ oure clergie ben drowned to helle. (pp. 5–6)

---

[53] References are to L. M. Swinburn, ed., *The Lanterne of Lighte* (London, 1917, EETS o.s. 151). The *Lanterne* was a 'notorious' Lollard text which 'played an important part in the trial and condemnation of the London skinner, John Claydon, in 1415'; Aston, *Lollards and Reformers*, p. 149. See also Hudson, 'Laicus Litteratus', pp. 230–231. Strikingly, Claydon is thought to have been illiterate, and paid for the text to be not only written and bound, but also read to him. The text was among the Lollard works publicized by early Protestant printers. It was printed, according to the imprint, by a certain 'Robert Redman' (*STC* 2nd edn. 15225). The date is uncertain, although the STC has a tentative date of 1535. It must surely have been printed before a list of prohibited books was published following the trial of Richard Bayfield in 1531, a list in which the *Lanterne* would almost certainly have been included if it was in print; see Aston, *Lollards and Reformers*, p. 220. Interestingly, the passage quoted below is subtly altered in the printed version, excising the reference to 'graduate men of schools'. It may simply be that the exemplar used was different to British Library MS Harley 2324, the one that Swinburn used for her edition, but being that the population of early Lutherans was considered to be largely university educated, it may plausibly have been a deliberate 'silent emendation' of the text. For the university associations of English Lutheranism in the 1520s and 1530s see Rex, *Lollards*, pp. 119, 132, and the testament of Skelton's 'A Replycacion Agaynst Certayne Yong Scolers Abjured of Late' in *John Skelton: The Complete English Poems*, ed. J. Scattergood (London, 1983), pp. 372–86.

[54] Hudson, 'Laicus Litteratus', p. 236.

The binary divides of this passage are rhetorically vital. The 'graduate men' in 'schools' are absolutely separated from the idealized figures of the apostles who, as the gospel puts it, 'take no care' for their speech but are suddenly inspired by the Holy Spirit into a kind of channelling of divine utterance, a language deliberately separated off from educated discourse. 'Heavenly lore' arrives 'unpremeditated' and is not to be confused with the 'deadly letters' that turn men into 'idiots' in God's eyes. While the citation of Augustine's *Confessions* here works as 'proof' for the author's privileging of the 'indoctie' over the 'clergie', one wonders quite what to do with Augustine's 'nos' at this point. For all the ostentatious intellectuality of the text, the writer aligns himself constantly with the 'symple and lowli' (p. 19), those like his reader, John Claydon, who face the persecution of a corrupt and over-educated 'antichrist'. The *Lanterne* foregrounds its own highly educated status whilst telling its reader flatly that all learning is essentially 'deadly'. The implication is that the text itself is literally 'ghost written', shaped and executed by the Holy Spirit. The formal education and compilation of Latin quotations the writer most likely had by his side is irrelevant, and is not to be associated with the 'graduate men' whose literacy comes presumably from a wholly 'worldly' source.[55]

This imaginative investment in a contradictory idea of 'untutored' eloquence was correlative with the assertion of material, as well as intellectual, simplicity. The 'simple and lowly' that the author of the *Lanterne* defends, eulogizes and ultimately attempts to embody was an archetypal part of Lollard self-fashionings as 'poor priests', 'true men' and 'poor men'.[56] Like Langland, the Lollards' aesthetic and theological sensibility was driven by an ascetic imperative, one that hinged on stripping away what had 'worldly reputation' in order to find revelation in what society denigrated. The 'holy fools', those whom conventional wisdom placed at the bottom of the social hierarchy, were those the Lollards strove to resemble. The image and voice of the agricultural labourer held a compulsive attraction for the combative Lollard; the Lollard textual self frequently has more than a little of the ploughman in it.

The most obvious example of this attraction is the text of *Pierce Ploughman's Crede*, a staunchly Wycliffite attack on the mendicant orders that directly appropriates Langland's iconic figure, and indeed the text itself, for the Lollard

---

[55] The frequency and breadth of patristic reference in the text leads Swinburn to suggest that the writer knew these sources, as was overwhelmingly the case in the period, from a *florilegium* compilation, rather than the 'original' texts (p. xv). The ability to cite and translate the texts appropriately nevertheless suggests that the author was a highly competent Latin scholar as well as a vernacular polemicist.

[56] See Hudson, 'Lollard Sect Vocabulary' in *Lollards and their Books*, pp. 165–80 and Peikola, *Congregation of the Elect: Patterns of Self-Fashioning in English Lollard Writings* (Turku, 2000).

cause.[57] Most importantly, the text figures the 'simple' ploughman as far 'simpler' than Piers ever is in Langland's text. We are aware of the class associations of Piers because of his vocation as an agricultural labourer, but Langland rarely concentrates his attention on the physical poverty of his ploughman. The closest that we come to a portrait of the physical surroundings of Piers is his inability to feed Hunger, the fact that he confesses 'I have no peny', quod Piers, 'pulettes for to bugge' (B6.279/C8.303). The Lollard ploughman, by contrast, is presented as appearing almost grotesquely poor. 'His hod was full of holes', his shoes are 'clouted ('patched') full thykke', yet the patches still do not shore up the holes that expose his feet: 'His ton toteden out as he the londe treddede' (ll. 423–5). His livestock is described as so undernourished that 'Men myghte reken ich a rib' (l. 432). The picture of his family is not much better:

> His wif
> Barefote on the bare ijs that the blod folwede
> And at the londes ende lay a litell crom-bolle,
> And thereon lay a litell childe lapped in cloutes …
> And alle they songen o songe that sorwe was to heren;
> They crieden alle o cry a carefull note. (ll. 433–41)

The modern reader might feel as if they have accidentally picked up one of the brutal anti-pastoral works of the eighteenth century, mistaking Goldsmith's 'Deserted Village' for a work of a period that rarely figures the physicality of rural poverty in such vivid terms. But the Lollard ploughman is a spiritual authority precisely *because* of his extreme and vivid poverty. What might seem to be anti-pastoral is in fact polemical pastoralism.

The poverty of the Wycliffite ploughman allows him to more directly criticize the quasi-urban buildings and ostentatious wealth of the clergy and mendicant orders.[58] The shadow of class oppression falls across the friars, as much as that of their fall from clerical ideals: a significant development in the Lollards' anti-

---

[57] All references are to the text in Barr, *The Piers Plowman Tradition*. Whilst much of the anti-fraternal satire in the text can not be said to significantly different to similar orthodox attacks, the assessment of the text as Wycliffite is warranted by the overt, eulogistic references to Wyclif himself (l. 528) and the Lollard Walter Brut (l. 657) tried for heresy in 1393. The text is literally attached to *Piers Plowman* in three of its extant copies: it introduces a copy of the C text in British Library MS Bibl. Reg. 18.B.XVII, an early sixteenth-century manuscript, and is appended to *Piers Plowman* in Owen Rogers' 1561 reprint of Crowley's edition (*STC* 19908). Barr's notes are slightly misleading here: Rogers reprinted Crowley's 1550 *Piers Plowman* and Reynor Wolfe's 1553 *Crede* (*STC* 19904) together, but Wolfe's edition was not originally appended to Langland's text. See Barr, p. 8, which conflates the texts.

[58] For Wyclif's own eulogizing of apostolic poverty, and the anticlerical uses of it, see Gordon Leff, *Heresy in the Later Middle Ages: the Relation of Heterodoxy to Dissent, 1250–1450* (Manchester, 1967), esp. pp. 527–8.

fraternalism to which we will return. But what is striking about this powerful, symbolic, polemical image is its probable distance from the historical reality of Lollardy as a social phenomenon. As Shannon McSheffrey's study of the social makeup of Lollards has shown, the vast majority of those who were recognized as Wycliffites were not ploughmen but artisans.[59] Despite doubts over the social reach of Lollardy into the gentry and aristocratic elite, 'no historian would any longer care to dismiss Lollardy as "proletarian"'.[60] The persistent claims of Wycliffite texts to be voiced by 'poor' individuals are open to comparative debate. Compared to the bishops and monarchs who took the initiative in hunting down and burning many of them, the Lollards *were* 'poor', but they were not as 'lowly' as their writers frequently fashioned them. Like Protestant self-fashioning, this is a textual process through which religious identity is created, yet it persistently appropriates the terms of social, class-bound oppression.

The Lollards' depictions of the labouring classes has been the subject of an important study by Helen Barr.[61] As Barr argues, Wycliffite writings, contrary to the assertions of conservative chroniclers, are 'unanimous and univocal in their declaration of obedience to secular authority'; in fact, they frequently replicate the conventional hierarchical 'estates theory' of society, stressing the need for political stability rather than reorganization. However, as Barr argues, their depictions of the third estate show two striking aspects. First, they persistently represent the labouring classes as a single estate of the peasant labourer, especially the rural poor, rather than the more accurate gradations of rural poor with artisans and peasant smallholders. Secondly, they are far less vitriolic in their denigrations of that estate than such writing habitually is; in fact, they often, as in *Crede*, eulogize rather than condemn this figure of the labouring poor. Barr's analysis is acute, and suggests immediately an important parallel with Fish's *Supplication* and the pastoralism of early Protestantism.

A good example of this rhetorical manipulation of the estates model in Lollard writing is the tract *Jack Upland*, a text to which we will return later in the context

---

[59]   McSheffrey, *Gender and Heresy*, esp. pp. 21, 45. The social makeup of the Coventry Lollards prosecuted in 1511–1512, for example, was overwhelmingly male and artisanal. Of 110 people recorded in the trials, 73 were male and almost all of them were artisans (pp. 24–5). The statistical makeup of this community leads McSheffrey to the conclusion that Lollardy was driven at least in part by social aspiration: 'To some extent, Lollardy may represent an attempt by artisan men to partake in a book-centred, self-directed piety just as their social superiors did' (p. 21).

[60]   Rex, *Lollards*, p. 101.

[61]   Helen Barr, '"Blessed are the horny hand of toil": Wycliffite Representations of the Third Estate' in Barr, *Socioliterary Practice in Late Medieval England* (Oxford, 2001), pp. 128–57, esp. pp. 128–9. The essay is reprinted in *Lollards and Their Influence in Late Medieval England*, ed. F. Somerset et al., pp. 197–216. The connection between Lollardy and political rebellion is discussed in Aston's seminal essay, 'Lollardy and Sedition, 1381–1431' in *Lollards and Reformers*, pp. 1–47.

of the controversy between Lollards and mendicants, and which was amongst the medieval heterodox texts printed in the early Reformation period. The text opens with the archetypal estates model, in an analogy with the trinity: 'So he [God] sette mannes state: in lordis to represente the power of the fadir; preestis to represente the wisdom of the sone; and the commons to presente the good lastynge wille of the Holi Goost'.[62] The stability of societal structure is described as the original created state of humanity, structured by God to echo the different aspects of the Trinity. It is the transgression of the clergy in particular, however, which has caused this structure to collapse. The first action of antichrist is to give 'leve to preestis ... to do lewid mennes office' (p. 119). The result is a catastrophic snowball effect: Lords begin to 'sle her britheren & brenne her housis'; labourers 'leve her trewe laboure & bicome idel men ful of disceites' (p. 120). The writer places the blame for societal breakdown firmly at the feet of the clergy for straying out of their 'estate', an action which is ultimately responsible for all other transgressions. The writer simultaneously speaks from an analytical position 'outside' the estates, diagnosing societal ills, whilst speaking in the voice of the rural labourer, 'Jack Upland', who is distanced from the 'commons' in the estates image, and instead appears as a suffering plaintive against the consequences of the breakdown of society. The Lollard polemicist shapes the image of the simple labourer in order to condemn, and vicariously share in, the material and spiritual suffering of the poor at the hands of an ambitious and corrupt clergy. Like Protestant writers from Fish to Foxe, the Lollard writer appropriates the language of class difference and oppression for the purposes of religious controversy. Jack Upland's political analysis, and the vital role of pastoral 'Upland'-ish, simple, beggarly voices here, is a direct antecedent of Reformation writing, and Reformation identities.

Mendicant Self-Fashioning, Lollardy and Protestantism

But the palpable similarity between Lollard and Protestant self-fashionings, their shared dependency on self-representation through polemical pastoralism, is not exclusive. Intriguingly, this form of self-fashioning was also the hallmark of the friars – a religious culture which strikingly produced both the most hostile opponents of Lollardy, but also many of the most prolific and vociferous of early English converts to reformism in the sixteenth century.

As scholars have argued, the mendicant orders, especially the Franciscans, were the *bête noire* of the Wycliffites. As Margaret Aston puts it, 'Those with similar aspirations and temperaments, if they are not the best of friends, always make the worst of rivals ... there was too much in common between the Lollards and the

---

[62]   References are to the edition in J. Dean, ed., *Six Ecclesiastical Satires* (Kalamazoo, 1991), p. 119.

mendicants'.[63] It was, I argue, their shared symbolic investment in 'simplicity' that was the most prominent aspect of this rivalry, rather than their similar emphasis on vernacularism and lay education, although these things surely intersect with the construction of simplicity in Lollard and Franciscan texts.[64]

The writing of Franciscanism, for example, was wrought with, in hindsight, some very familiar topoi. These topoi concerned the nature of idealized simplicity and its relation to textuality and intellectualism. Thomas of Celano's *Prima Vita*, for example, opens with a modesty topos which is more than the conventional claim to be a bit clumsy with words: 'I wish, however, that I might truly deserve to be a disciple of him who always avoided enigmatic ways of saying things and who knew nothing of the ornaments of language'.[65] Celano aims to make his own writing, his stylistic choices as a hagiographer, match the aesthetics and practice of plainness, poverty and simplicity that are the central aspects of St Francis' life. In the struggle to be the archetypal 'fool for God', Francis 'feared to be outdone by another' (*2 Celano*, p. 432).[66]

---

[63]   Aston, *Lollards and Reformers*, p. 17. It is worth noting as well that two of the most prolific early Protestant writers discussed in this book, Henry Brinklow and John Bale, were originally mendicants: Brinklow a Franciscan, Bale a Carmelite. Moreover, both Miles Coverdale and Richard Barnes were both ex-Augustinians, and William Roy, Tyndale's sometime assistant on his translation of the New Testament, was also an ex-Franciscan; see Rex, *Lollards*, p. 134. On the tradition of clerical satire on the fraternal orders, see Wendy Scase, *Piers Plowman and the New Anticlericalism*, esp. pp. 19–56.

[64]   As Andrew Cole and Laurence Clopper have noted, there often seemed to be a blurring between Lollardy and mendicant identities in late medieval writing. Cole suggests that Langland's use of the term 'lollere' is 'a fusion of Wycliffite and fraternal identities and practices ... it is an anti-Wycliffite expression of the first order that is nonetheless laden with anti-fraternal sentiment', and Clopper sees this blurring literally, as a confusion of English rigorist writing with Wycliffite texts. See Cole, 'William Langland and the Invention of Lollardy', p. 46 and Clopper, 'Franciscans, Lollards, and Reform' both in *Lollards and their Influence*, ed. Somerset et al., pp. 177–96. Interestingly, some Lollard writers were clearly aware of the fate of the Spiritual Franciscans, and of the continually embattled status of the order's rigorists. One writer says that: 'þei pursuen to þe deþ pore freris serabitis, þat kepen fraunseis rule and testament to þe rigt undyrstondynge and wille of aunceis wiþ outen glose of antecristes clerkis; þei ben false wyttenesse agens here patron and ben caymis breþren þat killyd his broþir' (*Matthew*, p. 12). Another laments how, 'biside Rome frere menours bi false name pursuen trewe pore freris to deþ, for as myche as þei wolden kepe fraunceis reule to þe lettere in pouert & mekenesse & in grete penaunce' (*Matthew*, p. 51). I assume that the correspondence between Lollard and Franciscan in these texts is a product of similar cultural self-definition, rather than a literal mistaking of one group for the other.

[65]   Marian Habig, ed., *St. Francis of Assisi: Writings and Early Biographies* (Chicago, 1973), p. 227. All references to Franciscan material are to Habig's edition, by page number.

[66]   For a fine study which emphasizes the 'competitive' problem of alms-giving and the different aspects of Franciscan voluntary poverty versus involuntary neediness, see K. B. Woolf, *The Poverty of Riches: St. Francis of Assisi Reconsidered* (Oxford, 2003).

Simplicity in material terms, the holy poverty that made Francis such a charismatic figure, was persistently correlated with intellectual simplicity, and often shaded into an outright hostility towards intellectualism which had to be softened and qualified. The *Speculum Perfectionis*, for example, reports Francis' castigation of a young friar who wanted to own a Psalter: 'Our concern is not with books and learning, but with holy deeds; for learning brings pride, but charity edifies ... there are so many who are eager to acquire learning, that blessed is the man who is content to be without it for love of the lord God' (*Speculum*, pp. 1130–1131). Francis' total focus on *the* central text, the gospel accounts of the *Vita Christi*, relegated all other texts, even the Psalms and Old Testament prophets, to a suspicious category of 'learning' that needed to be constantly regulated to prevent luxury and pride creeping into the order. In Celano's second hagiography, Francis' biographer narrates a remarkable episode in which a young friar asks to read from the Old Testament prophets and, after carefully complimenting scripture as a whole, Francis flatly replied: 'I need no more, son; I know Christ, the poor crucified one'.[67] Francis clearly gravitates here towards an ascetic distrust of textual proliferation. The Franciscan *Imitatio Christi*, in a way strikingly prescient of Lollard and Protestant polemic, was to be a plain re-writing of a divinely-authored text, but Francis was determined that there was ultimately only one text that needed to be copied. All others were peripheral, if not potentially dangerous.[68]

There is even in the texts of these testaments themselves a high level of scepticism and suspicion about the dangers of textual proliferation or multiplicity, a kind of asceticism about words themselves that recalls Celano's refigured modesty topos. *The Testament of St. Francis* ends with the command: 'I strictly forbid any of my friars, clerics or lay brothers, to interpret the Rule or these words, saying "this is what they mean". God inspired me to write the Rule and these words plainly and simply, and so you too must understand them plainly and simply' (*Testament*, p. 69). Similarly, the *Speculum Perfectionis* begins with the mantra: 'I wish the Rule

---

As Woolf puts it: 'People who were poor because of circumstances beyond their own control were not in a position to demonstrate that they held the world in proper disdain ... to disenfranchise, spiritually speaking, the poor who had not chosen to be poor ...[,] to distinguish between ordinary poverty and holy poverty in this way was effectively to translate the class distinctions that separated the rich from the poor in this world to the other world' (p. 26).

[67]   Habig, *St. Francis of Assisi*, p. 448.

[68]   One passage however, stands out in slightly shocking relief from the general wariness of books and learning in the Franciscan corpus. Celano writes of Francis reverencing and protecting the written word generally at one point: 'he was asked by a certain brother why he so diligently picked up writings even of pagans or writings in which there was no mention of the name of the Lord, he replied: "Son, because the letters are there out of which the glorious name of the Lord God could be put together. Whatever is good there does not pertain to the pagans, nor to any other men, but to God alone, to whom belongs every good"' (*1 Celano*, Habig, *St. Francis of Assisi*, p. 297). The passage stands in stark comparison with the majority of Franciscan writing.

to be obeyed to the letter, to the letter, without a gloss, without a gloss' (*Speculum*, pp. 1125–6). The danger of interpretative and textual proliferation is perceived as an omnipresent threat in Franciscan writing, in a way that interrogates our sense of the medieval period as an era of accretive culture and the Reformation as revealing a significantly 'new' emphasis on textual truth and literalism.[69]

The complex interplay of proximity and antipathy between mendicant and Lollard identities is in fact the underlying tension that shapes much of the most striking controversial exchanges between the Lollards and mendicants. The confrontation of 'Jack Upland' and 'Friar Daw' is concerned centrally with a conflict over the rhetorical ground of 'Holy Simplicity'.[70] The exchange demands to be seen in the terms of a written combat between 'Lollard tractarians' and 'orthodox pamphleteers', as a remarkable manuscript-era precursor of the voluminous and vituperative exchanges between Reformation figures like Tyndale and More.[71] Whilst some of the exchange at least seems to have been intended to be in alliterative verse, connecting it to the Langlandian tradition of *Mum* and *Crede*, the majority of the material is a closely connected series of prose arguments, answering the previous text point-by-point in the manner of later printed controversy.[72] As discussed above, *Jack Upland*'s attacks are not restricted to the friars, but encompass the regular clergy and monastic orders in a sweeping denunciation based on a rhetorical use of the estates model of society. But it soon centres on the mendicants, the 'fellist folk that ever Ante crist foond' (l.

---

[69]   For a particularly strong assertion of this idea, and a serious questioning of the 'novelty' of the Renaissance period as a whole, see Simpson, *Reform and Cultural Revolution*, esp. pp. 1–3.

[70]   I use the most recent editions of *Jack Upland, Friar Daw's Reply* and *Upland's Rejoinder*, found in Dean, *Six Ecclesiastical Satires*, which relies heavily on the work previously done by P. L. Heyworth, ed., *Jack Upland, Friar Daw's Reply and Upland's Rejoinder* (Oxford, 1968). The most recent, and best, critical work on the series has, however, seriously questioned the quality of both these editions, see Fiona Somerset, *Clerical Discourse and Lay Audience in Late Medieval England* (Cambridge, 1998), pp. 135–78.

[71]   Aston, *Lollards and Reformers*, p. 2.

[72]   The sequence of questions that Jack Upland rhetorically asks the friars are themselves drawn from a previous controversy; see Hudson, *Lollards and Their Books*, pp. 10–11. The *Reply* and *Rejoinder* are extant only in a single manuscript, Oxford, Bodleian Library, MS Digby 41. Bizarrely, the *Reply* is divided between prose and verse presentation. Roughly the first third is written as alliterative long lines, but the rest of the text is presented as continuous prose. Even more interestingly, the *Rejoinder* literally 'answers' the text of the *Reply*: instead of being presented as a separate work, it is actually written out in the margins of the previous text. The rubrication of the *Reply* similarly highlights the fact that it isn't a 'standalone' text, but a polemical response to *Jack Upland*. The key lines of Upland's texts in Dawe's response are underlined and highlighted in the manuscript almost as a reference tool to show the reader when Dawe is replying to a new accusation by Upland. For example, see lines ll. 84, 105: 'Jakke of þi foli þou feynest fife ordris', 'Jak þou sent þat we bilden the castels of Caym'.

69). The text rehearses some of the central anti-fraternal topoi one might expect: the mendicants are 'flateringe freris of al the fyue ordris', 'coveitous in marketis … caymes castel-makers': linguistically devious, commercially driven; associated with the secular pride and luxury of urban over-development. Similarly, the text reiterates the textual 'lateness' of mendicant rules in comparison with 'Crist's law' (l. 85), using this assertion to attack the idea of Lollardy's own novelty: 'ye clepen it the newe doctrine in sclaundringe of Crist?' (l. 190). Like later, precedent-seeking Protestant texts, Jack Upland's attack on the friars uses an attack on the comparative newness of the mendicant orders in order to reshape the idea of ecclesiastical history, allowing it to escape from the same slander which it aims at the mendicants.

The text drew a remarkable response in the form of *Friar Daw's Reply*, one that attempted to fight on Upland's ground, or at the least take Upland's rhetorical ground back from the Wycliffite writer. The text demonstrably tries to wrench the characteristic forms of Lollard polemical 'simplicity' back from Upland. Daw begins with a prophetic persona, the 'wailing of Jeremiah' that recalls the persistent attachment of Lollards to a combative prophetic voice. Indeed, one of Daw's first attacks comes in the form of a condemnation of 'Lollardis in her fals fablis', a deliberate use of a term laden with Lollard sentiments about the 'ungrounded' textuality of the mendicant orders, one that occurs constantly in Wycliffite writing (see, for example, *Matthew*, pp. 8, 50, 59, 124). The language of truth and falsity, of 'fabling', is clearly a language which is malleable and elastic, one that, regardless of the heavy anti-fraternal connotations, can be used by a mendicant and turned back on the scipturalist Lollard.[73] Indeed, Fiona Somerset sees each text 'redefining in its favour the terms of debate over each question, to bolster its own position at the expense of its predecessor … the participants are much concerned with the leverage they can gain by manipulating the terms of "lewed" and "clergie"'.[74] Somerset's discussion of the series is excellent, but it is this last point that I am most interested in, particularly the importance of 'lewedness' in the texts. Significantly, Friar Daw's own self-fashioning in the text is centred around intellectual 'simplicity'. Daw's self-fashioning is, as becomes increasingly apparent, an attempt to reposition Upland's rhetorical claim to idealized simplicity as ignorance in a pejorative sense. Daw asserts that 'lightly a lewid man' might take apart Jack's 'lewid … argument' (l. 45) and takes on some of the language of anti-sophistication in order to claim it for himself:

> And therefore shal no maistir ne no man of scole
> Be vexed with thy maters but a lewid frere
> That men callen 'Frere Daw Topias', as Lewid as a leke. (ll. 43–5)

---

[73] The association between the friars and 'fables' is explicit in, for example, *Crede*: 'folweth fulliche the feith and none other fables' (l. 274) and the 'Summoner's Tale': 'He served hem with nyfles and with fables', *Riverside Chaucer*, III. 1760.

[74] Somerset, *Clerical Discourse and Lay Audience*, pp. 140, 152–3.

The 'sotil witt of wyse men' might actually encourage Upland; the self-appointed fool must counter him instead. The fact that *Jack Upland* became an entrenched part of Chaucer's canon for the next century is somewhat ironic here. The friar plays on the name of Chaucer's deliberately awful doggerel romance, condemned as 'drasty rymyng' and 'nat worth a toord!', and on the name of the precious biblical gem stone, 'topez'. The point of Daw's own name is that he is more of a 'leek in the rough' than a diamond.[75] The poem's most recent editor notes: 'It is odd that the narrator of this supposedly polemical work refers to himself in the third person and characterises himself as "lewid as a leke"' (note 180). It might seem 'odd', but it seems to me to be very deliberate indeed. This, like so many other rhetorical claims to 'simplicity', is much more than a conventional modesty topos: it comes with a polemical purpose and a critical implication. If Upland is a rhetorical tool, Topias is one that allows the writer to interrogate the grounds of the ploughman's supposed 'humble integrity'. Strikingly, the writer, like Jack Upland, resurrects the image of the 'natural estates' of men, but does so to undermine Upland's use of it. Clerics, he says, are not 'to hewen … wede, corn, ne gras / Ne with Jakke Uplond ferme the dikes' (l. 55), in fact, God ordered the estates so they would not have to:

> For right as in thi bodi, Jake, ben ordeyned thin hondis
> For thin heed, and for thi feet, and forthyn eyen to wirken
> Right so the comoun peple God hath disposed
> To laboren for Holi Chirche and Lordships also. (ll. 59–62)

The writer takes Upland's estates model and reworks it back to a conventional model whose purpose is precisely to remind Upland that he should not be taking part in religious debate at all. Friar Daw's estates model takes the idealized, democratizing rhetoric which appropriates the lower classes as a model for proximity to God and re-writes it with a more traditional pejorative imperative for the ploughman to get on with labouring.[76] Simultaneously, the passage works to pry apart what *Piers Plowman* and the Lollards sought to meld together: the clerical vocation and the image of labour. Daw describes the estates in such a way that legitimizes the detachment from labour which Wycliffites so often criticized in the clergy. But this is only one aspect of a wider attempt to renegotiate the class symbolism used by the Lollards. The writer goes on to upbraid Upland with the words:

---

[75]   *Riverside Chaucer*, VII. 930, and see the notes to l. 717, p. 918. References to 'Topez' as a particularly bright gemstone are found in Job 28:19 and Psalms 118, 127.

[76]   Dean's suggestion that Friar Dawe is to be read as a generally 'anticlerical' figure who condemns himself with his own words does not strike me as being accurate; see Dean, *Six Ecclesiastical Satires*, pp. 145–6. Not only is the writer's 'simple' narrator a deliberate polemical counterpoint to Upland, but aspects of the text seem designed to be taken seriously. The condemnation of 'that wickide worme – wiclyf' (l. 71) has the ring of Hoccleve's *Remonstrance* or Lydgate's *Defence of Holy Church* to it.

> Who tythith bot ye the aret and the mente,
> Sterchynge your faces to be holden holi,
> Blaunchid graves ful of dede bones
> Wandrynge wedercokkes with every wynd waginge? (ll. 121–4)

The writer assembles a list of practices criticized by Christ as hypocritical. The Lollards are figured as 'tithing anise and mint', playing with numbers instead of dealing with 'weightier matters' (Matthew 23:23), disfiguring their faces to be held more holy, a reference to Christ's criticism of those who fast with a 'sad countenance' (Matthew 6:16), and as walking whited sepulchres (Matthew 23:27). The central accusation of hypocrisy and the association with the biblical Pharisees was a slander being constantly thrown at the friars (see for example the tract 'The Leaven of Pharisees' in *Matthew*, pp. 2–27), but here it is specifically designed to match the class associations of the Lollards. The addition of the image of the 'weathercock' as a metaphor for the Lollard's implied contrariness and lack of constancy suggests an underlying lack of substance, an inability to deal with the substantial issues that the Lollards 'feign' to even have an opinion on. There is also here an underlying attachment to materiality in Daw's depiction of the Lollard, an implication that the 'simple lollard ploughman' simply cannot reach the 'high' spiritual understanding that he claims. Daw cements with the scatological, and rather Chaucerian line: 'Th	ough quenching of torches in your taylend ye resseyve your wisdom' (l. 126). The association of the Lollards' claim to wisdom with excrement is a forerunner of Thomas More's gruesome abuse of Luther, and to some extent this kind of language was perhaps a regular and conventional aspect of religious controversy, but it seems to me to be done for a purpose. It takes the idealized, spiritualized rhetoric of simplicity found in the Lollards' self-fashioning as ploughman and 'poor men' and reiterates the tradition that associated those 'poor men' with the body, with the habitual, the domestic and the 'lowly'. Friar Daw, though 'lewid as a leek', attempts to destroy the aura of integrity around simplicity which the Lollards had persistently worked to construct.

Upland's Rejoinder, crammed into the margins surrounding *Friar Daw's Reply*, had two purposes: to unveil Friar Daw's self-fashioning, and to re-construct the idealized simplicity which the *Reply* had attempted to deconstruct.[77] The text's correspondingly abusive mode of attack – 'Daw, thou blaberest blasfemies' (p. 10) – is interrupted by a more striking comment: 'Daw, thou fablest of foxes and

---

[77]　The question of the *Rejoinder*'s 'Lollard credentials' is raised by Dean, as the writer seems to defend the secular clergy against the friars; *Six Ecclesiastical Satires*, p. 201. Dean comes to the conclusion 'By the time *Upland's Rejoinder* was written, "Jack Upland" had become a type representing those who opposed fraternal invasions of privileges traditionally enjoyed by secular clerics'. This may well be the case, but being that the *Reply* explicitly associates Upland with the 'wicked worm, wyclif' and consistently uses the term 'Lollard' to describe him, it would have taken a secular cleric who didn't mind tacitly supporting heresy to write it.

appliest hem to a puple of whom nether thou knowyst kunnyng, ne her conversacion' (pp. 14–15). Daw was not only 'fabling' again, but he was castigating, and to some extent impersonating, people he knew nothing about. The reference to 'conversacion' is compelling. It isn't simply that the *Reply* accused the uneducated 'Uplander' of being ignorant, what the writer of the *Rejoinder* objects to is that Friar Daw attempted to mimic the characteristic speech of a group of people, and did it badly. Towards the end of the text, the writer returns to the question of Friar Daw's 'persona': 'Thou saidist thou were no lettred man; thou prevest thi-self fals, For thou spekist of jerarchies, of heresies also' (p. 313). Friar Daw's generic choice of the Jeremiad, and his conflation of Lollardy with historical figures – 'Arrians, Wyclyfanes, Sabellyanes' (661) – are the signs of a formal education in both rhetorical writing and ecclesiastical history. The question of Daw's education is not peripheral for the *Rejoinder*, it is a central subject of attack. The *Reply* had slandered 'simplicity', and the writer of the *Rejoinder* was determined to unveil Friar Daw as a highly educated mendicant 'playing' at simplicity for devious and misleading polemical purposes.

Similarly, the *Rejoinder* attempts to resurrect the ideal of spiritualized simplicity that the *Reply* had attempted to undermine. The text comically echoes Friar Daw's scatological imagery, accusing him of taking the scriptures 'arseworde' (151). This is both a familiar point, accusing the friars of perverting the 'simple' sense of scripture for their own purposes, managing to turn it backwards; at the same time it is a judgement of Daw's entire text. As far as the writer is concerned, Daw gets everything 'arseward', most importantly the importance and integrity of 'simplicity'. The *Rejoinder* picks up on the image of 'Cain's castles' that originated in the first Jack Upland text, and writes: 'And thowgh thou saye ascorne a shepe house I have, that hath more grounde in Goddies lawe than alle your Caymes castelles' (222–3). Daw's 'scorning' of simplicity is answered with the reassertion of simplicity over the friars' quasi-urban castles, a point banged home by a sequence of scriptural quotations highlighting biblical support for the *Rejoinder*'s combative anti-urban stance: '*Non habemus hic manentem civitatem*', 'We do not have here a lasting city' (Hebrews 13:14); '*Et idem, Ve qui edificatis civitatem in sanguinibus*', 'Woe to you who build a city in blood' (Habakkuk 2:12); '*et Ve qui conjunctis domum ad domum*', 'Woe to you who join house to house' (Isaiah 5:8). The rubrication of the text in Oxford, Bodleian Library, Digby 41 is remarkably intense, and is obviously so at this point. The writer of the *Rejoinder* underlines and capitalizes his biblical citations without fail. Even in the often minute space afforded by the margins, each proof text is highlighted, giving the effect of an attempt to overpower the content of the central text on the page with the sheer density of its scriptural citation. At this point in the text, at the point of eulogizing the 'sheep house' that Daw has scorned, and condemning the urbanized mendicants, the effect is intensified: three different citations, from the minor Old Testament prophets to the Pauline epistles are underlined one after the other like a miniature casebook, a testament to the image of holy simplicity that Friar Daw attempts to wrest away from Jack Upland.

The uncomfortable proximity of self-fashionings in the Upand Series, the close rhetorical focus on the nature and ownership of pastoral 'simplicity', is tangible, and goes some way, I think, to explaining the sharp hostility between these two groups in the later Middle Ages. But the importance of the mendicants' polemical pastoralism is evident again when we turn back to the early English Reformation. In an important essay, Richard Rex has maintained that 'the friars remained a force in English religious life' right up to the suppression of the English mendicant houses in 1538–1539.[78] He also points out one of the most arresting facts about the early English reformers: that a large number of early Protestant writers and polemicists were converts from the mendicant orders. William Roye and Jerome Barlowe, authors of *Rede Me and Be Not Wroth* (1528), were converts from the Observant Franciscan Priory at Greenwich; Bernadino Ochino, whose conversion and English exile to the court of Edward VI was a cause célèbre in Siena, was similarly an Observant Franciscan; Henry Brinklow, a polemical contemporary of Robert Crowley, was likely also an ex-Franciscan; 'Little Germany', the famed hotbed of reformism in Cambridge, was peopled by Robert Barnes and Miles Coverdale, both previously Austin Friars; and it might not be coincidence that Martin Luther shared their mendicant background.[79]

Far more work remains to be done on this striking phenomenon, but Rex's suggestion that the friars, like the Lollards, transected substantially with early Protestantism is enticing and suggestive. It seems likely, as Rex puts it, that 'Interest in the latest currents of religious opinion is likely to have been found not among those who were disenchanted with the church but amongst those who were most zealous for reform within it'.[80] Rex suggests a number of reasons for the number of mendicant converts to Protestantism, amongst them their shared commitment to preaching, their usefully high levels of education and administrative capabilities, and their ability to write theological literature. It is this last point that interests me here, for mendicants had experience not only of writing controversial literature, but they also had, as we have seen in this chapter, experience of figuring themselves and their opponents using precisely the same strain of polemical pastoralism which was such a dominant aspect of early Protestant texts. It is worth here taking a brief look at another prolific early Protestant writer – and yet another convert from the mendicant orders – in the light of our exploration of pastoralism and religious

---

[78]   Richard Rex, 'The Friars in the English Reformation' in Marshall and Ryrie, *The Beginnings of English Protestantism*, pp. 38–59, 40.

[79]   On Ochino, see King, *Reformation Literature*, pp. 201–6, esp. 202. Wendy Scase has recently argued that Brinklowe's status as an ex-Franciscan, advertised on the title page of at least one of his works, is actually part of 'an old complaint tradition … the "feigned friar"', Scase, *Literature and Complaint*, pp. 159–60. Scase's argument though can hardly extend to the entirety of this group. I think it remains likely, if not provable, that Brinklowe was a convert from Franciscanism. On the importance of the Observant Franciscans in this group, and the Austin converts, see Rex, 'The Friars in the English Reformation'.

[80]   Rex, 'The Friars in the English Reformation', pp. 41, 58.

identity in Lollard and mendicant texts. For in some ways John Bale – antiquarian, historian, polemicist and playwright – is an exemplary writer of early Protestant self-hood.

This argumentative figure – 'Bilious Bale' – the writer of a vast number of prefaces, tracts and pamphlets for the Protestant cause, was also one of the major figures of Protestant antiquarianism that publicized Lollard texts.[81] It is striking that Bale's literary and antiquarian output is highly sensitized to the emotive, polemical significance of pastoral images, on the level of self-fashioning and even stylistic criticism. Indeed, in the midst of arguing for the continued compiling and printing of medieval texts, Bale argued that medieval chronicles should:

> Apere first of all in their owne simplycyte or native colours without bewtie of speche. The scriptures are not to be reiected, though they for the more part, want that same plesaunt order, which is commonly sought amonge prophane writers. God hath chosen (S. Paul saith) the folyshe and weake thynges of the worlde, to confounde the wyse and myghtye.[82]

The Pauline image of 'holy fools' is here entirely textual, concerning the stylistic choices of 'ordering', syntax and vocabulary. Medieval culture should be transmitted in its own 'plainness', the plainness of the Bible and those who cleave to it. In a nice reversal of the general consensus on the relative merits of medieval and Renaissance literary style, one that sounds from Puttenham and Sidney to the twentieth century, Bale makes heightened literariness 'common'. It is the 'foolish', persecuted text that is to be praised, not the 'profane' aesthetics of pleasure. The complimentary comments about 'plain' style are correlative with Bale's own combative self-fashioning. The *Vocacyon*, Bale's remarkable, almost Romance-like, autobiography, persistently returns to the image of 'plain simplicity' in its ruminations on the 'true' Church and the nature of the elect. Bale writes: 'The true churche of God had never sumptuouse hospitalles any longe tyme together but very simple cottages and caves if ye marke the sacred histories and auncyent cronicles'.[83] Likewise, Bale asserts that God 'called ... not the stought, sturdye and heady sort of men, but the lowly harted, simple and beggarly ydiotes ... these chose he out from the world to gyue knowledge of salvation to hys people' (p. 42). Bale's idealization of simplicity must have been dense with medieval heritage as well as the reformer's discourse about vernacular scripture.

Even more than Bale's antiquarian work, though, his plays are an extremely rich subject of discussion because of the way his strikingly polemical and politicized

---

[81]   He was also almost certainly the source for Robert Crowley's information about Langland. See Chapter 3.

[82]   *The Laboryous Journey and Serche of Johan Leylande, for Englandes Antiquities* (London, 1549), sig. C3v–C4r.

[83]   Peter Happé and John N. King, eds, *The Vocacyon of Johan Bale* (New York, 1990), p. 37.

drama crystallizes key aspects of Protestant identity.[84] Bale's foregrounding of the issue of textuality goes even further than the construction of the vernacular as the plain antithesis to sophistic Latin, making textual debate a central aspect of the plays. Moreover, Bale's figurations of biblical characters highlights the process in which the latent figures of landscape associated with polemical asceticism were redefined by the Protestants. The pejorative associations of urbanism that can be traced back to Langland, if not earlier, are heaped onto the demonized fallen city of Rome, whilst the Protestants constructed themselves as anti-urban prophetic figures. Indeed, in their negotiation of biblical figures such as John the Baptist, Bale's plays demonstrate the creative process by which such wilderness prophets were synthesized with the Protestant's own sense of simplicity. Vitally, Bale renegotiates not only the awkward connotations of the Mystery Play format from which his plays are formed, but can even be seen in the remarkable process of reconstituting the significance of biblical figures in a striking and precarious way.

Bale foregrounds the act of reading and interpretation itself in the plays, to the extent that some passages seem intended as extended 'reading lessons' in vernacular scriptural debate – lessons that foreground again the powerful significance of reformist simplicity. For example, in *King Johan*, Clergy 'proves' the legitimacy of the variety of Catholic orders by citing another Psalm, this time 44:10: '*Astitit Regina a dextris tuis in vestitu / deaurato circumdata varietate /* A queen, sayth Davyd, on thy ryght hond, lord, I se, / Apparrellyd with golde and compassyd with dyversyte' (ll. 434–7). After a dense list of different orders that lasts for over 20 lines, 'Civil Order' cuts in to contradict Clergy's reading: 'Me thynkyth yowre fyrst text stondeth nothyng with yowre reson / For in Davydes tyme wer no such sectes of relygyon' (ll. 461–2). Not only the oblique use of scripture, but the ensuing argument about its truthfulness, serves to assert the necessity of constantly defending the 'simple' truth of the text from the 'darkening' of it by the clergy.

Bale's 'brefe comedy', *The Temptation of Our Lord*, is centrally concerned with the same process of embattled 'right-reading'. At the key moment of the scriptural passage on which the play is based, Satan 'tempts' Christ to throw himself off the temple, citing Psalm 91 as proof that if he is the Son of God, he

---

84   Bale's drama has, perhaps unfortunately, not had a great press of late. James Simpson sees Bale as the exemplar of 'a new, exclusionary historical practice whose exclusions are at once formal and doctrinal'; Simpson, *Reform and Cultural Revolution*, pp. 502–57, 528–9. In an earlier work stretching across the fourteenth to sixteenth centuries, Ritchie Kendall characterized Bale's drama as an exemplary case of the violence of reformist judgmentalism: 'All that he feared in the stage, he sequestered among his enemies and their creations; all that he could safely love, he appropriated as his own. The result is a severely limited art'; Kendall, *The Drama of Dissent: The Radical Poetics of Non-Conformity, 1380–1590* (Chapel Hill, 1986), p. 131. The least dismissive of recent scholarship on Bale's drama is by Paul Whitfield White in *Theatre and Reformation: Protestantism, Patronage and Playing in Tudor England* (Cambridge, 1993), pp. 12–41.

cannot be harmed.[85] Bale's text is worded so closely to the scriptural text that one can imagine an audience ready for Christ's reply: 'Get thee behind me Satan'. Certainly, a later Protestant use of the episode does follow the scriptural text, with only a characteristic emphasis on particular verbs. Milton's *Paradise Regained* figures the episode, following the narrative of Luke, rather than Matthew, as follows:

> Cast thyself down: safely if Son of God
> For it is written, he will give command
> Concerning thee to his angels, in their hands
> They shall uplift thee, lest at any time
> Thou chance to dash thy foot against a stone.
> To whom thus Jesus; also it is written,
> Tempt not the lord thy God, he said and stood
> But Satan smitten with amazement fell. (*Paradise Regained* IV. 555–62)[86]

Barring the excision of Christ's imperative command and the use of the heavily laden Miltonic verbs 'stood' and 'fell', the passage is an extremely close rendition of the biblical passage.[87] Bale's text however, suddenly departs radically from its scriptural source. 'In no wyse ye ought the scriptures to deprave, / But as they lye whole so ought ye them to have' (ll. 215–16), says Bale's Christ, and so ensues a lengthy debate about Satan's reading of the Bible. 'Whye, is it not true that soch a text there is?', complains Satan; 'Yes, there is soch a text, but ye wrast it all amys', replies Jesus (ll. 221–2). Bale delays the biblical dismissal of Satan and instead foregrounds the fact that the scriptural passage is based itself on a debate about scriptural meaning, with Satan using Psalm 91 as a 'proof text' and Christ replying with a passage from Deuteronomy 6:16. The temptation becomes entirely about interpretation, about the need to fend off deceptive 'glossing' of a text which is 'whole', 'simple' and self-sufficient.

Moreover, the vital imagery of intellectual and interpretative integrity in opposition to a sophistic papist threat is part of a remarkable demonstration of how the symbolism of landscape associated with sophistication and luxury, the two demons of asceticism, was reconfigured by Protestantism. Monks, according to 'Sedition' in *King Johan*, are 'urban sects', ('fynd me in every towne / Where as is fownded any sect monastycall' (ll. 257–8)), something repeated by

---

[85]   There are in fact a choice of passages to follow; the Temptation is recorded, with the 'tests' in different order, in both Matthew 4:1–11 and Luke 4:1–13. Bale uses the former. See Happé, ed., *Complete Plays*, II p. 13.

[86]   J. Carey, ed., *The Complete Shorter Poems* (London, 1968, repr. 1997), p. 508.

[87]   For the importance of the verbs 'stood' and 'fell' see *Paradise Lost* III. 99: 'Sufficient to have stood, though free to fall' and Sonnet 16, l. 14: 'They also serve who only stand and wait'; A. Fowler, ed., *Paradise Lost* (London, 1968), p. 148; Carey, ed., *Complete Shorter Poems*, p. 333.

'Dissimulation's prophecy of Papal activities: 'He wyll also create the orders monastycall / Monkes, chanons, and fryers with gaye coates and shaven crownes / And buylde them places to corrupt cyties and townes' (ll. 995–7). The hypocrisy suggested in the combination of 'gay coats' and 'shaven crowns' is not just the product of the urbanized friars, but all the orders associated with Catholicism, including the traditionally withdrawn monastic orders. At the same time as the pejorative associations of the city are laid on the clergy, King Johan himself is eulogized by 'Veritas' after his death because he 'made both in towne and cytie / Grauntynge great lyberties for mayntenaunce of the same / By markettes and fayers in places of notable name' (ll. 2209–11). King John is the fulfilment of Fish's plea to the charitable, protective aspect of monarchy who cares for the 'sore, syke, halte and lame' (l. 2208). The topos of the urban has been divided: one half is associated with charity and the mutual benefits of Protestant monarch and his 'poor' people, the other retains all the ancient connotations of the fallen city and seems to be populated entirely by monks and friars. This sudden divide is aided by a geographical movement of the sin-laden city south-east, across Europe, to Rome. 'Blody Babulon', King Johan calls Rome, 'the grownd and mother of whordom – / The Romych Churche I meane, more vyle than ever was Sodom' (*King Johan*, ll. 368–70). In *God's Promises*, God himself, the character 'Pater Coelestis', attacks 'ye tyrauntes of Sodoma! … Dyscontent I am with yow beastes of Gomorra' (*God's Promises*, ll. 689–91) for their 'ydolatryes' (l. 688). The Roman Church, imagined as a pit of immorality in central Italy, is perceived to be evangelizing its quasi-biblical urban status with the reach of its friars and monks. The growing nationalism of English Protestantism struck upon the expedient image of the urban monster of Rome, shifting its apocalyptic conception of the fallen city onto a foreign object which had to be fought off.[88]

The idealized opposite of the legendary fallen city was also reconfigured in Bale's plays. The prophetic figures of Christ and John the Baptist, with their connections to wilderness asceticism, underwent a transformation. Bale's reworking of Christ's 40 days and nights in the wilderness is a case in point. The *Temptation* portrays Christ in the desert being accosted by Satan who, significantly, appears as a monk. Bale's stage direction has '*Hic simulate religione Christum aggreditur*', making the connection between Satan and monasticism visually palpable. Satan identifies himself as 'A brother … of thys desart wyldernesse' (l. 83), and compliments

---

[88]   Bale's *Image of Both Churches* was the first full-length Protestant commentary on Revelation. Following Luther's reading of the text as a prophecy of the Reformation, Bale appropriated Joachim de Fiore, the thirteenth-century writer who had such a marked influence on radical Franciscan thought, as a proto-Protestant, applying Fiore's identification of the antichrist with the papacy to the Reformation. Rome became the archetypal fallen city of Babylon. As John King writes, Bale's 'apocalyptic historical vision was ingrained in the Renaissance consciousness through assimilation into such major texts as the Geneva Bible, Foxe's *Acts and Monuments* and Book 1 of Spenser's *Faerie Queene*'; King, *Reformation Literature*, p. 61.

Christ for his choice of 'so vertuouse a lyfe ... / As here thus to wander in godly contemplacyon / And to lyve alone in the desert solytarye' (ll. 79–81). Christ replies bluntly: 'Your pleasure is it to utter your fantasye' (l. 82). Bale sets up the play as a denunciation of ascetic practices associated with monasticism. Christ remains in the wilderness, but his first purpose is to maintain that the whole endeavour of 'contemplcyon' practised by the 'desart solytarye' is 'fantasye'. Bale splits the significance of the wilderness, retaining the prophetic associations and jettisoning the connections to monastic asceticism. The same occurs in Bale's depictions of John the Baptist in *God's Promises* and *John the Baptist's Preaching*.[89]

John the Baptist's calling in *God's Promises* is a classic example of the attractions of the figure for the Protestant writer. Asked to 'pave the way' for the messiah, John replies, quoting a previous prophetic figure: 'Unmete lorde I am, *quia puer ego sum*, / And other than that, alac, I have no scyence / Fyt for that offyce, neyther yet cleane eloquence' (ll. 871–3). God's reply suggests that John's 'boyhood' and lack of 'science' and 'eloquence' are immaterial: in fact they are the things that God rightfully endows. It is because the Baptist is so 'simple' that he receives the gifts of 'grace / Eloquence and age, to speake in the desart place' (ll. 874–5). Bale underlines the direct inspiration of the vatic speaker by having the act of inspiration happen physically on stage. Bale's stage direction is '*Hic extendens dominus manum, labia Joannis digito tanget ac ori imponet auream linguam*'; God literally reaches out to John, touches his lips and gives him 'golden language'.[90] This moment when the 'poor', 'simple' prophet is endowed directly with the untutored eloquence of God can be seen as analogous to Bale's own self-fashioning in the *Vocacyon*. Indeed, the Baptist's prophecies in *Johan Baptystes Preachynge*, that 'The Mountayns and hylles shall be brought downe full lowe ... / Mekenesse wyll aryse and pryde abte by the Gospell. / The symple fysher shall now be notable / The spirytuall Pharyse a wretche detestable' (ll. 75–9) is in many ways more of a testament to Bale's hopes for the Reformation in England than a recapitulation of biblical history which will be fulfilled in Bale's following play.[91]

---

[89] The figure probably held a special attraction, and difficulty, for Bale because of his mendicant past: 'Bale's notebooks show a compulsive interest in the Baptist, whom legend held to be a Carmelite', Happé, ed., *Complete Plays*, I. 8.

[90] Quite how this 'golden language' would be represented is unclear. T. Blatt suggests in her edition that an emblematic tongue might have been placed in John's mouth. See T. Blatt, ed., *The Plays of John Bale* (Copenhagen, 1968), p. 91. Practically, however, the actor would have had to have taken the tongue out before speaking his next line. It seems possible that the 'golden language' could have been signalled by the exchange of a symbolic object, possibly even an English Bible.

[91] It seems logical that *Temptation* would follow *John Baptist's Preaching* in performance, enacting a continuous biblical narrative that echoed but sought to replace the traditional mystery cycles. See Happé, ed., *Complete Plays*, I. 12. Moreover, the printed organization of the texts suggests the interconnectedness of the two plays. Whilst *God's Promises*, *Preaching* and *Temptation* were all printed in 1547, the latter two plays were printed in a double volume, presenting them to the reader together. Bale's *Vocacyon*

The Baptist's own self-fashioning in the mould of Isaiah, as the 'vox clamantis in deserto' in *Preachynge* was almost a narrative of Bale's own historical self-understanding: 'I am the cryars voice / But he is the worde and message of rejoyce. / The lanterne I am, he is the very lyght' (ll. 203–5). The isolated, simple medieval antecedents with their own investment in John's image of the 'lanterne of light' had paved the way for the 'very light' of the Reformation whose own sense of being compassed round with darkness was about to be reinforced by the violent state policy of the Marian years.

But John the Baptist's image as the wilderness prophet to surpass Isaiah had to be carefully negotiated just as that of the ascetic, eremitical Christ had to be. Bale's didactic tendency to place a detached voice at the close of his plays to make sure the audience derived the right meaning was in some ways necessary. While we might be struck now by the overpowering conviction of Bale's dramaturgy, it is equally important here to see how precarious it is. The Baptist's association with the wilderness could easily be taken as a tacit support for the 'men's traditions' of monastic asceticism that Bale was so hell-bent on eschewing. Consequently, the voice of 'Baleus Prolocutor' begins to sum up the import of the preceding drama with the words: 'The waye that Johan taught was not to weare harde clothynge / To saye longe prayers, nor to wandre in the desart / Or to eate wylde locusts. No, he never taught soch thynge. / Hys mynde was that faythe shuld puryfye the hart' (ll. 472–5). The declamatory tone suggests that Bale thought he was quite likely to get an argument about it. Very overtly, and very pointedly, Bale steered the essential 'meaning' of John the Baptist away from the traditional associations of the wilderness with monastic ascetic practice, positing instead an active, embattled and isolated figure which reflected the dynamics of Bale's own self-image.

The isolation of the wilderness prophet in Bale's plays is perhaps what *is* new about this example of pastoral self-fashioning. James Simpson has written that the narrative of Protestant Reformation always posited three 'players': the 'people', Catholic institutions, and evangelical liberators.[92] But this formulation, I think, fits Bale far more than other early Protestants. Whilst the Lollards, Foxe, Fish and Tyndale all to some extent posited the image of a community of the 'simple fools of God', an image which centred on the self but assumed a common ground with others, persecuted though they might be, Bale's plays make the divinely inspired 'simple' prophet utterly singular and completely alone. Like Milton's Abdiel,

---

suggests that all three plays were performed as a day-long cycle on at least one occasion: 'The yonge men in the forenone played a Tragedye of God's Promises in the Olde Lawe at the market cross ... In the afternoone agayne they played a Commedie of Sanct Johan Baptistes preachinges of crist's baptisynge and of his temptacion in the wildernesse to the small contentacion of the prestes and other papists there'; *Vocacyon*, p. 59. One suspects that 'small contentacion' was a polite euphemism for the reaction Bale's deliberately contentious plays received from a largely Irish Catholic audience. There is little wonder that he was physically chased from his bishopric in Ossorie.

[92]   Simpson, *Burning to Read*, pp. 58–62.

'encompassed round with foes' (*Paradise Lost*, V.876), the glory of Bale's solitary testament to the truth was not to be compromised by some timely moral support. It is significant that among the many fissuring manoeuvres in Bale's drama, one is the dividing of the rhetoric of the 'poor' and 'simple' between the lone prophet and the 'people'.

In *King Johan*, the increasingly isolated proto-Protestant martyr-king is separated from the 'commynnalte' which he governs. The 'people' are certainly 'poor', ravaged by 'blyndnes' and 'poverte' because of the 'nowghty gydes' of the Catholic Church. To some extent, like Fish's beggars, Bale's picture of the 'Commynnalte' works as a polemical image of the victimized flock persecuted by a parasitic and predatory clergy. But the divide between the 'poor' inspired prophet and the '*Turba Vulgaris*' in *John Baptist's Preaching* demonstrates the underlying isolation of the 'simple faithful' from the 'poor commons' who had nurtured him. The weight of destiny lies on the shoulders of a single figure, poor though he may be, whose role it is to influence the recalcitrant vulgar crowd towards enlightenment. One image of simplicity is empowered whilst the other is curiously stripped of the spiritual efficacy that it had often been afforded.

In nascent form, Bale's isolated figures of simplicity suggest the central problem that Protestantism was to face in the latter part of the sixteenth century. As Diarmaid MacCulloch suggests, the arrival of political success, of a Protestant government, 'caused considerable problems for the self-image of … reformers … how difficult they found it to abandon the self-image of a persecuted little flock, which was implicit in the Lollard heritage, even whilst they were taking over an established national church and persecuting other little flocks'.[93] But by 1563, the year Bale died and his companion John Foxe published the first edition of the *Acts and Monuments*, the reflections of these cultural sympathies became an inherent part of national consciousness and were institutionally empowered. The formation of religious identity through these types of polemical pastoralism was now a central part of the way that Protestant England came to think about itself. Crowley's visions of Langland 'cry[ing] oute agaynste the worckes of darckenes', and Foxe's nostalgic imagining of the Wycliffite 'Christian days', became vital components of Protestant identity across the entire Tudor period.

---

[93] MacCulloch, *Tudor Church Militant*, p. 142.

Chapter 3

'The Living Ghost of *Piers Plowman*': The Ploughman in Print, 1510–1550

Significantly, the two most famous biblical scholars of the early sixteenth century chose to imagine the final effect of their endeavours as the meeting of ploughmen with scripture. Desiderius Erasmus, in his preface to his 1516 *Novum Testamentum*, now frequently identified as the 'paraclesis', stated 'I would ... that the farmer sing some part of them at the plow, the weaver hum some parts of them to the movement of his shuttle'.[1] In a long line of rhetorical phrases ('I would ... I would), the agricultural labourer takes his place amongst the figures of the lowest classes Erasmus could imagine. The 'lowliest woman', and 'farmer ... at the plow', the 'weaver': all are linguistic tools in a passage intended to throw the rhetorical weight of democratization behind a new edition of the New Testament. William Tyndale, according to Foxe, would famously say to an anonymous Catholic academic, with a rather more determined air, that 'If God spare my life ere many years, I will cause a boy that driveth the plough, shall know more of the scripture than thou dost'.[2] The different forms of the verbs are all important. Erasmus' 'I would' was the wish of the central figure of continental humanism, a figure who managed to negotiate various urbane networks of contacts around a European intellectual elite that stood on the periphery of the Reformation. Tyndale's resolute 'I will' had him executed. Of course, the fact that any 'plowboy' attempting to read Erasmus' text would have needed a more than workable knowledge of Latin, whilst Tyndale's could have, literally, learned scripture through contact with his vernacular work, didn't help. However, what is interesting is the presence of the ploughman, the rhetorical importance of the agricultural labourer in the discourse of two of the most formidable intellectuals of the period whose own labour centred around the study and translation of classical languages. Neither author can reasonably be assumed to have been particularly knowledgeable about the lives of the labouring classes, unless it was to castigate the unsettling aspects of groups such as the Anabaptists. But the ploughman is nevertheless *active* in both cases, his presence does something for the passages. The ploughman is a rhetorical figure, saturated with biblical ideas of social inversion. He is a sign of the democratization of spirituality, a sign that a whole nation could be steeped in scripture, suggesting the possibility of a Christian community echoing the Israelites of the Old Testament.

---

[1]   Erasmus, 'The Paraclesis' in *Christian Humanism and the Reformation: Desiderius Erasmus, Selected Writings*, ed. J. C. Olin (New York, 1965), pp. 92–106, 97.

[2]   *A&M*, IV. 117.

Above all else, the ploughman appears in these two famous passages because he has rhetorical efficacy, because he has picked up from the Bible, and from the pastoral tendency of much Protestant writing, a certain literary *power*. In the last chapter, I outlined how vital polemicized pastoralism was to early Reformation writing, and some ways in which it had precedents and parallels in earlier controversial writings. In this chapter I turn to one specific figure which is testament to the power of radical pastoral in the early Reformation period: the ploughman.

Of course, the ploughman had a complex history well before the Reformation. Paul Freedman has described how this 'complex image', at times analogous to the wickedness of Cain – the first man to till the earth – came in some cases to be a powerful symbol of peasant agency, piety, integrity and humility.[3] In a pair of important studies of Langland's *Piers Plowman*, Elizabeth Kirk and Stephen A. Barney have outlined the way in which Langland's ploughman developed rather suddenly in the later fourteenth century into a deeply pious quasi-clerical figure, and eventually into what Sarah Kelen has called 'the figural antithesis of the priest'.[4] Chaucer's matched siblings of parson and ploughman, some of the very few 'positive' portraits of the *General Prologue*, demonstrate what many critics have seen to be a striking debt to Langland's pious figure and at the same time an idealization that might thinly veil a sharply contemporary critique.[5] To scholars of medieval literature, then, the ploughman is an arresting and complex symbol well before we reach Tyndale's and Erasmus' rhetoric.

And indeed my discussion of the ploughman figure in early printed literature here is indebted to, and often analogous with, a raft of recent work by medievalists. Sarah Kelen and John Bowers have both recently produced books on the post-medieval literary history of Langland – both of which reach all the way into the nineteenth century, when the poem was edited for the first time since 1550.[6] Other medievalists have worked to shut down the avenues of enquiry which Kelen and Bowers have pursued. As I discussed in Chapter 1, Anne Hudson famously proclaimed that Langland's poem was essentially 'more honoured in the name than in the reading' in the sixteenth century.[7] More recently, James Simpson's hostile account of early Protestant writing has brought him to proclaim, twice, that the poem was 'unreachable' to Reformation writers too bound up with their

---

[3]   Freedman, *Images of the Medieval Peasant*, pp. 223–9.

[4]   Kelen, *Langland's Early Modern Identities*, p. 46; Stephen A. Barney, 'The Plowshare of the Tongue: The Progress of a Symbol from the Bible to *Piers Plowman*', *Mediaeval Studies*, 35 (1973), 261–93; Kirk, 'Langland's Plowman and the Recreation of Fourteenth-Century Religious Metaphor'.

[5]   The relation between Chaucer's portrait and Langland's poem has long been noted, but see in particular Helen Cooper, 'Langland's and Chaucer's Prologues', *YLS*, 1 (1987), 71–81. On the latent critique hidden by these idealized figures, see Christopher Dyer, 'Piers Plowman and Plowmen', *YLS*, 8 (1994), 155–76.

[6]   Kelen, *Langland's Early Modern Identities*; Bowers, *Chaucer and Langland*.

[7]   Hudson, 'Epilogue: The Legacy of *Piers Plowman*', pp. 251–66, 263.

tyrannical theological ideas to grasp the 'decentralized' theology Langland was apparently preaching.[8] But I am less concerned here with broad-brush theological or cultural history, and less interested in circumscribing this chapter strictly within the bounds of a history of *Piers Plowman* reception. What we see in the early printed depictions of the ploughman is, as Andrew McRae puts it, the 'struggle over the identity of a cultural icon'.[9] This struggle produces a figure who is often a great deal more ambivalent and various than one might expect.

In early printed ploughman literature we discover first the complexity of the ploughman figure in the earlier Henrician period – especially in the 1520s. The end of this decade, however, brought with it the Reformation Parliament, and the resulting transformation of the figure into a reformist polemicist. The satirical and anticlerical possibilities of the ploughman figure – already latent in the 1520s – then became absolutely central to this icon of Protestant pastoralism.

I then go on to show how this figure was utilized for polemical purposes between 1530–1550, in particular in the controversies over the historical precedent of Lutheranism, and the mid-century agrarian crisis. Finally I return to the most-discussed of sixteenth-century ploughman literature: Robert Crowley's editions of *Piers Plowman* (1550). But here, I argue, as much as we can detect the influence of this market for ploughman polemic, we can also see Crowley swimming against that tide, producing editions of the poem which are high-kudos, institutionally-respected examples of an eclectic Edwardian literary canon shaped as much by contact with the vernacular version of humanist writing which appeared in the mid-century as by the polemical ploughman.

'Priest shall I never truste agayne': Diversity and the Henrician Ploughman

The earliest example of 'ploughman literature' in the Henrician period is a remarkable text entitled *A Lyttle Geste how the plowman lerned his Paternoster* (1510).[10] This short text is a 'gesting' moral piece that seems to have been almost entirely ignored by critics. Anne Hudson awards it the most attention and calls it simply 'strangely un-edifying'.[11] However, the text utilizes some important images

---

[8]   Simpson, *Reform and Cultural Revolution*, pp. 328–30; the point is also made in Simpson, 'Grace Abounding: Evangelical Centralisation and the End of *Piers Plowman*', *YLS*, 14 (2000), 49–73.

[9]   Andrew McRae, *God Spede the Plough: The Representation of Agrarian England, 1500–1660* (Cambridge, 1996), p. 2.

[10]   *A Lyttle Geste how the plowman lerned his Paternoster* (London, 1510). References incorporated in the text.

[11]   Hudson, 'Legacy', p. 258. The text is described, very briefly, by Kelen in *Langland's Early Modern Identities*, pp. 71–2; see also the brief account in Nicholas Watson, '*Piers Plowman*, Pastoral Theology, and Spiritual Perfectionism: Hawkyn's Cloak and Patience's Pater Noster', *YLS*, 21 (2007), 83–118.

of material wealth and physical, and more importantly spiritual, idleness – images and ideas which will come to underpin much of the reformist ploughman literature of the 1530s to 1550s. However, these ideas are 'inverted', they do not consolidate the ploughman figure but undermine him, siphoning off the clerical aspect of the ploughman to create a pro-clerical morality tale at the expense of the laity.

De Worde's ploughman is not quite what we expect. Whilst he works 'To mowe and repe bothe grasse and corne' and knows 'all thynge that to husbandry dyde fall', these labours do not produce a character, they are not ontological characteristics but labour which produces pay: de Worde's ploughman lives in a market driven society, and one in which the labourer is aspirational and potentially wealthy. The labour is not in itself a role or identity, but a means: 'By these to ryches he was brought / That golden ne sylver he lacked nought' (sig. A1v). Significantly, this wealth is demonstrated not with the actual currency, but through the produce it buys. The sign of the ploughman's wealth is the plethora of food on his table. Whilst Langland's ploughman is unable to offer Hunger anything 'neiþer gees ne grys … I haue no salt bacon / Ne no cokeney … coloppes to maken!' (B6.280–284/C8.304–8), de Worde's ploughman has *everything*. Langland's imagined labourers who would accept 'no peny ale … no pece of bacoun / But if it be fressh flessh' (B6.308–9/C8.332–3) have reappeared: the ploughman has become aspirational and wealthy. His house's 'rofe was full of bacon flytches … full of egges butter and cheese … onions and garlicke had he … and good crème and mylke of the cow' (sig. A1v). The build up of names of the different foodstuffs is quick and effective, building an image of overabundance and luxury which is consolidated by the context of famine, 'of corne is grete skarsnesse' (sig. A2r). This is the image that the author uses to lead the reader into the text's real 'mater', the ploughman's ignorance of the Lord's Prayer. A correlation is made between this specifically glutinous luxury, and a spiritual laziness, and there is a sense that a more significant type of labour has been neglected.

This is the central matter of the text and one underlined by the priest, and the importance of the *Pater Noster* is obvious: 'without it saued canst thou not be' (sig. A2r). What underlies this short narrative is a latent argument over the cause of this ignorance which is, from the perspective of either medieval dissent or the sixteenth-century Reformation, absolutely vital. The ploughman's defence is one of total ignorance: 'what thynge is that which ye desire to here so sore I herde neuer therof before' (sig. A2r). The idea of the ploughman's complete ignorance of the Lord's Prayer is important. It brings with it the veiled possibility of anticlerical discourse; it raises the interpretative possibility that complete ignorance of the essential articles of faith in the laity is caused by the failure of the pastoral duty of the clergy. It is this protested ignorance that the priest first attacks, pondering 'I meruayl right gretly That thy byleue was neuer taught the' (sig. A2r). The 'marvel' is of course extremely pointed, and the ploughman, when offered the opportunity to learn the *Pater Noster* from the priest, condemns himself with his own obstinacy: 'I wolde threshe sayde the plowman yeres ten rather than I it wolde leren' (sig. A2r). The ploughman confirms his reluctance to learn an essential article of faith and exposes his previous claim to ignorance as a blatant evasion. Instead of learning the prayer, the ploughman attempts bribery, a kind of inverted simony in which he offers the priest 'fourty shelynges in grotes rounde' if he will show the ploughman 'how I maye heven reach' without having to labour at the prayer. Interestingly, it is simony that is the standard centre point of any anticlerical discourse, whether it be in Dante, Chaucer, Tyndale or Spenser. Here the possibility of simony is directly placed in the actions of the lay ploughman. The priest significantly makes no reply to the offer anywhere in the text. Instead the priest must teach the ploughman his *Pater Noster*, playing on his greed and forcing him to recite the words of the prayer one at a time as if they were names of poor debtors who owed the ploughman corn or money.

The text uses this latent possibility of anticlericalism contained in the ignorance/ obstinacy argument concerning the ploughman's ignorance, but uses it to defend the efficacy of the clergy's pastoral care by locating the culpability for spiritual poverty, material corruption and doctrinal ignorance in the insensate laity. The text ends in a striking way, in a court scene in which the official support for the well-intentioned guile of the priest produces a vindictive aside from the ploughman: 'priest shall I never truste agayne' (sig. A4v). It is a curious way to end the ploughman's role in the text, and curiously prophetic of the ploughman literature which will develop over the next 40 years, as if the conservative sensibilities of the text are aware of the radically different potential for the ploughman figure and seek to pre-empt and undermine the assumed integrity of the ploughman's voice that will become more and more evident.

Of Gentylnes and Nobylyte (1525),[12] a dialogue printed by John Rastell, brother-in-law to Sir Thomas More, is an exemplary text in early Henrician depictions of the ploughman. The text's depiction of the ploughman is extremely ambivalent yet very suggestive. At times shockingly radical, at others openly quietist, sometimes openly legitimized and at others clearly undermined, the figure of the ploughman in Heywood's text amply demonstrates the complexity of the icon in the Henrician period. To some extent, this difficulty in identifying the ploughman's status and role in the text might be explained by the form of the text itself. Any reader familiar with Thomas More's *Utopia* (1516) can expect a humanist dialogue 'with divers toys and gestis addyd', as the title has it, to be formidably difficult to pin down, and likely to refuse ideological closure through constant recourse to linguistic and structural irony. However, the text itself seems to vacillate extensively over what the ploughman really *means*, as if the 'struggle over a cultural icon' that McRae described is enacted, without closure, in the text itself.

---

[12]   *Of Gentylnes and Nobylyte* (London, 1525). The authorship of the text is unclear. The final page note 'Johanes rastell me fieri fecit', before the usual 'cum privilegio regali' has obviously created some problems. Both the STC and EEBO treat Rastell as the author rather than the printer. Here I use the edition of the text in *Three Rastell Plays: Four Elements, Calisto and Melebea, Gentleness and Nobility*, ed. Richard Axton (Cambridge, 1979). Axton attributes the play to Heywood.

The 'gesting' dialogue ostensibly concerns 'who is a very gentylman and who is a noble man'. The subject of the text is class authority. The lines of the debate are drawn between a merchant, a knight and the ploughman. However, the dialogue opens with the ploughman absent, in an argument between the 'old' and 'new' money of the mercantile and aristocratic figures. The merchant opens and controls the debate with a self-congratulatory air: 'I am magnyfyed and gretly regardyd, / And for a wyse and noble man estemyd' (ll. 9–10). Immediately the knight replies from a different perspective, that of inherited wealth, the feudal perspective, contesting the merchant's 'presumpsion' by asking 'what your auncestours were' (ll. 12, 14).

Interestingly, the merchant seems to have usurped the rhetoric that is traditionally that of the labourer, a discourse of self-sufficiency. He states 'that whyche I haue got by myn own labour and wit' (l. 25), and proclaims 'I call hym a gentylman that gentilly / Doth gyf unto other men lovyngly … myn auncestours haue giffyn alwey / to thyne auncestours such thynge as they / By their labours did trewly get and wyn' (ll. 45–6, 51–3). The merchant has reinvented himself as the generous provider, or at least someone able to claim inherited dignity from them; those who would, as Langland's ploughman did, 'swynke and swete and sowe for us bothe' (B6.25). Amusingly the ploughman enters to break up this upper class wrangle, not as the dignified labourer, but as a Bakhtinian figure who enters 'with a short whyp in hys hand' and launches into a far from weighty reprimand: 'Now here is bybbyll babbyll clytter clatter! / I hard never of so folysh a matter' (ll. 175–6). His comical role is underlined by his immediately egotistical engagement in the 'matter' that he attacks: 'to speke the troth, / I am better than other of you bothe' (ll. 177–8). This is far from the assumed dignity of Langland's Piers the Plowman. But it is complicated by the ploughman's constant presence in the discourse of the moneyed classes. Every time the merchant and knight embark upon an argument, the ploughman interrupts to be bluntly insulting: 'Two proude folys make a crakkyng, / And when it commyth to point, dare do no thing … By God all the reasons syth ye began, / That ye have made therof, be not worth a fly' (ll. 202–3, 209–10). Just before this tirade begins, a Latin stage direction reads '*Et verberat eos*', 'he beats them'. The 'gentyl' debate is constantly interrogated by the ploughman prototype of Lear's fool; undignified, sneering, funny, and not entirely wrong.

But this role is suddenly revoked, and the ploughman enters the debate with what seems like a tangential question: 'What is the noblest thynge that can be?' (l. 279). The answer, somewhat surprisingly, comes in a discussion of theological and philosophical proportions in which the discourse of self-sufficiency and productive labour are wrested back from the merchant. The most noble thing that can be is God 'which reynith etern in blysse' because he 'is in him self so suffycyent, / And nedyth the helpe of no nothyr thyng' (ll. 283, 288–9). 'Sufficiency' is back in the debate, but now controlled by the ploughman, and used to attack both merchant and knight: 'I cannot see whi ye ought or mai / Call your self noble because ye were it, / Which was made bi other menis labour and wit' (ll. 322–4).

The collocation 'labour and wit', familiar from the merchant's opening speech, is repossessed by the ploughman, who then strikes off into a discussion of natural science and philosophy, concluding that man, though 'impotens' in his body is rightfully master of creation 'by hys soule, beyng so excellent' and because of 'hys soule intyllectyve' (ll. 378–9). The Bakhtinian fool has transformed into a disputant with a theological and philosophical agenda far beyond that afforded to the merchant or knight. Likewise, the sheer amount of space accorded to his discourse by the author is impressive. The ploughman is suddenly at the centre of the dialogue, and working at its highest register.

The figure has shifted in seriousness and register, but now he combines a philosophical disputation with a stream of increasingly radical ideas surrounding social levelling which are deeply reminiscent of the ploughman's rebellious past and polemical future:

> Thou thynkest thy self a gentylman to be;
> And that is a folyssh reason, semyth me.
> For when Adam dolf and Eve span,
> Who was then a gentylman? (ll. 483–6)

Whilst I do not wish to argue that the text itself is Wycliffite, and that Rastell is merrily printing illicit texts in 1525, it seems that Lollardy, or at least the record of John Ball's sermon recorded by Thomas Walsingham, had found its way into Renaissance literary culture, and done so in the company of the iconic ploughman.[13] The ploughman goes on to attack the knight, with the words 'Thy blood and the beggars of one colour be' (l. 521), a surprisingly close parallel of Langland's 'breþeren as of oo blood, as wel beggeres as erles' (B11.199). Although it is tempting to assert a direct literary connection, what is most important is the certainty that there is a connection here between the ploughman figure, religious discourse and potentially radical ideas concerning social levelling. The 'living ghost' of *Piers Plowman*, if not of the text, then at least of the Langlandian literary culture of the 1381 rebels, is clearly present. What becomes more interesting is that the text itself seems extremely unsure about what to do with this newly radicalized and Langlandian ploughman. At first the figure becomes blunter in his attacks, leaving ideas of social levelling behind and directly attacking the propertied classes. He confronts the knight with the words: 'By Gogges swete body, thou lyest falsely; / All possessions began furst of tyranny' (ll. 597–8), and that 'such extorsyoners had oppressyd / The labouryng people' (sig. B2r). The direct attack on the 'tyranny' of property, and those who possess it, sounds somewhere in between St Francis and

---

[13]   The couplet was supposedly John Ball's text for a sermon delivered to the insurgents of 1381; see Dobson, *The Peasants' Revolt of 1381*, p. 374. Versions of this rhyme were, however, also proverbial and widespread. See, for example, the use of it in an excellent fourteenth-century lyric, R. T. Davis, ed., *Medieval English Lyrics: A Critical Anthology* (London, 1963), p. 143.

Gerard Winstanley. More importantly, it sounds a great deal like the attacks on enclosure that proliferate in the later Henrician and Edwardian years. The figure has passed simply attacking the abuses of luxury or ostentation and is attacking the very idea of private property itself.

The text continues to focus on the ploughman, yet it both magnifies him and seeks to dampen his radicalism and subsume his stature within the structure of the dialogue. The text actually gives the 'stage' to the ploughman at one point; whilst the merchant and knight disappear, the ploughman enters a lengthy monologue which includes the almost millenarian desire to see a time when 'our governours may intend / Of all enormytees the reformacyon, / And bryng in theyr handis the rod of coreccyon' (ll. 997–9). The reforming outburst is the culmination of the ploughman's character after his transformation from fool to philosopher, and it is also the aspect that the text foregrounds as the spokesman of the 'poor', a genuinely self-sufficient labourer who debates theological points beyond the grasp of merchant or knight. He is no longer to be discounted. Yet the ploughman is suddenly silenced. His final words potentially discount the force of everything he has said. For all his desire for 'reformacyon', he ends on a note of deliberate impotence:

> Gestyng, and raylyng, they mend no thyng.
> For the amendement of the world is not in me. (ll. 1003–4)

Then he disappears, almost instantly, from the text. He is replaced by the knight and merchant who comment on how they are 'glad that he is gon' (l. 1014), that they should 'let churllys bable' (l. 1094). There is a massive ambiguity here about how this moment should be interpreted. The ploughman is the only figure to have a soliloquy barring the 'Philosopher' who stands outside the dialogue and provides closure, moving the debate over 'gentylnes' out of the discourse of class and into an abstract 'virtue' – much like the debates that concern other Tudor drama like Medwall's *Fulgens and Lucres* (c. 1510). The ploughman's closing speech is clearly not intended to sound foolish or ineloquent. If anything it is designed to make the speaker seem less politicized than he seems to be. Yet the returning figures ridicule him as if we were still dealing with the Bakhtinian figure of the ploughman's entrance, and the dialogue swiftly shifts into one concerning opposing political theories of elected and inherited government. The structure of the text seems to subsume the ploughman, keeping him within the aimless, egotistical comic world of the class-bound debate, yet he stands in the centre of the text, alone, speaking with a sophistication and radicalism which has developed virtually out of nowhere. The text seems to have imbued the figure with iconic authority yet apparently attempts to confine and silence that authority as quickly and effectively as possible.

As mentioned above, the 'experimental' nature of the dialogue form in this period, a form that rejects the wholesale support of particular voices through self-reflexive irony, could be seen to be part of the reason for the baffling complexity of the text.[14] But what seems clearer is that the very status and identity of the ploughman figure is deeply uncertain and sharply contested. The buffoonish, sneering and immoral figure of de Worde's panegyric to Catholic pastoral practice transforms, in a rather hallucinatory, Langlandian fashion, into a clearly unsettling and radical voice for social reformation that is both legitimized and silenced by the culture that produced it. John Heywood, the likely playwright, has been characterized by Greg Walker as one of a number of writers who were part of a pre-Reformation Henrician 'culture of enquiry and counsel'. This culture is characterized as a self-confident culture pushed into psycho-social dysfunction by Henrican tyranny after the Reformation Parliament.[15] Walker's study is arresting, but one wonders here about the state of Heywood's nerves whilst he wrote *Of Gentleness and Nobility*. For Heywood's representation of the ploughman is full of power, but also full of hesitation and self-effacement, as if the engaging social critiques of the figure are a little too pressing, as if that reformist voice is simultaneously enthralling and revolting, as if Heywood's play is fraught with the tensions between reformist id and conservative ego.

In these early texts, then, the ploughman appears as a complex and even rather confused figure whose significance is not yet clearly defined. There is a sense that the figure is indeed caught in the midst of a 'struggle over the identity of a cultural icon'.[16] His cultural status, characteristic style and religious associations are deeply ambiguous. At moments he seems to be a figure with a burgeoning literary, rhetorical and polemical efficacy. Yet, simultaneously, the power of the figure is suppressed, allowed to dissipate into bawdy comedy or be subsumed within a traditional hierarchy of class and 'wisdom'. There is an anxious hesitation about Heywood's endorsement of the agitational aspect of the symbol of ruralism. Such nervousness regarding the symbolic figure becomes more apparent in cases where the phenomenon of direct governmental censorship or authorization surround the production of 'ploughman literature' in the period. This literature also, significantly, begins to demonstrate the ferocious polemical potential and reformist pedigree of the figure's voice.

Significantly, of course, the dividing line between the diversity of the Henrician ploughman detailed above and the polemical ploughman of much later writing is the Reformation Parliament. From 1528–1529 onwards, the momentum of state reform of England's ecclesiastical culture – much of it including violence to people and property – increases at a frightening rate. The 1530s witness a striking phenomenon. The ploughman becomes synonymous with the aggressive pursuit of reform as quickly as devotional practices and institutions such as monastic and mendicant houses could be culled by the Henrician government.

---

[14]   On this form see in particular the classic study by Joel B. Altman, *The Tudor Play of Mind: Rhetorical Enquiry and the Development of Elizabethan Drama* (Berkeley, 1978).

[15]   Walker, *Writing under Tyranny*, esp. pp. 5–26, 20.

[16]   McRae, *God Spede the Plough*, p. 2.

The speed of this process is neatly demonstrated by the differences between Heywood's *Of Gentleness and Nobility* (1525) and the two 'Chaucerian' pieces *The Plowman's Tale* (*c*. 1532) and *Jack Upland* (1536). Neither of them contains anything remotely approximate to Chaucer's writing in terms of style or subject matter, barring their anticlerical stance, and some uncertainty over their authorship is apparent even in the sixteenth century.[17] However, the frontispieces of both texts assert Chaucer's authorship. The printing of these texts in the guise of Chaucerian literature is part of what is described below as an ideologically-motivated antiquarian project, an attempt to endow the text's overwhelming anticlericalism with the authority of age and literary quality. But the specificity of these texts as 'Chaucerian' is significant. By attaching them to the name of such a 'respectable' author, one who had been a centrepiece of the socially and religiously conservative period of early print culture in England, the fierce anticlerical critique contained in them stood a much greater chance of surviving the rigour of both the censor and the marketplace.

The figure of the ploughman in these texts has changed radically from that of the *Lyttle Geste* (1510), picking up on the indignant, polemical aspect of Heywood's figure and excising his hesitations and qualifications. Significantly, the ploughman here is no longer presented in the company of a noble or merchant: he is an image of severe privation. He is imagined as

> forswonke and all forswat
> Men might have sene through both his chekes
> And every wang toth and where it sat.[18]

Similarly, his livestock is 'feble ... of hem nys lefte but bone and skinne' (ll. 5, 15). This is a far cry from the aspirational figure of the earlier text, and a great deal closer to the meagre household of Langland's Piers, who complains to Hunger that 'I have no peny ... palettes for to bugge' (B6. 179) and to the more deprived image of *Pierce the Plowman's Crede*, in which Piers' wife appears 'Barfote on the bare ijs' and his cattle so thin that 'Men mighte reken ich a rib'.[19] The texts which seek in some way to constrain or contradict the efficacy of the ploughman

---

[17]   John Bale, for example, allocates a text he calls variously 'narrationem agricole' and 'Aratoris narrationem', almost certainly the *Plowman's Tale*, to Chaucer, but states plainly that 'Joannes Wiclef scripsit Iack Uplande'; John Bale, *Index Britanniae Scriptorum*, eds C. Brett and J. Carley (Cambridge, 1990) pp. 75, 76, 274.

[18]   Mary Rhinelander McCarl, ed., *The Plowman's Tale: The c. 1532 and 1606 Editions of a Spurious Canterbury Tale* (London, 1997), ll. 13–16. All references are to McCarl's edition of the *c*. 1532 text, incorporated in the text. Quotations from *Jack Upland* are from James Dean's edition in *Six Ecclesiastical Satires*.

[19]   *Pierce the Plowman's Crede*, in H. Barr, ed., *The Piers Plowman Tradition*, ll. 436, 432. The late fourteenth-century text is claimed by the writer of the *Plowman's Tale* (ll. 1066) as his own work, but the massive difference in verse form and style make this

all provide him with substantially more wealth. When his polemical potential is unleashed he is elevated by his privation to the position of a legitimate spokesman for dissent and reform. The self-deprecating aspects of the figure, his financial, and increasingly his linguistic insufficiencies, work to form the strength and integrity of his speech. There is here, as there was in archetypal form in *Piers Plowman*, a vaticinal aspect to the ploughman. This image allows his voice to leave behind the 'bybbyll babbyll' of the *Lyttle Geste* and become a 'vox clamantis in deserto', a powerful ethical voice in the mould of John the Baptist or Isaiah. It is this voice that the ploughman will increasingly speak with in the literature of the mid-century.

Significantly, the ploughman appears without the qualifying voices of other figures, and is instead supported by a reconfigured Chaucerian host. The *Plowman's Tale*'s use of this character in its prologue is significant. It both serves to 'graft' the tale into the form of a 'Canterbury Tale', and it forms the reader's identification with the figure. The entrenched conservatism of Chaucer's host who claims to 'smell a loller in the wynde' when he encounters the 'Parisshe Prest' who will narrate, or rather preach, the 'Parson's Tale', has disappeared.[20] Instead he becomes a narrator himself, the perspective through which the reader sees the ploughman, and a kind of witness to his elevated status. Similarly, his comments on the ploughman's own narrative are characterized by total approbation rather than edgy criticism. He requests that the ploughman 'Come nere and tell us some holy thyng' (l. 45), and politely requests that he 'Say on … I the beseche' (l. 49).

The vision of the ploughman that we see through the host's eyes is one which highlights aspects of the figure which would clearly be attractive to a reformist readership in the 1530s. He is described as 'sunne ibrent' (l. 18), and as 'a man wont to walke about / He was nat alwaie in cloister ipente' (ll. 21–2). This negative description of the figure is vital. He appears as a kind of Godly doppelganger to the clergy who are 'in cloister ipente'. This is an early formulation of Milton's scathing attack on 'cloistered virtue'.[21] The ploughman is defined by his labour, and by the physical effects of it. The opposing image of the clergy is implied to be over-protected and indolent. Like Langland's quintessentially rural figure, the ploughman is formed in opposition to the clergy who are figured by *Jack Upland* as specifically urban, as 'coveitous in marketiis … and caymes caste-makers' (ll. 69–70). The construction works to identify the sixteenth-century reformist reader with the ploughman, endowing him with a similar identity through their shared anticlericalism.

---

difficult to believe. See McCarl, *Plowman's Tale*, p. 228. The text was printed by Reynor Wolfe in 1553.

[20]   Chaucer, 'The Man of Law's Epilogue' in Benson, *The Riverside Chaucer*, II. 1173.

[21]   Indeed, *The Plowman's Tale* was clearly the most important aspect of 'Chaucer' for Milton, as it was for Spenser. See John Milton, *Of Reformation* in *The Works of John Milton*, 18 vols, general ed. F. A. Patterson (New York, 1931–1938), III. 44, in which Milton quotes at length from the *Plowman's Tale*.

One of the central aspects of these texts, their foregrounding of a socially conservative 'estates model' view of society, is likewise something that would have been peculiarly attractive to a reformist reader in the 1530s, as state Protestantism found its way through the vexed question of temporal authority over the Church during the years of the Anglican break with Rome. The ploughman's vitriolic anticlericalism is formed through an idea of the breakdown of a natural societal organization, the usurpation of power, status and social roles not assigned to the clergy in this political model. At the opening of *Jack Upland*, the rural narrator outlines this estates model in the Langlandian allegorization of the Trinity:

> So he [God] sette mannes state: in lordis to represnte the power of the fadir; prieestis to represente the wisdom of the sone; and the commons to presente the good lastinge wille of the Holi Goost. (ll. 5–10)

The appropriate offices of the estates are directed at the point of creation by the creator. To transgress against this order is to figuratively take the forbidden fruit again. Societal structure and the correct 'degree' of the people who live within it is part of a structure with cosmological scope. In this context, the main thrust of the ploughman's anticlericalism becomes not one of overbearing authority but of illicit usurpation, that the clergy have been influenced by the antichrist 'to do lewid mennes office' (l. 15). Such a negative perspective on the Church's temporal power could not but be attractive to a reformist reader in the decade that saw the English state dissolve the culture of monasticism in England and defy papal authority to the extent of virtually excommunicating itself.

The structure of the *Plowman's Tale* is constructed to a similar purpose. In the mode of a debate poem, the text describes two opposing figures: the Pelican, a Christocentric allegory of those 'symple and small' (l. 57), against the Griffon, a symbol of those 'great growen … Popes cardinals and Prelates' (l. 58, 62) who are notably described as 'sharpe as fyre' (l. 91). The ostensible violence of the Church figure suggests the fires of the trials of reformists and the burning of books that were part and parcel of orthodox culture in England from Arundel's *Constitutions* onwards. The development of these opposing figures is the central shaping idea of the text. The 'symple and small' championed by the ploughman are images of Christ-like virtue who like 'a lambe … lykeneth Christ over all' (l. 98): they are fashioned in the image of the '*agnus dei*' of John's gospel. The image that defines the clergy's power is again scriptural, but has important repercussions for the social vision of the ploughman:

> Christ sayd: *Qui gladio percutit*
> With swerde he shall dye
> He bade his preestes peace. (ll. 245–7)

The biblical episode of a disciple's attempt to protect Christ by force in Gethsemane is taken as an image of the ideal, pacifistic clergy. But it is also a traditional image of temporal power, of the governmental and military aspects of secular, noble authority. The clergy are not only falling from an ideal by 'taking up the sword', they are transgressing against a divinely bestowed social role; they will 'lede … lordes lyues' (l. 273) through the sword when 'A swerde no sheperde usen ought' (l. 583). Clerical power is figured as a usurpation of a God-given social role which causes the unleashing of the antichrist and the collapse of moral society. It is an image which takes the apocalyptic aspect of anti-fraternalism at the close of Langland's poem and fits it more fully to the question of ecclesiastical authority as a whole. It is also an image which would be equally attractive to a fifteenth-century Wycliffite and a sixteenth-century reformer, both of whose calls for clerical disendowment made them, at least temporarily, allies of secular government.

The nature of these texts in terms of their dates is ambiguous, especially the former, and only a tentative critical consensus exists. They are both most likely fifteenth-century Wyclifite texts, with the *Plowman's Tale* having a sixteenth-century 'prologue' attached to graft it into the text of the *Canterbury Tales*.[22] However, the concerns of authorship and provenance, largely the focus of modern scholarship on the texts, must be subsumed within an analysis whose assumptions are both simpler and more forceful. These were the texts printed, bought and read in the 1530s. In the case of the *Plowman's Tale*, it was a central attraction of Chaucer's works from 1542 until Tyrwhitt excised it in the late eighteenth century. In McCarl's words, this was 'the accepted Chaucer, the Chaucer of Spenser and Milton'.[23] Regardless of problematic questions of date and authorship, it is necessary to realize that, whilst we recognize Chaucer's anticlericalism, we must also recognize that the anticlericalism was presented here as brutal, prolific and, vitally, similar to reformist sentiment. Whilst it seems garishly anachronistic, this was the central aspect of Chaucer's identity for over two centuries. This was the image of Chaucer that the sixteenth century bequeathed to literary history. Moreover, what is important about this image of the 'father of English poetry' is that it places him in the disconcerting shadow of his contemporary: his image

---

[22]   Some very eminent critics assume that the text is entirely a product of the sixteenth century. See A. G. Dickens, 'The Shape of Anti-clericalism and the English Reformation' in *Politics and Society in Reformation Europe: Essays for Sir Geoffrey Elton*, eds E. Kouin and T. Scott (New York, 1987), pp. 379–410, 382; and Alistair Fox, *Politics and Literature in the Reigns of Henry VII and Henry VIII* (Oxford, 1989), p. 222. Fox also asserts, without any evidence, that Thomas Godfray, the printer of the text, was also its author. Previously Andrew Wawn had argued, using the evidence of vocabulary analysis, that the majority of the text could be dated to the fifteenth century; see 'The Genesis of the Plowman's Tale', *Yearbook of English Studies*, 2 (1972), 21–40. Although, unlike *Jack Upland*, there is no extant manuscript of the text that predates the sixteenth century, the text's most recent editor follows Wawn's thesis; see McCarl, *Plowman's Tale*, pp. 16–41.

[23]   McCarl, *Plowman's Tale*, p. 14.

is distinctly Langlandian.[24] The brief portrait of the ploughman in the 'General Prologue', a minor aside, possibly a pointed reference to Langland's work, becomes a central character of the *Canterbury Tales*, and a figure as closely bound to the perceived image of the author as Piers the Plowman is to Langland. The deft, self-conscious sophistication of Chaucer is utterly refigured in the image of an extremely polemical version of Langland's icon.[25]

The controversial aspect of the ploughman in these texts has been augmented by the spectre of state censorship and authorization that has been persistently detected by critics and commentators from the late sixteenth to late twentieth centuries.[26] The enigmatic absence of the *Plowman's Tale* in *Chaucer's Works* (1532), edited by William Thynne and printed by Thomas Godfray, has produced a vexed issue of censorship concerning the text. Indeed, its *not* being included lends weight to the most recent, and most thorough, work on Thynne's 1532 edition, which sees Thynne swimming against the tide of reformist appropriation, as a representation of Chaucer as 'a moderate, consensual, figure, not a radical one'.[27] The *Plowman's Tale* was printed as a single, separate edition around 1532–1535, yet it does not appear in the text of the *Canterbury Tales* until 1542, where it would stay until 1775.[28] The cause of this curious bibliographical phenomenon could well be something as pragmatic as the tight deadlines of a busy printer's shop, or

---

[24]   This is, as John M. Bowers has argued, an important period in the history of the Chaucer/Langland traditions in which the two writers – unusually – become proximate with each other. See Bowers, *Chaucer and Langland*, p. 225.

[25]   On this polemicized version of Chaucer, see for example Carolyn Collette, 'Afterlife' in *A Companion to Chaucer*, ed. Peter Brown (Oxford, 2000), pp. 8–22, esp. 11–13; John J. Thompson, 'Reception: Fifteenth to Seventeenth Centuries' in *Chaucer: An Oxford Guide*, ed. Steve Ellis (Oxford, 2005), pp. 497–511, esp. pp. 505–7.

[26]   The major modern commentators on the *Plowman's Tale*, Andrew Wawn and Mary Rhinelander McCarl, both suggest a propagandist purpose. See Wawn, 'Genesis of the *Plowmans Tale*', pp. 21–40 and 'Chaucer, The *Plowman's Tale* and Reformation Propaganda: The Testimonies of Thomas Godfray and *I Playne Piers*', *Bulletin of the John Ryland's Library*, 56 (1973), 174–92, and pp. 37–41 of McCarl's introduction to *The Plowman's Tale*. Thomas Heffernan also propounds this theory, see 'Aspects of the Chaucerian Apocrypha: Animadversions on William Thynne's Edition of the *Plowman's Tale*' in *Chaucer Traditions: Studies in Honour of Derek Brewer*, eds R. Morse and B. Windeatt (Cambridge, 1990), 155–67. The problems of Thynne's account, and of the assumption that the state was directly involved in the production of the text, are explored below.

[27]   Walker, *Writing under Tyranny*, pp. 29–99, 33.

[28]   The year of publication was not printed with the text and its exact date is unknown. Wawn originally assumed the date of publication to be 1533, but later tentatively asserts a date as late as 1536, implying that the *Plowman's Tale* and *Jack Upland* were produced in close succession. McCarl, however, suggests a date shortly following the printing of Thynne's *Works* in 1532. See Wawn, 'Genesis', p. 21 and 'Propaganda', p. 175; McCarl, *Plowman's Tale*, p. 16. For a recent discussion of the text, see Kelen, *Langland's Early Modern Identities*, pp. 66–8.

as ideologically enticing as a growing demand for 'reformist medievalism' in the decade – something to which we will return – but the most notorious supposition originates with an account written by William Thynne's son at the close of the sixteenth century.

Francis Thynne's *Animadversions* (1598) states that

> this tale, when king Henry the Eighth had read, he called my father unto him, saying, 'William Thynne! I doubt this will be allowed; for I suspect the bishops will call thee in question for it' ... my father was called in question by the bishops, and heaved at by cardinal Wolsey, his old enemy ... but for all my father's friends, the cardinal's persuading authority was so great with the king, that though by the king's favour my father escaped bodily danger, yet the cardinal caused the king so much to mislike of that tale, that Chaucer must be new printed.

Thynne adds that when the tale was passed as part of Chaucer's *Works* (presumably the 1542 edition), it did so 'with much ado', and

> in such sort that in one open parliament ... when talk was had of books to be forbidden, Chaucer had forever been condemned, had it not been that his works had been counted but fables.[29]

The remarkable image of Henry VIII's personal reading of Thynne's edition of Chaucer, and certainly the somewhat comic image of Wolsey 'heaving' at his 'old enemy' make for entertaining reading, but serious question marks must be placed beside Thynne's account. As Walker writes, Thynne's account is 'fraught with difficulty, and cannot be accurate in the detail of many of its assertions'.[30] First and foremost it conflates two pieces of Chaucerian apocrypha. At the beginning of Thynne's enormous prose periods he is referring to the 'Pilgrim's Tale', by the end the text in question has become the 'Plowman's Tale'. The text under consideration is an entirely different one from the 'Pilgrim's Tale' which found its way into *The Court of Venus*, a compilation of Chaucerian texts compiled by Robert Singleton and printed by Thomas Gibson between 1536 and 1539.[31] Secondly, the chronology of this anecdote is deeply problematic. If the episcopal censorship of the *Plowman's Tale* that Thynne's account narrates refers to the

---

[29]   Francis Thynne, *Animadversions upon the Annotations and Corrections of some Imperfections of Impressions of Chaucer's Works*, eds G. Kingsley and F. Furnivall (London, 1865, EETS o.s. 9), pp. 9–10.

[30]   Walker, *Writing under Tyranny*, p. 66.

[31]   *The Courte of Venus* (London, *c.* 1538). A modern edition exists in R. Fraser, ed., *The Court of Venus* (Cambridge, 1955). Wawn notes some borrowings from the *Plowman's Tale* in this text, and it has similar anticlerical concerns, but it remains a different work. See Wawn, 'Propaganda', pp. 175–6.

1532 edition, which it seems to, then a serious problem arises. Wolsey's fall from favour at the close of the 1520s is, and was, notorious. By December 1530 he was dead from a rather mysterious illness and his position as Chancellor had been taken up by Thomas More. It seems highly unlikely that Wolsey would have had any great 'persuading authority' in the years closely preceding Godfray's printing of Thynne's text in 1532. It seems far more likely that Francis Thynne was endeavouring to use the popular, overwhelmingly pejorative, image of Wolsey, and of Catholicism in general, that swept England in the decade following the attempted invasion of the armada to shape a positive image of both Protestant family pedigree and favour in the 1590s.[32] Repeatedly he returns to an assertion that his father was 'in great favour with his prince (as many yet living can testify)', and portrays Henry as being a kind of long-suffering neutral having to fend off aggressive episcopal censoriousness in order to support Thynne's endeavour. Rather than being a reliable source of information regarding the ideological status of ploughman literature in the 1530s, Thynne's *Animadversions* reads very much like familial history as self-fashioning, even self-congratulation.

A far more likely context for the appearance of the ploughman in these Chaucerian texts is the rise of reformism guided by Thomas Cromwell's ascendancy in the 1530s, a context that scholars have repeatedly suggested. However, the tone of these suggestions must again be questioned. Andrew Wawn argues that the *Plowman's Tale*, and the later *Jack Upland*, were produced for 'a calculated and official propagandist purpose', and P. L. Heyworth views the commonplace formula 'cum privilegio Regali' on the frontispiece of *Jack Upland* as 'royal assent to what is essentially an act of policy'.[33] More recently Thomas Heffernan asserts the idea that the texts were produced so that 'whatever else they might provide … Tudor readers, [they] … should be able to evidence a healthy disrespect for church authority, especially that of the Bishop of Rome'.[34] Alexandra Gillespie suggests that the *Plowman's Tale* and *Jack Upland* 'may … have been meant to be linked in some way', possibly as a polemical pairing of Chaucerian works.[35] That the newly galvanized anticlerical voice of the ploughman would have been useful to a regime attempting to defend both the Act of the Submission of the Clergy (1531) and Act of Supremacy (1534) is undeniable. Henry's 'Great Matter' needed all the support it could get whilst his own Chancellor was willing to die rather

---

[32] George Cavendish's Marian biography/hagiography, *The Life and Death of Cardinal Wolsey*, made some ground in salvaging Wolsey's reputation, but his precarious relationship with Henry was still apparent in the early seventeenth century in the overwhelmingly hostile portrait of Shakespeare's and Fletcher's *Henry VIII*.

[33] P. L. Heyworth, 'The Earliest Black-letter Editions of *Jack Upland*', *Huntingdon Library Quarterly*, 30 (1967), 307–14, 313.

[34] Wawn, 'Propaganda', p. 175, and Heffernan, 'Aspects', p. 159. See also Simpson, *Reform and Cultural Revolution*, p. 331.

[35] Alexandra Gillespie, *Print Culture and the Medieval Author*, pp. 196–201, 198.

than acquiesce to it.[36] However, whilst the emerging sense of the ploughman's polemical and reformist character can be correlated conveniently with this broad stroke of 'reformist/orthodox' tides in the Henrician period, we should perhaps be wary of assuming such a direct cause-and-effect agency between these texts and state religious policy in a time when, as one Venetian ambassador put it, 'it was not possible to tell what religious belief would prevail from one day to the next', and in which the iconic figureheads of both orthodox and evangelical polemic, More and Tyndale, could be publicly executed – albeit not both in London – almost within a year of each other.[37]

What is problematic about these critical accounts is their unqualified emphasis on direct state agency, their use of terms like 'official' and 'act of policy'. This is a part of the traditional 'top-down' approach to the analysis of print culture that has recently been brought into question.[38] It requires that we imagine a scene curiously similar to Francis Thynne's, but with Cromwell and Cranmer taking the place of Wolsey, and hostility being substituted for approbation and positive initiative. It also necessitates a view of the sixteenth-century print shop as virtually a government-run newspaper utilized for the purposes of propounding the latest turn of state policy.

Such official relationships did indeed exist, but in the form of patents for the production of primers, Psalters and Bibles such as those held by John Day and William Seres. As well as allowing the state to control the form of these most read of printed books, they had the equally important purpose of controlling costs and quality.[39] It is this economic perspective which is lacking from any thesis which regards the production of ploughman literature like *The Plowman's Tale* as an 'official act of policy'. A print shop was in essence an economic body. There was no point producing copy after copy of texts which would not sell, however important they might be in hindsight in terms of the history of Henrician government, religious policy, or indeed literature. The printing of ploughman texts had to be driven, at least to some extent, by an economic imperative: people had to want to buy them. Whilst it led to a certain 'short-termism' compared to the

---

[36]   Indeed, More's foremost modern scholar, Alistair Fox, writes that 'More's execution was a serious political miscalculation on the government's part, for it aroused much disaffection' and notes that some evidence points to a connection between public reaction to the execution and the Pilgrimage of Grace. See A. Fox, *Thomas More: History and Providence* (Oxford, 1982), p. 253.

[37]   Brian Cummings, *The Literary Culture of the Reformation*, p. 8. More was executed on 6 July 1535, Tyndale in early October, 1536. See Fox, *History and Providence*, p. 253, and Daniell, *William Tyndale*, p. 382.

[38]   Most effectively by Ian Green in his excellent *Print and Protestantism in Early Modern England* (Oxford, 2000). Greg Walker has also reassessed the long-held assumption that Thynne's 1532 edition of Chaucer's works was 'semi-authorised royal propaganda', see Walker, *Writing under Tyranny*, p. 35.

[39]   See Green, *Print and Protestantism*, pp. 15–16.

investment of time in printing 'steady-sellers' such as primers, one way to thrive commercially was, as Green puts it, 'to enter the lists of controversy, or to latch onto the coat-tails of a current cause célèbre'.[40] The short-termism that Green ascribes to profits from such polemical works could perhaps be offset if they came in a consistently attractive form. The proliferation and endurance of ploughman texts over the period, all of them 'controversial', is such an example. Instead of churning out governmental propaganda, the printers can be seen to be taking advantage of the ideological situation to meet a demand for polemical ploughman literature and the increasing grip of a developing 'zeitgeist' figure on the popular imagination. However useful the texts may have been to a propagandist campaign originating from Cromwell, this idea must be balanced with a more economic, and wider cultural, consideration. What allowed printers to survive financially was not only protection and patronage, but attention to the movements of the market, and the emerging figure of the polemical ploughman was becoming a serious draw for solvent, book-buying members of the public.

'I Judge the Earth': The Polemical Ploughman, 1530–1550

The rhetorical potential of the ploughman figure as the voice of polemical critique which characterizes the 'Chaucerian' texts of the 1530s was to become its central function. Amongst the diversity of the Henrician portraits of this symbolic rural figure, it is possible to see a rising tide of associations around him, a growing clarity of delineation. The fiery anticlericalism, reformist perspective and vaticinal aspects come increasingly to the fore. In line with this process, there is an understandable lacuna in the printing of ploughman literature between the Cromwellian ascendancy in the 1530s and the apex of the fortunes of the 'commonwealthsmen' working under the protection of Somerset in the 1540s. Barring the rather paradoxical appearance of the *Plowman's Tale* in Thynne's 1542 edition of Chaucer, and an Edwardian reprint of the *Plowman's Tale* in 1548, there is no distinctive ploughman polemic printed in the Henrician period after the Act of Six Articles (1539), which virtually reversed the reforms of Cromwell and instigated a reactionary form of Anglo-Catholicism. Indeed, a number of the printers associated with ploughman polemic were imprisoned or fined throughout the 1540s as the orthodox restrictions on the content of printed books tightened again.[41]

This period of silence, however, is a brief interval in what was a prolific time for the printing of ploughman literature. Even in the fluid and tumultuous decade of the 1530s and again in the more radically Protestant Edwardian reign,

---

[40]   Green, *Print and Protestantism*, p. 19.

[41]   John Gough, the printer of *Jack Upland*, Richard Grafton, the future printer of Crowley's editions of Langland, and his associate Edward Whitchurch, were all subject to state punishment for producing prohibited works during the years after Cromwell's fall from grace in 1540; see Green, *Print and Protestantism*, p. 19.

the ploughman becomes overwhelmingly associated with a combative reformist discourse. In particular, an analysis of two texts with problematic printing histories demonstrates that the ploughman was becoming a central part of an enthusiasm for what might be called 'reformist medievalism'. In the high temperature of religious controversy both in England and the continent, ploughman polemic became a central pillar in reformism's use of antiquarianism as a strategy of authorization and 'marketability', in a defence against orthodox attacks on the movement's perceived novelty.

However, at the same time as the literary outline of the ploughman figure becomes clearer, the subject matter of the literature diversifies into a constellation of associated concerns. In Chapter 1, I discussed the way that reformist writers took on the mode of polemical anti-urban satire which they found so arresting in Langland's text. But they also took on the polemical potential of antiquarianism, and launched prophetic critiques about the state of agrarian society in the sixteenth century. This synthesis of different discourses with the ploughman's early combative stance towards the clergy works to blur boundaries of politics, economics and religion. It also constructs the ploughman as *the* agitational champion of Protestantism before Foxe's *Acts and Monuments* (1563) raised the Protestant martyr to a comparable status.

Mid-way through the text of *Jack Upland*, the narrator complains that the clergy have attacked his belief that 'the Gospel schulde be prechid to the trwe' with the accusation of modishness: 'ye clepen it the newe doctrine' (ll. 192–3). It is a highly significant accusation. In the discourse of religious controversy in the sixteenth century, such an idea of novelty carried serious connotations for the reformist movement. The authority of the Catholic Church rested not simply on doctrinal debates or biblical arguments about apostolic succession, but on its sheer cultural stature. It was a faith supported not only by its control over the dissemination and meaning of the Vulgate Bible or its central place in the mechanics and experience of daily life, but by a spiritual, social and intellectual tradition that reached back for centuries. The first waves of Protestantism were extremely vulnerable to the question of precedent and authority in such terms. Whilst some orthodox polemicists occasionally referred to the burgeoning evangelical movement as an old heresy 'writ large', it was far more effective to accuse it of novelty, to ask 'where was your faith before Luther?'.[42] In the shadow of an ancient orthodox institution, Protestantism ran the risk of being perceived as an intellectually slight and socially dangerous enthusiasm. There was a distinct need to defend the legitimacy and historical pedigree of the Protestant faith. As Bruce Gordon puts it, 'there remained for the evangelical cause the imperative of locating and explaining its historical place ... the nascent reform movement

---

[42]   The question became a stock in trade of orthodox polemic. See, for example, S. J. Barnett, 'Where was your Church before Luther? Claims for the Antiquity of Protestantism Examined', *Church History*, 68 (1999), 14–41.

could not turn its face against God's historical plan'.[43] This imperative could force Protestants to make the claim of 'first principles', a return to the perceived integrity of the early Church, in the same way that monastic reform movements and the mendicant orders did between the eleventh and thirteenth centuries. But it could also drive reformers to look closer to home in their search for historical precedent, to any dissenting voices in the English Middle Ages which could be utilized to form a tradition or founding history of reformism. Whilst this ideologically motivated antiquarianism roved far and wide, it persistently returned to the fashionable genre of ploughman literature.

One such text is the *Prayer and Complaynt of the Ploweman unto Christ* (1532).[44] This tract has recently been described by Wendy Scase as the 'first Protestant book originally published abroad to be printed in England'.[45] As Anne Hudson notes, the text is surrounded by 'considerable obscurity' in terms of its publication.[46] The *STC* notes that it was printed, possibly in Antwerp, in 1531 (*STC* 2nd edn 20036) before being reprinted in London the following year (*STC* 2nd edn 20036.5). Question marks surround all attempts to date its publication or identify an author or printer for it. However, two things strike the reader on a first glance. The first is the advertisement of the frontispiece which identifies it as 'written nat longe after the yere of our Lords. M and three hundred'. The second is the substantial preface entitled 'W. T. to the reader'. The initials are extremely enticing. The *STC* notes the possibility that Tyndale was the author of the preface, whilst some critics have automatically assumed his authorship.[47] However, there is nothing extant to finally prove or disprove his involvement. One might as well search for the identity of Shakespeare's enigmatic 'Mr. W.H'. But what is significant in terms of the book itself, whether Tyndale had a hand in it or not, is the marketability of the suggestion of both his involvement and the text's 'antiquity'. Six years after the printing of Tyndale's New Testament (1526),

---

[43]   Bruce Gordon, 'The Changing Face of Protestant History and Identity in the Sixteenth Century' in *Protestant History and Identity in Sixteenth Century Europe*, ed. B. Gordon, 2 vols (Aldershot, 1996), vol. 1: *The Medieval Inheritance*, 1–22, 2. See also, in the same volume, Alec Ryrie, 'The Problem of Legitimacy and Precedent', pp. 78–92.

[44]   The work exists in a modern edition, from which I quote here, by page and line number. See Douglas H. Parker, *The praier and complaynte of the ploweman vnto Christe* (Toronto, 1997). Parker remains neutral on the question of Tyndale's possible role as editor (pp. 41–51).

[45]   Scase, *Literature and Complaint*, pp. 154–6. Scase argues that the title, which she views as editorial, works to 'frame the whole tract as peasant plaint' (p. 155). The text is discussed in terms of its Lollard character in Anne Hudson, '"No newe thyng": The Printing of Medieval Texts in the Early Reformation Period' in *Middle English Studies Presented to Norman Davis in Honour of his Seventieth Birthday*, eds Douglas Gray and E. G. Stanley (Oxford: Clarendon Press, 1983), pp. 153–74, esp. 157.

[46]   Hudson, 'Legacy', p. 257.

[47]   For example, Ryrie in 'The Problem of Legitimacy and Precedent in English Protestantism', p. 80.

and shortly after editions of his Pentateuch began to arrive in England, Tyndale's notoriety, even celebrity, could not have been stronger.[48] But the ostentatious assertion of the text's age is as important as the suggestion of its editor's identity. As Sarah Kelen has noted, the text presents itself as 'simultaneously ancient and relevant'.[49]

The preface begins with a narrative of Christ's conflict with the Pharisees, with a heavy emphasis on the accusations of the Pharisees: they 'cryed alwayes: What new lerninge ys this? These fellowes teache new lerninge' (108/22–4). The term 'newe lernynge' is repeated over and over again in the preface (108/23, 24, 25–6, 39), often within the same sentence, endowing it with an almost sarcastic tone, working to chip away at the efficacy of the phrase. The use of biblical history is matched by the scholarly assertion of the antiquity of the text itself. The editor emphasizes the 'untouched' nature of the text, and asserts that he has altered nothing:

> chaingynge there in nothinge as ferforth as I coulde obserue it other the english
> or ortographie/ addynge also there to a table of soch olde wordes as be now
> antiquate and worne out of knoulege by processe of tyme. (110/107–110)

What is foregrounded is the text's authenticity and its antiquity. The rhetorical image of language 'worn out by time', and the editor's ostensible refusal to modernize medieval linguistic and orthographical forms are designed to throw a light of legitimacy across the following text. The appearance of authenticity achieved through the grafting of ploughman literature into the Chaucerian canon by Godfray and Gough is here advanced through the humanistic claim to a genuine antiquarian process of discovery and editing. As we shall see in the later example of Crowley's editions of *Piers Plowman*, such a combination of authenticity and humanistic endeavour was an effective strategy to use in the attempt to bolster the cultural status of Protestantism and, simultaneously, an effective way to advertise a book.

What is equally significant about this antiquarianism is that it is a form of self-fashioning, a means by which an identity could be formed. The author of the preface makes a direct historical link between Christ's lifetime and the sixteenth century, through the oppositional figures of the Pharisees:

> And so with these olde clokes of their fathers the phereses byshops and prestes /
> fyrst they persuade the people the worde of god to be heresye ... Even as the old
> phareses with the bischops and prestes presoned and persecuted Christe and his
> Apostles. (109/76–8, 80–82)

---

[48]   See Daniell, *William Tyndale*, p. 283.
[49]   Kelen, *Langland's Early Modern Identities*, pp. 52–8, 58.

The biblical episode becomes a historical archetype for the actions of contemporary history. Similarly, the ploughman's text itself is made up of a patchwork of biblical quotations and paraphrases, most often from the Old Testament prophets Isaiah and Ezekiel. His authority is shaped not only by his apparent 'antiquity', but by the way he too utilizes authoritative texts. The vaticinal aspect of the ploughman is reconfigured within biblical history. The antiquarian and biblical strategies of the text form the reformist ploughman as a trans-historical figure: both 'medieval' and sixteenth century, both apostle and Protestant, simultaneously John the Baptist and William Tyndale.

The antiquarian strategy for presenting ploughman texts was widespread. In 1553, the last of these texts to be printed before the Marian reign, *Pierce the Plowman's Crede*, was prefaced by Reynor Wolfe with a short poem:

> To read strange newes, desires manye
> Which at my hande they can not haue
> For here is but antiquitie
> Expressed only, as tholde booke gaue
> Take in good part, and not depraue
> The Ploughmans Crede, gentil reader
> Loo, this is all that I requyer.[50]

Wolfe's little piece asserts that the text is above all worth reading. It is not the 'strange news' that would develop into a craze for sensationalist 'journalistic' cheap print in the later sixteenth century. Indeed, it is precisely the text's 'plain antiquity' which endows it with authority. The assertion that the printed text is also faithful, adding nothing to 'tholde booke' is also strikingly similar to the claims of the *Prayer and Complaynt of the Ploweman unto Christ* prologue. There is a concentration on the idea of 'an old copy', an absent material object, which is demonstrable 'proof' of both the text's authority and authenticity.

A close contemporary text of the *Prayer and Complaynt of the Ploweman, A Proper Dyalogue Betwene a Gentillman and a Husbandman* (*c.* 1530) similarly uses this kind of antiquarian strategy, but its use of ancient texts is more curious; it uses these texts as polemical ammunition both following the scheme of the

---

[50]   *Pierce the Plowmans Crede* (London, 1553), sig. A2v. The literary taste of the Marian years did not, understandably, have a place for such texts. Indeed, as John N. King notes, it was characterized by an 'old fashioned ... literary taste ... the huge outpouring of modishly radical Protestant literature that marked her late brother's reign dried up as printers abandoned the Protestant favourites – Chaucer and Langland – to turn to publishing safely non-controversial medieval "classics" like *Le Morte d'Arthur*', John N. King, *Tudor Royal Iconography: Literature and Art in the Age of Religious Crisis* (Princeton, 1989), p. 186. Wolfe's poem was re-printed when ploughman literature came back into vogue. On the re-printing of the text with *Piers Plowman* in 1561, see Chapter 4.

Prayer, and as an intra-textual device, a literary strategy within its dialogue form.[51] Again, the identification of the text's printing history is extremely difficult. It has a transparently false imprint at the close of the text, identifying the printer as 'me, Hans Luft' and the place of publication as 'Marborow in the lande of Hessen' (sig. D8r).

The name is famous as the false imprint of Martin de Keyser of Antwerp, the printer of Lutheran texts in the 1520s and 1530s, as well as a number of Tyndale's works.[52] Its alternative title, 'An A.B.C. to the Spiritualte' suggests that it was marketed as a kind of alternative, polemical primer for an English reformist readership. What is striking about this text is that, in the middle of a text firmly in the dialogue genre utilized by Heywood and More, the husbandman suddenly produces a book (see Figure 3.1). It is, he says, 'an olde treatyse made aboute the tyme of Kynge Rycharde the Seconde' (sig. B4r).

The book appears with the express purpose of disproving the clerical attack on 'Lutheranes / Whom they saye is a secte newe fangled / With execrable heresyes' (sig. B3v). Interestingly, the text is not separate from the dialogue as such, but described as a physical object, becoming the subject of the dialogue itself before it is 'read out' by the ploughman and becomes part of the fabric of the wider text. The ploughman describes the book as:

> Aboue an hundred yere olde …
> But alas the boke we want
> Hauynge no more left than a remenant
> From the begynnyge of the vi. Chapter verily. (sig. B3v–B4r)

The Gentleman dismisses the fragmented state of the text with the words 'it maketh no matter', but it is in fact extremely important. The book is dated by the reader, though not entirely consistently: if the text is supposed to be Ricardian, it would have been at least 131 years old. What is important though is the ancient, authoritative nature of the book: its efficacy comes partly from its very obscurity. The exact details of the text have been 'worn out of knowledge by process of time'. What has also been 'worn out' is the physical form of the codex itself.

What was the purpose and effect of the ploughman's claiming that the book was only a 'remenant', a fragment, and that the text it contained is not extant 'from the begynnynge of the vi. Chapter'? It is perhaps possible to take the dialogue

---

[51]   Scase similarly notes the 'strategy of re-using old complaint material' within the text, see Scase, *Literature and Complaint*, p. 156. For other brief descriptions of the text see: Simpson, *Reform and Cultural Revolution*, pp. 331–2; M. Aston, 'Lollardy and the Reformation', *History*, 49 (1964), 149–70; Hudson, 'No newe thyng', p. 159. As both Hudson and Scase note, the in-laid text *is* actually a Lollard work: a text known as *The Clergy May Not Hold Property*. See Matthew, *The English Works of Wyclif hitherto unprinted*, pp. 362–404.

[52]   See Daniell, *William Tyndale*, p. 156.

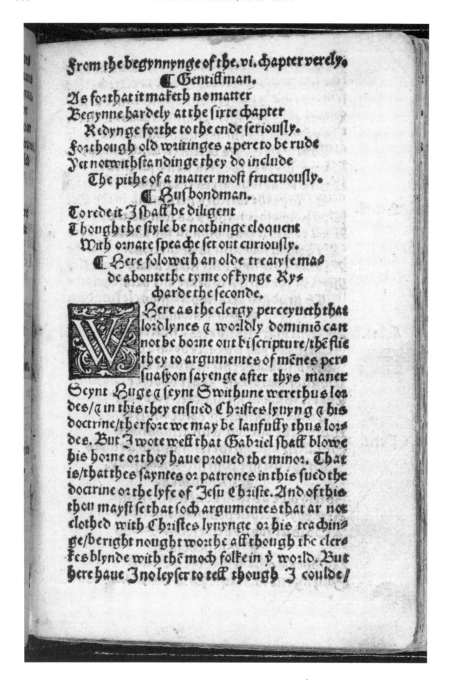

From the begynnynge of the .vi. chapter verely.
¶ Gentillman.

As for that it maketh no matter
Begynne hardely at the firte chapter
    Redynge forthe to the ende seriouſly.
For though old wrytinges a pere to be rude
Yet notwithstandinge they do include
    The pithe of a matter moſt fructuouſly.
        ¶ Huſbondman.
To rede it I ſhall be diligent
Though the ſtyle be nothinge eloquent
    With ornate ſpeache ſet out curiouſly.
        ¶ Here foloweth an olde treatyſe made
        aboute the tyme of kynge Rycharde the ſeconde.

Here as the clergy perceyueth that
lordlynes ꝗ worldly dominiō can
not be borne out bi ſcripture/they flie
they to argumentes of mēnes per
ſuaſyon ſayenge after thys maner
Seynt Huge ꝗ ſeynt Swithune were thus lordes/ꝗ in this they enſued Chriſtes lyuyng ꝗ his
doctrine/therfore we may be lauſully thus lordes. But I wote well that Gabriel ſhall blowe
his horne or they haue proued the minor. That
is/that thes ſayntes or patrones in this ſued the
doctrine or the lyfe of Jeſu Chriſte. And of this
thou mayſt ſe that ſoch argumentes that ar not
clothed with Chriſtes lyuynge or his teachinge/be right nought worthe althoug the clerekes blynde with thē moch folke in ꝥ world. But
here haue I no leyſer to tell though I coulde/

Figure 3.1   *A Proper Dyaloge between a Gentillman and a Husbandman* (London?: William Barlowe?, 1530), sig. B4r. © The British Library Board.

character at his word, to see the 'inset text' as a way for the *Dyalogue*'s author to publicize a piece of Ricardian prose anticlericalism found in a fragmentary codex. But this approach ignores the textual flexibility and rhetorical purpose of the polemical enterprise. What is important is the strategy through which *the idea* of this text is created. The ploughman's narration of the physical state of his book is a claim to veracity, one made through the expression of knowledge of its physical detail. It works in much the same way as Geoffrey of Monmouth's claim that his *Historia* is based on 'a certain very ancient book' given to him by the Archdeacon of Oxford.[53] The specificity of the physical codex endows the author with the aura of veracity and transparency. It also lends him considerable cultural kudos, a point that the ploughman's interlocutor reinforces with his comment: 'though olde writings apere to be rude / … they do include / The pithe of a matter most fructuously' (sig. B4r). The point of this matter is demonstrable: it is to disprove the accusation that Lutheranism is 'newe fangled'. A point that the Gentleman makes quite explicit:

> Is it so olde as thou doest here expresse
> Reprouynge their pompous lordlynes
> So it is than *no newe found heresy*. (sig. B3v, emphasis added)

The label of 'heresy' remains entirely unquestioned. What is important is not to defend the doctrine itself as legitimate but to defend it against the implications of its novelty. The antiquarian drive to defend the 'new learning' is again apparent at the latter end of the text, where a separate text is appended to the dialogue, entitled 'A Compendious olde treatyse shweynge howe that we ought to haue the scripture in English' (sig. C8r. The text runs from here to sig. D8r). Instead of being introduced, the text here introduces itself in a short two-stanza poem, again emphasizing its age and veracity. Though it is 'olde clothed in barbarous wede', it says, 'yet I tell the trouthe' (sig. C8r). The polemical purpose of this curious type of antiquarian self-fashioning is set out in a prose preface similar to that of the *Prayer*. Again it emphasizes the continuity of religious controversy between the medieval past and the sixteenth-century present, in the form of altercations over the vernacular Bible. It records how the 'prelates … barke against the worde of God, and specially the new testament translatyd and set forthe by Master William Tyndale' (sig. C8v). The contemporary relevance of the medieval text is underlined. In particular, it is a piece of evidence set down to combat the accusation that Tyndale's translation was 'sore corrupte'. The editor has therefore

> Put in prynte a treatyse written aboute the yere of oure lorde a thousande and foure hundryd. By which thou shalt plainly perceyue that they wolde yet neuer

---

[53]   Geoffrey of Monmouth, *The History of the Kings of England*, trans. L. Thorpe (London, 1966), p. 51.

from the begynnyng admyte any translation … so that it is not the corrupte
translation that they withstonde. (sig. C8v)

The actual linguistic problems of vernacular translation that More and Tyndale
fought over, the doctrinally important alterations of words like 'ecclesia',
'church', and 'sacerdos', 'priest', in the Vulgate to what Tyndale claimed to
be more philologically accurate Hebraic terms 'congregation' and 'elder' are
noticeably absent.[54] The argument instead uses the 'ancient' text as proof that
orthodox opposition to vernacular translation of the scriptures is driven by a
tyrannical institutional desire to withhold control of a sacred text from the non-
clerical faithful. The question of philological rigour and its doctrinal ramifications
is implied to be a convenient channel through which the Church could focus its
broader hostility to the proliferation of interpretation and intellectual authority that
the translation threatened.

It is the textual consciousness of this polemic which is striking; the attempt to
use a medieval text as a weapon in the controversies over another text, the body of
the Bible itself. The epithet of Protestantism as the 'religion of the book', though
now qualified, seems extremely appropriate here.[55] Correlatively, the figure of
the ploughman has become a curiously 'textual' figure, able to marshal obscure,
ancient texts and biblical knowledge in the aid of his polemical and prophetic
status. Similarly, the texts themselves are peculiarly self-conscious about their own
'market' as texts, the status and associations that surround them. The 'Compendious
olde treatyse' has marginal notes printed beside the body of the main text, which,
like much marginalia in this period, is highly significant. In the text itself, the
ethical education of reading is eulogized, interestingly through the figures of
Seneca and Bede. In another humanistic turn, the 'subtle science of trouthe' (sig.
D1v) in a religious sense is argued to be supported and strengthened by the reading
of ancient texts, regardless of the ideological or religious inconsistencies that might
arise from the process. The passage places the treatise, and the ploughman text as a
whole, within an erudite field of antiquarianism and scholarship.

By the side of the passage is printed: 'Reade robyn hode saye oure masters' (sig.
D1v). It is a striking note, more so as the text does not mention the Robin Hood
ballads, or any written versions of them, at any point. It seems like a reference to
the texts as Langland envisioned the Robin Hood narratives, as 'pub-literature',
as a distracting opposite to the serious work of reading morally edifying works.
The 'masters' here are guilty of a deliberate obfuscation of ethical reading and
meaning through their recommendations in literary taste. It is something that
reappears in another, later, ploughman text, *I Playn Piers* (1550) in which the

---

[54]   See Fox, *History and Providence*, pp. 147–66.

[55]   'Print was in no sense the prerogative of Protestantism', although, despite the
efforts of the counter-Reformation, the two would become increasingly correlated. See
Cummings, *The Literary Culture of the Reformation*, pp. 19–20. See also Green, *Print and
Protestantism*, pp. 1–40.

rural figure angrily states that the clergy would 'allowe, they saye. Legenda aurea, Roben Hoode, Beuys and Gower, and al baggage besyd, but God's word ye may not abyde'.[56] The antiquarianism of these ploughman texts is extremely aware of the reputation and cultural status of literary texts, and implies that the medieval ploughman is the most capable and ethical reader. Tyndale's promise to educate the 'plowboy' to a comparable level to the clergy is ostentatiously borne out by this polemical antiquarianism.

This argumentative strategy extends further even than these rather ingenious uses of texts, to become a process that encompasses the narrative of English history itself. Amidst the *Proper Dyalogue* the reader is directed to the 'text' of native regal history.[57] It is a history overwhelmed with alleged clerical conspiracy. The French campaign of Henry V is viewed as a clerical sleight of hand to avoid suppression, and it is suggested that the clergy 'put him to a confusion evene as they dyd other kynges before' (sig. C6v). The list of other conspiracies is astonishing, including not only the notorious example of King John, but the figures of Stephen, Henry II and Richard II. The reign of Henry V is described as a time of horrific persecution in which the clergy set about a virtual orgy of punishment, throwing laymen into 'sharpe gayles and horrible doungeones / Causynge many to be brent in fyre' (sig. B2v). The rest of the fifteenth century is shaped into a prophetic history of divine punishments for this persecution. The loss of French territory under Henry VI is only the first of a sequence of disasters which includes the entire course of the Wars of the Roses. The wars are figured as a punishment for iniquity on a biblical scale, 'With great effusion of English bloode / Frende against frende brother against brother ... Moste terrible plages of fearfull vengeaunce / And endless sorowe to oure nacion' (sig. B2v). The historical 'text' of the past is used as a polemical warning to the England of 1530, lest it suffers 'The same vengeaunce for like offence' (sig. B3r).

This prolific strategy of antiquarian support for the legitimacy of the 'new learning' had become a powerful process of historical self-fashioning and prophetic historiography taking in swathes of the medieval past. The figure of the ploughman, erudite, indignant and authoritative, was at the heart of this process. One might even suggest that we see in this polemical antiquarianism a sequence of embryonic versions of Foxe's *Acts and Monuments*; none, of course, as voluminous, scholarly

---

[56]   *I Playne Piers which cannot flatter* (London?, 1550), sig. E3v. All references to it are from the early printed text, incorporated in the text. Kelen describes the text in *Langland's Early Modern Identities*, pp. 61–3. The text is mentioned briefly in Simpson, *Reform and Cultural Revolution*, p. 331 and Hudson, 'Legacy', pp. 258–9. On the important re-printing of this text as a Marprelate polemic, see Chapter 4.

[57]   The *Dyalogue* is densely packed with this appropriative history. It is a shame that it isn't explored in Julian Lock's otherwise excellent essay 'Plantagenets against the Papacy: Protestant England's Search for Royal Heroes' in *Protestant History and Identity*, ed., B. Gordon, I. pp. 153–73.

or influential, but all of which point towards that monumental work of Elizabethan Protestant historiography.

The ploughman literature of the early sixteenth century was not only a part of this politicized antiquarianism though. The ploughman was equally central to the anxious and controversial discourse of agrarian complaint. This subject was one of particular concern in a period which has been termed variously a time of 'agricultural revolution', of the 'agrarian problem' and as the 'age of plunder'.[58] The literature associated with this era has only recently been given much attention, traditionally being passed over with the epithets 'dull' or 'bombastic'. It is now beginning to be viewed in the more favourable and productive light of a 'magnificent literature of protest, vibrating with the righteous indignation of what Tawney called "an age that had rediscovered the Bible"'.[59] This was a milieu in which ploughman literature could, and did, thrive. The agrarian and economic developments of the early sixteenth century which will be broadly outlined below produced the perception of a social crisis, an extraordinary anxiety over agriculture which made it one 'of the most controversial topics in sixteenth-century England'.[60] The furore concerned issues such as enclosure, engrossment, the redistribution of land after the Dissolution, and the widespread problems of vagrancy and impoverishment that came in their wake. The social problems associated with these issues are strikingly similar to those that vexed Langland in the latter half of the fourteenth century. Once again the issues of labour and vagrancy were topics of great concern. In this context the ploughman became the central spokesman for agrarian, as well as Protestant, interests, as he was a central figure in defending the 'novel' faith and attacking Catholic doctrine on the Eucharist. Much of the ploughman literature of the period makes direct reference to the agrarian and socio-economic issues of the mid-century, playing on the symbolic possibilities of the figure as an authority on such matters, even whilst the writers and printers of these works were predominantly living and working in an urban context.

The various aspects of the sixteenth-century 'agrarian problem' have been explored in detail by a number of scholars, but a provisional outline based on their work is helpful to put the agrarian complaints of these ploughman texts in context. The socio-economic repercussions of the massive drop in population in England after the sequence of pandemic diseases in the mid-fourteenth century

---

[58]   See R. H. Tawney, *The Agrarian Problem in the Sixteenth Century* (London, 1912); E. Kerridge, *The Agricultural Revolution* (London, 1967); W. G. Hoskins, *The Age of Plunder: The England of Henry VIII, 1500–1547* (London, 1976).

[59]   Keith Wrightson, *Earthly Necessities: Economic Lives in Early Modern England* (New Haven, 2000), p. 151. Wrightson's work, along with Joan Thirsk's, provides the most persuasive and detailed account of the economic history of the period. McRae's *God Spede the Plough* is the most cogent exploration of the connection between agricultural discourse and literary culture.

[60]   Joan Thirsk, *The Agrarian History of England and Wales*, vol. 4, 1500–1640 (Cambridge, 1967), p. 200.

were to remain a shaping factor in the social conditions of the country for at least the following 150 years. Perhaps only by the very end of the fifteenth century were population levels rising again, and it was not until we reach the sixteenth century that they resemble pre-Black Death figures.[61] The resurgent population levels resulted in a rising demand for both land and produce, a demand that was not, perhaps could not, be met quickly enough. The prices of basic consumables rose tremendously in the first half of the sixteenth century, utterly out of proportion to the wages that were paid in an increasingly competitive labour market. Langland's labourers might have been seen to wander around the country in search of higher wages because of the greed and laziness that came from the country's dependence on them in a population decimated by plague, but the vagrants of the mid-sixteenth century wandered out of sheer poverty. Whilst wages increased by two-thirds between 1520 and 1550, the average price of grain trebled.[62] The habitual burdens of providing food and shelter became increasingly onerous, to the extent that many simply could not sustain rent payments whilst depending on the uncertainties of wage labour, higher prices and an increasing number of dependants.

At the same time, the period saw the living standards of some classes improve massively. Since Marx this has been seen, perhaps rather paradoxically, as the era of 'the genesis of the capitalist farmer', who arose in a situation that 'enriched him just as speedily as it impoverished the mass of the agricultural people'.[63] The financial division between rich and poor, if not previously garish, was now immense. The economic opportunities for those with an income large enough to keep up with the 'price revolution', especially in the 1540s, often came in the form of agricultural enterprise. One such scheme was 'engrossment', the amalgamation of a number of farms into one. Such a practice was regularly mentioned in the same breath as 'enclosure', the fencing off of traditionally arable or common land, predominantly for its conversion into pasture. The expansion of the cloth industry in the Henrician years provided economic opportunities to those who could graze enough sheep to produce large amounts of exportable fabric.[64] The wide-scale transferral of arable and common land to more economically promising pasture inevitably exacerbated a highly wrought social situation. People needed more land to grow food and graze livestock, especially if they depended on uncertain employment, whilst less was available. Thomas More's much quoted complaint that 'your sheep … are becoming so greedy and wild that they devour men themselves' was not intended to be entirely funny, neither was it an unusual perspective.[65] Added to which was the spectacle of a 'feeding frenzy' amongst the landed classes after the Dissolution, an event which has been called the 'greatest

---

[61] Wrightson, *Earthly Necessities*, p. 146; Thirsk, *Agrarian History*, p. 202.

[62] Wrightson, *Earthly Necessities*, p. 146.

[63] Marx, *Capital. A Critical Analysis of Capitalist Production*, 2 vols, trans. S. Moore and E. Aveling (New York, 2003), I. 694–5.

[64] Thirsk, *Agrarian History*, p. 218.

[65] Thomas More, *Utopia*, ed. and trans. R. Adams (London, 1992), p. 12.

transfer of property in England and Wales since the aftermath of the Norman Conquest'.[66] The ostensible motivation for this astonishing action, the image of monastic corruption and the reforming intentions of Henry VIII, all too quickly evaporated into the more cynical rationale of enhancing both the royal estate and the property portfolios of established landowning families, along with a significant proportion of 'new men'.[67] The dissatisfaction with the outcome of the dissolution went far beyond John Bale's complaint that the monasteries' new owners were using medieval manuscripts to clean their boots.[68] What may have seemed like an opportunity to lessen the pressures on common land produced by encroaching engrossment and enclosure became instead an addendum to the stock complaints about rapacious landlords.

That engrossment and enclosure were 'as ancient as farming itself' cannot be denied.[69] A continuity can be drawn between the growth of the slave-run 'latifundia' which decimated the culture of the Roman smallholder in Virgil's Italy and John Clare's lament in the early nineteenth century that 'Inclosure came and trampled on the grave / Of labours rights and left the poor a slave'.[70] But in the sixteenth century these practices, coupled with the increasing economic divides of the country, led to an 'electric atmosphere … of popular agitation', to the extent that almost all of the major civil unrest of the period can be traced back to the agrarian crisis in some way.[71]

The ploughman literature of the period is deeply concerned with this perceived agrarian crisis, and repeatedly makes direct references to it. Even as early as 1530, the *Dyalogue* contains a complaint about engrossment: 'But nowe for their ambicious suttlete / Maketh one fearme of two or thre' (sig. A6v). By 1550 the complaint was joined by a wave of similar observations. *Pyers Plowman's exhortation* (1550) exclaims that

> A fewe riche men haue ingrossed up so many fermes and shepe pastures and haue decayed so many whole townes that thousands of the poore comens can not get so much as … any little house to put their head in. (sig. A2r)

It also describes how landlords are 'driuen by their insaciable couertousnes to conuert al their groundes unto the pasturing of shepe' (sig. A7r). In an ingenious

---

[66]   Wrightson, *Earthly Necessities*, p. 142.

[67]   Wrightson, *Earthly Necessities*, pp. 142–4; Thirsk, *Agrarian History*, pp. 338–53.

[68]   John Bale, *Laboryouse Journey*, sig. B1r, cited in *Index Britanniae Scriptorum*, eds Carley and Brett, p. xii.

[69]   Thirsk, *Agrarian History*, p. 201.

[70]   See E. J. Kenney, 'The Age of Augustus' in *The Cambridge History of Classical Literature*, ed. E. J. Kenney (Cambridge, 1982), pp. 297–332. John Clare, 'The Mores', ll. 19–20, in *John Clare*, eds E. Powell and E. Robinson (Oxford, 1984).

[71]   Thirsk, *Agrarian History*, p. 224; see also D. MacCulloch and A. Fletcher, *Tudor Rebellions* (London, 1997).

twist on More's image of predatory sheep, the author describes the landlessness caused by the process of enclosing land for sheep pasture in the image of a 'flocke of labourers' (sig. A7v) roaming the countryside.[72]

Lacking the tools of modern economic analysis, the Edwardian writer figures these notorious agrarian problems in the terms of social morality, and the ploughman figure as the biblical, prophetic critical analyst.[73] Whilst the ploughman of the *Exhortation* does demonstrate some strikingly sober ideas for the remedy of the agrarian crisis, the ploughman more often does not mutter economic figures but bellows 'heare ye therefore, O, ye kynges, and understonde that I judge the earthe' (*I Playn Piers*, sig. B3r). The critique of the agrarian situation is figured in the familiar terms of a transgression against the natural state of the commonwealth, imagined in the image of the estates model. The Edwardian ploughman remembers a kind of agrarian golden age in which it was possible to lead

> A goodly lyfe, a household then to keep and feed, both with broth and bacon and bread of the bible, to tell forth Christes trade. (*Playn Piers*, sig. A6r)

The association of the rural household, rural labour and the work of 'Christ's trade' creates, as Langland had done, a spiritualized, moral image of physical labour as 'Godly', as the natural created state intended for humanity at the moment of creation. It is the image of an Edenic state shaped by what Milton would call man's 'daily work ... which declares his dignity'.[74] But whilst Milton is careful to suggest that this work can be 'of body or mind', the Edwardian writer is determined that the labour of dignity is the work of rural production. Langland's commands to 'swynke and swete and sowe' (B6.25) are mirrored in the *Exhortation*'s demands that to labour should be to 'bryng furth corne ... making of cloth ... thynges necessary both for themselues and for all those other' (sig. A4v). The rapacious economic self-interest of the mid-century is seen as a transgression against natural labour, and the ploughman denounces it in the terms of a raging and elegiac lament for the destruction of the Christian commonwealth.

However, the Protestant ploughman's persistent anticlericalism now overwhelmingly defines the terms of his rural ideology and his reaction to the agrarian crisis. The accusations of covetousness and greed that should have been aimed more accurately at the landed classes and even the crown were placed by the ploughman at the door of his ever-present opposite, the clergy. The *Exhortation* conflates the 'fatte priestes' (sig. A1v) of the pre-Dissolution period with the 'fatte marchauntes' (sig. A2r) that engross and enclose land to the detriment of the poor commons. The state of agricultural England is seen to have been caused by the

---

[72]   On this text, see also the discussions in Scase, *Literature and Complaint*, pp. 165–9; Kelen, *Langland's Early Modern Identities*, pp. 59–60. Scase argues that the text 'draws on the old tradition ... of peasant plaint' (p. 169).

[73]   Wrightson, *Earthly Necessities*, p. 149.

[74]   Milton, *Paradise Lost*, IV. 618–19.

ongoing effects of a Catholic culture of idleness. Before the Dissolution, 'a great parte of the men of thys realm' were in religious orders, they had 'idle liuings', whilst the rest of the population were too busy with 'going of pilgrimages', 'gyldyng of Images', and 'keping of so many supersticcious holydays' to work, to the extent that 'the third part of the men of thys realm had then continuallye lyued in Idleness' (sig. A4r). After the Dissolution, the indolence and its catastrophic economic effects are still apparent, but have simply moved out of the cloister and into vagrancy. The massive unemployment of the lower-wage earner is imagined as the effects of the appearance of a redundant ex-clerical class in the labour market. It is this image that constitutes a threat to the commonwealth, rather than the state's own predatory instincts or those of the landed classes. 'If more woorke be not prouided for thym', warns the writer, 'what can ensue but extreame pouertie beggary and miserie' (sig. A3v). The ploughman conflates the economic situation with clerical abuses, under the pressure of his constantly reinforced anticlericalism. He effectively throws the battered culture of monasticism in England under the wheels of the careering bandwagon of agrarian protest.

This strategic rhetorical 'taint' of Catholicism was to have a long history, threading its way through the Marprelate tracts to the literature of the Exclusion Crisis more than a century later. As has been suggested throughout this chapter, what this appropriation of the ploughman figure enabled was the construction of an oppositional identity for the sixteenth-century Protestant, an identity in which he could imagine himself to be the natural heir of the medieval ploughman. The emotive attractions of controversial pastoralism outlined in the last chapter come to be sharply focused on this one figure. Even whilst the texts which enacted this appropriation were necessarily printed, and probably written and read, in a metropolitan context, the Protestant writer/editor could take his cultural place in the tradition of politicized pastoralism, in which 'the poore printer also, which laboreth but for his lyuynge' (*Playn Piers*, sig. C2r) was as much the victim and opponent of the perceived corruptions of the clerical and land-owning estates as the rural labourer.

Negotiating Langland: Robert Crowley's Editions of *The Vision of Piers Plowman* (1550)

The developing enthusiasm for Langlandian 'ploughman literature' in the sixteenth century suggested by the printing of these polemical texts is confirmed – but also complicated – by what should be seen as one of the most ambitious and most intriguing literary printing ventures of the mid-century. Up until fairly recently, the traditional scholarly interest in the Latinate humanists, More and Erasmus, has had the unfortunate effect of hiding Robert Crowley's editorial work under the shadow of Thomas Chaloner's translation of *The Praise of Folie* (1549) and Ralph Robinson's English version of More's *Utopia* (1551).

John N. King's work was for a long time the most substantial discussion of Crowley's editions of *Piers Plowman*.[75] The critical view traditionally offered of Crowley's editing of Langland's text frequently presented him as at worst a blundering, obtuse, propagandist appropriator, and at best a heavily partisan reader of *Piers Plowman* who just about shows some cursory care as an editor. King writes that Crowley's editorial additions to Langland's text produced a 'powerful revolutionary attack against monasticism and the Roman Catholic hierarchy', and Charlotte Brewer similarly described Crowley's venture as 'a direct contribution to controversy'.[76]

To some extent these claims were quite right. The printing of so many 'ploughman' texts before 1550, some of them ferociously polemical, must have had an effect in shaping the cultural landscape in which Crowley's editions appeared. There was clearly an extremely active market for the 'propagandist ploughmen literature' with which Crowley's editions have been associated. However, the overemphasis on the propagandist nature of Crowley's editions does a great disservice to them. Whilst both King and Brewer gesture at the status of Crowley's editions as an early attempt at a critical edition of a 'classic' English text, and Thorne and Uhart's article serves to correct some of the textual details upon which King relies, their collective critical interest in the partisanship of the texts obscures the often complex synthesis of different purposes and effects at play in the editing and printing of the work.[77]

More recent scholarship has already complicated this picture, asserting how little of Crowley's editorial activity is actually as intrusive as had been thought, relating the editions to traditions of prophetic writing, and generally focusing much more closely on the bibliographical aspects of the editions.[78]

---

[75]   King, *English Reformation Literature*, pp. 319–57; see also J. R. Thorne and Marie-Claire Uhart, 'Robert Crowley's *Piers Plowman*', *Medium Aevum* 55:2 (1986), 248–53; Charlotte Brewer, *Editing Piers Plowman: The Evolution of the Text* (Cambridge, 1996), pp. 7–19.

[76]   King, *Reformation Literature*, p. 322; Brewer, *Editing Piers Plowman*, p. 16.

[77]   King, *Reformation Literature*, p. 328; Brewer, *Editing Piers Plowman*, p. 12. Thorne and Uhart, tracing the probable manuscript tradition of B-texts that Crowley used, argue that one of the key pieces of evidence for King's idea of 'ideological editing', the excision of B10.291–303, on Gregory the Great, was caused by accident rather than intent. They argue that the lines do not occur in the manuscripts Crowley was probably using. See Thorne and Uhart, 'Robert Crowley's *Piers Plowman*', p. 252.

[78]   The best work from a very detailed bibliographical angle is that of R. Carter Hailey, 'Geuyng Light to the Reader', and also 'Robert Crowley and the Editing of Piers Plowman (1550)', *YLS*, 21 (2007), 143–70. For revisionary accounts of Crowley's editorial work, his marginal annotation in particular, see Larry Scanlon, 'Langland, Apocalypse and the Early Modern Editor' in *Reading the Medieval in Early Modern England*, eds David Matthews and Gordon McMullan (Cambridge, 2007), pp. 51–73, and Michael Johnston, 'From Edward III to Edward VI: *The Vision of Piers Plowman* and Early Modern England', *Reformation*, 11 (2006), 47–78. On the connections between Crowley's editions and traditions of prophetic

This section explores the presentation, prefacing and marginalia of the editions in order to demonstrate how Crowley enacts a complex negotiation of interpretative encouragement, some of it partisan, but also a process of interpretative control or constraint, as well as an interest in marketing the text in a way that differentiates it from the polemical literature that preceded it. In place of the idea of the margins of the text as a place solely of religious polemic, the space that allows Crowley to forcefully wrench *Piers Plowman* into a 'revolutionary attack', the margins of Crowley's editions are instead viewed as the site of a 'complex construction of literary community'.[79] While Crowley's editions are indeed touched by the ecclesiastical and social concerns which produced much of the ploughman polemics I have discussed in this chapter, it is vital, I think, to differentiate Crowley's editions from this tendency towards polemic. I argue instead that Crowley's *Piers Plowman* editions were presented as an institutionalized, high-kudos vernacular literary classic. Langland became a name to conjure with, in the same way that Erasmus and More were, in an Edwardian literary culture whose diversity and complexity is still not fully recognized.[80]

Crowley's editions are remarkable even in the superficial sense of the speed and copiousness of their production. The first edition spawned two further reprints in the same year. The second edition adds 'summaries' of the passus and a massive amount of marginal annotation to the first. The third edition is more ambiguous, being identified as a second edition on the title page. It can therefore be identified only by small differences in the marginal additions and title page (Crowley is spelt 'Crowlye' on the title page of the third edition, for example). The most regularly quoted part of Crowley's editions, what Walter Skeat called in passing 'the most

---

writing, in both manuscript and print, see Lawrence Warner, 'An Overlooked *Piers Plowman* Excerpt and the Oral Circulation of Non-Reformist Prophecy, *c*. 1520–55', *YLS*, 21 (2007), 119–42, and Wendy Scase, '*Dauy Dycars Dreame* and Robert Crowley's Prints of *Piers Plowman*', *YLS*, 21 (2007), 171–98. On the importance of prophetic discourse in Kett's Rebellion (1549), and that rebellion as an unacknowledged but vital context for Crowley's editions, see my essay, '"Thys is no Prophecye": Robert Crowley, *Piers Plowman*, and Kett's Rebellion', forthcoming in *The Sixteenth-Century Journal*.

[79]   Evelyn B. Tribble, *Margins and Marginality*, p. 8. For a fuller exploration of the transition of Humanism from Latinate elitism to vernacular populism see David Weil Baker, *Divulging Utopia: Radical Humanism in Sixteenth-Century England* (Amherst, 1999).

[80]   John N. King's trail-blazing assertions about the inclusiveness of Edwardian literary culture in *Reformation Literature* have perhaps still not been widely acknowledged. A volume as representative as the *Cambridge History of Early Modern English Literature* still characterizes Edwardian literature in the following terms: 'the social violence and iconoclasm of the literature of Edward's reign proved newly excessive ... the preponderantly negative and polemical tonality of English Reformation literature at mid-century coalesces in angry laments over the dissolution of community, in which there is very little positive social vision or portrayal', Janel Mueller, 'Literature and the Church' in *The Cambridge History of Early Modern English Literature*, eds Janel Mueller and David Lowenstein (Cambridge, 2002), pp. 257–309, 293, 297.

interesting part', is something common to all three; a preface added by Crowley to the beginning of the text, titled 'The Printer to the Reader' (sig. *2.r).[81] What Skeat, King and Brewer single out for attention is the following passage. As Scanlon quips, 'Then comes the sentence that everyone quotes':

> In whose [Edward IIIs] tyme it pleased God to open the eyes of many to se hys truth, geuing them boldenes of herte, to open their mouthes and crye oute agaynste the worckes of darckenes, as did John Wicklefe, who also in those dayes translated the holye Bible into the Englishe tonge, and this writer who in reportynge certaine visions and dreames … doeth moste christianlye enstruct the weake, and sharply rebuke the obstinate blynde. (sig. *2r)[82]

Whilst Crowley's attempt at dating the poem is incorrect (something we will return to shortly), this is an extremely effective piece of rhetorical writing – indeed I used it as an epigraph to Chapter 2 for precisely this reason. The sense of the passage depends on the stock images of Protestant rhetoric, of dichotomies between darkness and light or enlightenment, silence and speech or 'speaking out' which find their notorious completion in the famed mixed metaphor of Milton's 'Lycidas'. The 'blind mouths' of rhetoric work in a familiar manner to construct an image of Catholicism as simultaneously an obscure, empty language and a kind of institutional conspiracy of silence from which the Protestant writer and reader breaks free. The language of enlightenment is similarly used by writers intent on invoking an idea of the divide between the 'dark' past and the Renaissance. Philip Sidney, in eulogizing Chaucer's *Troilus and Criseyde*, writes that he is unsure 'whether to marvel more, either that he in that misty time could see so clearly, or that we in this clear age go so stumblingly after him'.[83] At the same time, like the apocryphal 'Chaucerian' pieces *The Plowman's Tale* and *Jack Upland*, and the *Praire and Complaynt*, the passage seeks to produce a mythologized tradition of reformation, a chronological and cultural bridge between the fourteenth and sixteenth centuries. Well before Hudson's *Premature Reformation* or even Foxe's *Acts and Monuments*, Crowley imagines the chronologically disparate reigns of Edward III and Edward VI as times when 'it pleased God to open the eyes' of the people, when God is imagined to have acted directly in the ecclesiastical affairs of England to bring about a fracture with the 'darkness' of Rome.

This rhetoric of reformation as enlightenment is evidently prevalent in Crowley's imagination. He returns to it in both the preface, and the summaries added to the second and third editions. The summaries and marginal notes are

---

[81]   Walter Skeat, ed., *The Vision of Will, regarding Piers Plowman*, 2 vols (Oxford, 1886), II. lxxiii.

[82]   Robert Crowley, ed., *The Vision of Piers Plowman* (London, 1550). The three different editions are 19906 (first edition) 19907a (second edition) and 19907 (third edition). All references are incorporated in the text.

[83]   Philip Sidney, *A Defence of Poetry*, ed. J. van Dorsten (Oxford, 1966), p. 62.

placed there, says Crowley on the title page of the second edition, for the purpose of 'giuyng light to the reader'. In the preface, Crowley describes the difficulties of the poem's language as making

> the sense somewhat darcke, but not so harde, but that it may be understande of suche as will not sticke to breake the shall of the nutte for the kernelles sake. (sig. *2v.)

The image of darkness/enlightenment is here combined with an image of the act of readership itself, the need to decode or 'break' the surface of the written text to grasp the kernel of meaning within. This image is one produced by a writer peculiarly concerned with the practice of reading. Crowley introduces the image because of the indebtedness of his rhetoric to the vocabulary of controversies that are similarly focused on the image of reading practice, those over the vernacular Bible and their associated construction of a specifically Protestant image of the act of scriptural interpretation. The image of reading that Crowley invokes is heavily laden with reformist ideology: it is of the individual reader *working* at interpretation in a way that echoes the reformist cries of 'sola scriptura'. Bound up with this image is the idea of the individual Christian developing spiritual understanding based upon a personal 'hands-on' reading of (vernacular) scripture and the inspiration of the holy spirit and individual conscience, rather than through the mediation of an ecclesiastical hierarchy and the dictates of interpretative tradition.

Some of Crowley's additions to the text, both in the form of summaries and marginalia, are distinctly partisan, seeking to reform the text itself to the tastes of the reformist reader. Marginal comments such as 'The fruites of popishe penaunce' (Ed. 2. sig. C4v) and 'The suppression of abbayes. Good counsell' (Ed. 2. sig. F1r) are plainly opportunistic, taking Langland's attacks on insincere confession (B3.50–55) and wealthy monastic houses (B5.40–50) and wrenching them into significance for a culture which had managed to institutionally abolish both the sacrament of confession and the vast culture of monasticism in England. Similarly, the summaries Crowley appended to the second and third editions reinforce these intrusive editorial interpretations. A good example is the summary of Langland's prologue (Ed. 2. sig. *3r). The marginalia for the opening lines simply lists the professions of the figures that Langland's vast opening plateau presents, and the summary begins by doing the same. In a long sequence of repeated constructions, Crowley lists the figures: 'Some to be gallant Some to contemplation … Some to iesting Some to beggyng' and so on, until, that is, he comes to Langland's mention of bishops. Then Crowley's cursory list slows pace and halts for a separate paragraph:

> Than it declareth the great wyckednes of the byshoppes, that spareth not to hange their seales at euery Pardoners proxes, and what shameful Simony reigneth in the church. (Ed. 2. sig. *3r)

Langland's satire does of course encompass bishops and simony, but Crowley distends and rearranges the sense of the prologue's lines drastically. The image of the corrupt bishop who actively 'hangs his seal' on pardoners reverses the agent of Langland's text. The image of the seals is perhaps suggested by Langland's description of pardoners who 'Broughte forth a bulle with bisshopes seles' (B.Prol. 69), but here it is the pardoner, not the bishop, who is actively corrupt, 'bringing forth' corruption to 'deceyve the peple' (B.Prol. 79). Crowley makes the bishop the prime culprit of ecclesiastical corruption, and simultaneously 'over-represents' the particular importance of the bishops amongst the baffling plethora of action and topics and figures in Langland's text to lay extra emphasis on those aspects with more significance for the Protestant reader. This is a deeply partisan strategy by Crowley, and as King and Brewer have asserted, part of Crowley's editorial intention is demonstrably to make the social and ecclesiastical satire of *Piers Plowman* more relevant and attractive to a mid-sixteenth century readership than it would otherwise have been.

However, whilst Crowley does sometimes instigate an intrusive editorial practice encouraging the reader to view Langland as a fellow-spirited reformist writer, this aspect of Crowley's work needs to be offset against attention to other aspects of the editions. There are many intentions at work; the editions are not simply presented as polemical works, but are shaped by what might be called multiple strategies of interpretative guidance. In other words, they are 'marketed' not to a monolithic, abstract Protestant readership solely interested in controversial marginalia but to a complex community of readers with multiple interests and affinities.

A vital part of a reader's first impressions of *Piers Plowman* in 1550 was Crowley's own self-fashioning as an antiquarian in the preface. Here the antiquarianism is represented as less immediately polemical and controversial. Crowley fashions himself as a responsible and erudite mediator between the text and reader in a role correlative with that of a humanist editor or translator. In the second edition, Crowley tells his reader that on the title page that he has 'added certayne notes and cotations in the mergyne, geuyng light to the Reader'. His role as editor, one of 'bringing to light' the work, is important: not only does it echo the heavily Protestant rhetoric of spiritual enlightenment, but it delegates to the editor the responsibility for explicating the spiritual and moral meaning of the work. But Crowley's role is not limited to commenting on a well-known text. His work is first to 'bring to light' the classical text itself. Whilst some manuscripts of *Piers Plowman* certainly circulated in the sixteenth century, the frontispiece of the first edition is quick to claim that Crowley's edition is, importantly, original.[84]

---

[84]   Four manuscripts containing *Piers Plowman* are known to date from the sixteenth century: British Library MS Royal 18. B. XVII, a C-text; British Library MS Digby 145, an A/C conjoined version copied by Adrien Fortescue around 1531–1532; the former Sion College MS, now Takamiya 23; and Cambridge University Library MS G. 4. 31, both B-texts; see Brewer, *Editing Piers Plowman*, p. 10. See also Kelen, *Langland's Early Modern*

It is 'the first time imprinted'. Such a slight and self-evident comment might seem unimportant, but it must also be seen as a significant 'selling point' for the editions. They are advertised as a luxurious new addition to the growing corpus of vernacular works. What is asserted is the originality and excitement of a newly rediscovered classic. Crowley's self-fashioning in his preface, retained in all three editions, is important in forming both the text's status and his own. Crowley presents himself as

> Beyng desyerous to knowe the name of the Autoure of this worthy worke (gentle reader) and the tyme of the writynge of the same: I did not onely gather togyther suche aunciente copies as I could come by, but also consult such men as I knew to be more exercised in the studie of antiquities, then I myselfe haue ben. (sig. *2r)

The self-presentation is one of a curious and responsible amateur scholar, speaking to a leisured, equally curious and notably 'gentle' reader, for whom he has taken it upon himself to undertake a project of research, collecting manuscripts and consulting with experts. The status of the antiquarian and the implied difficulty of his labour is heightened and moulded to resemble that of the humanist philologist, editor and translator. There is something rather 'Erasmian' about Crowley's persona.

If the reader were in any doubt about the academic nature of Crowley's interest in *Piers Plowman*, Crowley goes to some length to persuade him. The 'polemical' interpretation on spiritual enlightenment in the England of Edward III, so often quoted as the highlight of Crowley's preface, is preceded by a passage that rivals it in length which details Crowley's evidence for dating the poem. What is striking about this passage is its detail. Crowley narrates that he has seen a dated manuscript 'in the later ende wherof was noted, that the same copye was written in the yere of oure Lorde .M.iiii.C. and nyne' (sig. *2r). He moves on to internal evidence, noting that there is a reference to a 'dere yere ... in the second side of the lxviii. Leaf of thys printed copye', a reference, he writes, to 1350. Like a modern editor attempting to deduce a *terminus a quo* and *terminus ad quem* for a text, Crowley details his evidence, both external and internal, and comes to the conclusion that he 'may be bolde to report that ... we may justly collect therefore that it was first written about two hundred yeres paste, in the tyme of Kynge Edwarde the thyrde'. Even by the standards of the most recent attempts to date the poem, Crowley's effort is far from disastrous. Whilst we recognize Langland now as a Ricardian author, the broad dates that Crowley works between, 1350 and 1409,

---

Identities, p. 3, who counts three fragmentary sixteenth-century manuscript copies as well as the four listed here. On Fortescue, see Thorlac Turville-Petre, 'Sir Adrian Fortescue and his Copy of *Piers Plowman*', *YLS*, 14 (2000), 29–48.

are reasonably, even strikingly, accurate.[85] Even regardless of accuracy, Crowley's detailed, referenced search for historical veracity is impressive, and importantly, was meant to seem so. The sheer detail that Crowley relates makes the passage significant, and it gives his editions an aspect of academic, even pedantic gravitas: the editions are set up not as a convenient polemical appropriation of a text, but as a serious antiquarian project.

Another aspect of Crowley's preface is suggestive of the antiquarian editor/mediator role in which he writes: his introduction to the language and metre of the poem itself. Crowley introduces the metre as

> not after the maner of our times that write nowe adayes (for his verses ende not alike) but the nature of hys miter is, to haue thre wordes et the least in euery verse whiche beginner with some one letter. (sig. *2r)

And concerning the language, Crowley writes of it being 'somewhat dark', as noted, but 'not so hard' for the Protestant reader prepared for the interpretative toil of reading. Whilst the idea of reading has been argued above to be part of a particular discourse about interpretation familiar to a Protestant readership, it is also active in Crowley's editorial introduction as something of a more aesthetic nature. By explaining the nature of alliterative verse, comparing it to sixteenth-century rhymed forms and warning the reader of the 'somewhat dark' vocabulary, Crowley acts as a kind of knowledgeable aesthetic mediator between the 'ancient' text and the expectations of the early modern reader. Again, he seems as concerned with positioning himself as an educated scholar-editor as he does a polemical historiographer. The antiquarian persona that Crowley assumes is not, as in the case of the Chaucerian texts or the *Prair and Complaynt*, a thinly veiled strategy to legitimize a brutally combative polemical text. Crowley's presence is at once more historically aware, and more aesthetic in its preoccupations.[86]

One aspect of Crowley's editions which has engaged the most critical interest apart from the preface is his marginal annotation. Some of these annotations are, as shown above, undeniably polemical, wrenching Langland's text rather surreally into a post-Dissolution context. But the nature of Crowley's annotations has been misconstrued to a large extent by critical emphasis on the more controversial of them. What a closer analysis of the marginalia makes clear is the complexity of the process, a complexity that destabilizes any idea about the bald propagandist intent of the editor. There are clearly multiple purposes at work, and whilst the

---

[85]   Crowley's consultants, those 'more exercised in the studie of antiquities' almost certainly included John Bale (or at least Crowley had access to Bale's catalogues). The identification of Langland as 'Roberte Langlande, a Shropshire man borne in Cleybirie, about viii. Myles from Malverne hilles' is that of Bale in his *Index Britanniae Scriptorum*, eds C. Brett and J. Carley, p. 383.

[86]   On Crowley's unusual emphasis on Langland's historicity, see also Rebecca L. Schoff, '*Piers Plowman* and Tudor Regulation of the Press', *YLS*, 20 (2006), 93–114, esp. 96.

marginalia does, in the tradition of reformist biblical annotation, encourage polemical interpretation, it also at points acts to constrain and control interpretation at potentially critical moments.

As Thorne and Uhart note, the first edition contains far fewer annotations than the subsequent editions, the majority of them packed into the prologue and passus 1.[87] Charlotte Brewer would seem to be right when she says that Crowley 'warmed to his editorial task as his familiarity with the poem increased' in the later editions.[88] Crowley added a massive amount of annotation to the second and third editions, along with the passus 'summaries'. What is striking about these annotations, however, is not so much their sporadically political intent, but their utilitarianism. The vast majority of them are scriptural references, and the bulk of the remainder are what might be called 'plot summaries'. Crowley notes a passage in passus 10 with 'The thief was saved before any of the prophets' (sig. N4r), and Langland's extended imagist explications of the trinity with 'A description of the trinitie' (sig. Z1v). The marginal notes are, for the most part, aids to guide an early modern reader through what is, as any modern reader of *Piers Plowman* will recognize, a sometimes formidably confusing text, helping them grasp particular scenes and sequences and doing the scholarly work of tracking the Vulgate quotations down; a process which both foregrounds the scriptural richness of Langland's poem and prevents the less Latinate reader from becoming alienated. Whilst it seems less remarkable than the marginalia that critics have singled out, the vast majority of Crowley's annotations are of this sort: they are utilitarian rather than ideological.

Having said this, there are moments in which we can see Crowley in a more intrusive editorial mode. Yet the point of these interventions is just as often to discourage as encourage the suggestion of contemporary political relevance. The marginalia becomes at points a strategy to control interpretation, and Crowley can be seen in a process of constraining the potentially 'radical' meaning of the text. One particularly important moment occurs in Crowley's marginal addition to Langland's prologue, lines 196–210. The passage utilizes a quotation from Ecclesiastes 10:16: '*Ve terre ubi puer est rex*', 'Woe to the land where a boy is king'. It is one of Langland's moments of coy, assertive defensiveness regarding the political valence of his text: 'What þis metels bymeneþ … Devyne ye, for I ne dar, by deere God in heuene' (B. Prol. 209–10). The refusal to fully interpret the passage is purposefully careful, and understandably so. Richard II was barely 10 years of age when he acceded to the throne in 1377, and Langland, writing not long afterwards, knew he was sailing precariously close to the wind. So, it would seem, was Crowley. In an intriguing mirroring of Langland's evasion, Crowley attempts in his marginal comment to explain away the same potential threat. Crowley only writes two marginal comments in Latin; one refers to Meed's

---

[87] Thorne and Uhart, 'Robert Crowley's *Piers Plowman*', p. 248.

[88] Brewer, *Editing Piers Plowman*, p. 16. A statistical account of the annotations is available as an appendix to Scanlon's article, see 'Langland, Apocalypse, and the Early Modern Editor', pp. 72–3.

marriage, the other states: 'Omnium doctisumorum suffrago, dicuntur, hec de regibus, fatuis, aut ineptis principibus, non de etate teneribus quasi dicat, ubi rex puer est' (sig. A3v). It is a paradoxically scholastic moment for a Protestant writer. Refusing the vernacular, Crowley defers to the 'doctors' and states that a history of biblical commentary asserts that the passage from Ecclesiastes is referring to lazy, inept, 'childish' princes, rather than the prince's literal age. The potential for seditious interpretation is obvious at this point. Just as Langland saw the inequities of fourteenth-century society as deriving, to some extent, from the lack of a stable, mature monarch, a reader of *Piers Plowman* in 1550 would have seen the internecine strife behind the young Edward VI's throne boil over into the deposition of Seymour by John Dudley in 1549. Crowley, perhaps more so than Langland, moves to defuse the potentially 'radical' meaning of the biblical quotation and allegorical vision. His marginal comment works here to constrain, not to invoke, polemical interpretation.[89]

Finally, one of the most important aspects of these editions is one that the recent interest in book history and the 'materiality' of texts has foregrounded: the particular physical appearance and format of the editions. A brief outline of the print culture in which Crowley worked is helpful in suggesting the peculiar status of his editions of *Piers Plowman*. Crowley's print shop opened in 1549 at Ely Rents in Holborn, and proved to be a prolific centre of activity. Crowley managed to publish 19 texts in the space of three years, including 10 of his own works or editions. An important partnership enabled this output. Richard Grafton, who regularly worked with Edward Whitchurch and succeeded Thomas Berthelet as 'King's Printer', printed almost all of the texts which bear Crowley's name, including *Piers Plowman*.[90] He is, a little bizarrely, never acknowledged. But he was part of a loose knit group of printers, scholars and writers who seem to have enjoyed governmental and aristocratic support and protection in the Edwardian years. Such support was not novel: Wynken de Worde and Pynson depended heavily on royal and ecclesiastical favour in the 1520s, as did Berthelet in the following decade.[91] What is new is the wholehearted institutional support for the reformist cause that makes the Cromwellian phenomena of sanctioning anticlerical polemic look like a slight form of opportunism. The precarious status

---

[89]   As Thomas Betteridge has argued, 'Crowley's poetics simultaneously demand an iconoclastic reading while at the same time seeking to make any other reading impossible'. See *Literature and Politics in the English Reformation*, p. 105.

[90]   See L. Hellinga and J. B. Trapp, 'Introduction' in *The Cambridge History of the Book in Britain*, vol. 3. eds L. Hellinga and J. B. Trapp (Cambridge, 1999), p. 11. Hellinga notes that the first 'King's printer' was Richard Pynson, appointed in 1506. Pamela Neville-Sington argues in the same volume that Pynson was in fact the second, after William Faques was appointed 'Impressor regius' in 1504. See 'Press, Politics and Religion' in *The Cambridge History of the Book in Britain*, vol. 3, pp. 576–607, 579.

[91]   See David Loades, 'Books and the English Reformation prior to 1558' in *The Reformation and the Book*, ed. Jean-Francois Gilmont (Aldershot, 1990), pp. 264–91, 268.

of printers in the Henrician and later Marian years is not apparent. King writes of Grafton and Whitchurch operating what were 'virtually government presses' and Crowley's shop in Holborn as a 'conduit for controversial works favouring the new regime'. The institutional enthusiasm for print culture also seems to have emanated outwards to encompass printers or scholars such as John Day, William Seres, John Bale and William Baldwin.[92]

What also seems unusual about this community is its emphasis on producing certain types of books. Whilst the earliest years of English printing can be characterized by Caxton's aristocratic folio editions, Crowley's era is notable for the proliferation of the inexpensive octavo format, in a way that seems highly suggestive of both a change in the demographic of his readership and perhaps a pointing of the way towards the innovation of the pocket-sized editions of the Geneva Bible (1560). The vast majority of Crowley's publishing work appears in just this octavo format. A small number of works were published in the larger, more expensive quarto form. Of Crowley's quarto texts, *The Vision of Piers Plowman*, of which three separate quarto editions appeared in a single year, was clearly the most popular. Only Crowley's octavo format translation of *The Psalter of David* (1549) and *The True Copye of a Prolog Wrytten about two C. Yeres Paste by John Wyclyfe* (1550) rival the editions of Langland in terms of length. It is one of the, if not *the*, biggest and most prestigious venture of Crowley's career as an editor/publisher.

The prestigious nature of the editions, an aspect which critics have generally undervalued, is conspicuous when some attention is paid to the actual physical appearance of the editions, particularly the frontispiece of the first edition. High-status literary works, such as Sir Thomas Chaloner's translation of Erasmus's *Praise of Folly* (1549), were published with an eye to marketing their authoritative classical status. An ornate architectural façade regularly surrounded the title and epigraph. The effect is both to conjure up images of the cultural weight of the ancient world and its artistic and philosophical achievements, whilst bestowing on the text a feeling of intellectual gravitas. The designs figure the texts as Chaucer figures Virgil's *Aeneid*: written in stone or metal, inscribed in the permanent record of an intellectual tradition.[93]

A cursory look at the frontispieces of one of Crowley's first edition of Langland and analogous items shows quite clearly how Crowley and Grafton wished to market their text.[94]

---

[92]   See King, *Reformation Literature*, pp. 76–121.

[93]   Chaucer, *The House of Fame* in *The Riverside Chaucer*, ll. 140–150.

[94]   See Figures 3.2 3.4. R. Carter Hailey has argued suggestively that the first edition, some copies of which were printed on vellum rather than paper, may well have been produced with a different readership in mind to the consequent editions. As Hailey points out, this might also explain both the peculiar use of the engraving on the title page in the first edition, and the proliferation of marginalia in the second and third editions. See Hailey, 'Geuyng Light to the Reader', esp. pp. 492–5.

Crowley's *Piers Plowman* is again presented within the authoritative structure of a classical façade which is perhaps cleaner and neater than that used for Chaloner's Erasmus. Associated ploughman texts come with no such support, their large black-letter type standing rather sparsely on the page, as if their status as topical, polemical complaint is matched by their cursory presentation.

The monumental distance between those texts and Crowley's is the distance between permanence and transience. The polemical texts which do, as Brewer says of Langland, make 'a significant contribution to current religious and political issues' appear almost too 'current', as if their production depended far more on immediate relevance than on sustained authority. Crowley's editions of Langland, for all their relevance, are designed to appear 'classic', to be, with Aristotle and Erasmus, works of enduring intellectual worth. Whilst the 'propagandist' feel of some of the preface, summaries and marginal notes seem to locate the editions in the same 'market' or implied readership as works like *I Playn Piers* or the *Exhortation*, Crowley and Grafton clearly went to some trouble to present Langland's *Piers Plowman* as *different*. It was not to be viewed as an ephemeral political complaint, but as a work of institutionalized 'high' culture, comfortable in the company of humanistic classics such as Erasmus's *Praise of Folly* and More's *Utopia*.

Indeed, the institutional feel of Crowley's first edition can be ascribed also to the specific device that was used to advertise it. For the device we see surrounding Crowley's title of the work would be very familiar to readers from one of the most important institutional texts of the mid-century: the *Book of Homilies*, named on the title page as *Certayne Sermons, or homiles* (see Figure 3.4).[95]

A reader seeing Crowley's first edition of *Piers Plowman* would have to try rather hard not to be reminded of the *Book of Homilies*, which three years previously had appeared in a sequence of prints and which would – albeit with different devices on the title page – appear again in 1562 and 1571.

The editions are not, then, simply the product of a predatory and polemical culture, but are part of a striking literary and cultural canon. It is important to recognize the nature of this canon, as the literature of the Edwardian period has not tended to have the easiest of rides from scholars. It has been viewed as 'excessive', and as having a 'preponderantly negative and polemical tonality'. At other points it has been characterized as being part of a revolutionary Reformation which killed off cultures of either reformist literature or of political counsel.[96] We can instead

---

[95]   See Ronald B. McKerrow, *Printers' & Publishers' Devices in England & Scotland, 1485–1640* (London, 1913), pp. 137–8. The device is McKerrow's number 108. According to McKerrow, the device was used for the first time in 1547, and passed to John Wayland at the beginning of the Marian reign in 1553. Its final recorded use was in 1581.

[96]   Janel Mueller, 'Literature and the Church', p. 297. I refer here also to the representation of Protestant culture provided by James Simpson's polemical *Reform and Cultural Revolution* and *Burning to Read*, and Greg Walker's more considered *Writing under Tyranny*. For a far more positive view of Edwardian Protestant literary and intellectual culture, see Betteridge, *Literature and Politics in the English Reformation*, pp. 88, 112–13.

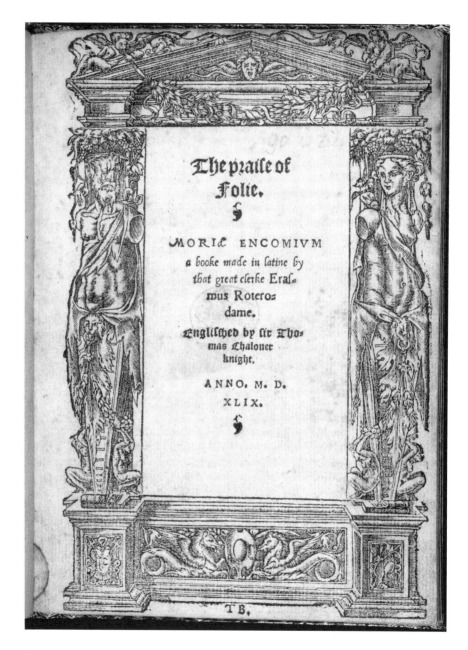

Figure 3.2   Title page of Sir Thomas Chaloner's translation of Erasmus, *The Praise of Folly* (London: Thomas Berthelet, 1549). © The British Library Board.

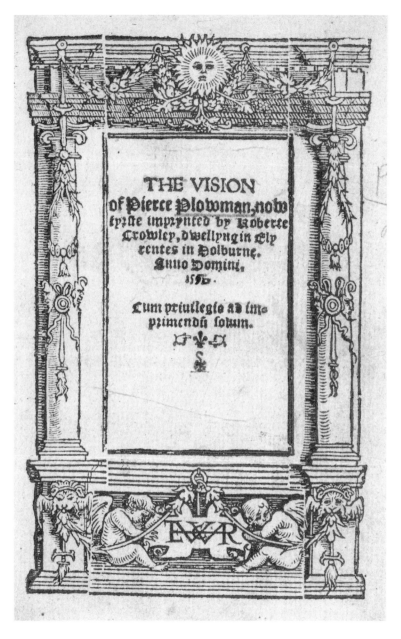

Figure 3.3   Title page of *The Vision of Piers Plowman* (London: Robert Crowley, 1550). © The British Library Board.

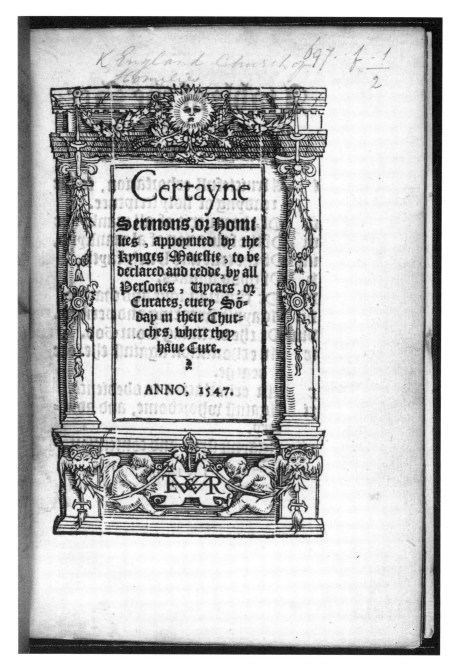

Figure 3.4   Title page of *Certayne Sermons, or homiles* (London: Edward Whitchurch, 1547). © The British Library Board.

see here, I argue, a rich and complex literary culture which can be characterized as being simultaneously: reformist, utopian, antiquarian, vernacular, humanist, and inclusive of the pre-Reformation past. The Edwardian reign saw Erasmus and More reach a new vernacular readership, and it also negotiated the rich variety of attractions offered by the 'living ghost of *Piers Plowman*'.

Chapter 4

The Elizabethan Ploughman:
From 'Piers Marprelate', to *Pierce Penniless* and back to Piers Plowman

To the Reader
To read strange newes, desires manye
Which at my hande they can not haue
For here is but antiquitie
Expressed only, as tholde booke gaue
Take in good part, and not depraue
The Ploughmans Crede, gentil reader
Loo, this is all that I requyer.[1]

I have addressed this present history, intending, by the favourable aid of Christ our Lord, not so much to delight the ears of my country in reading of news, as most specially to profit the hearts of the godly in perusing antiquities of ancient times.[2]

The sixteenth-century enthusiasm for radical pastoral writing did not wither in the fires of the Marian years; it emerged strongly in the Elizabethan period in remarkable new forms. Whilst some of its influence is palpably present in what have been regularly seen as distinctly new 'Renaissance' forms, particularly Spenser's *Shepheardes Calender* (1579) and Nashe's *Pierce Penniless* (1592), its continued significance was fuelled by the ongoing circulation of Langland's text and the tradition of politicized forms of pastoral self-fashioning found in Foxe's *Acts and Monuments* (first edition, 1563).[3] At a time when Protestant writers such as Foxe, Crowley and Bale were returning from enforced exile on the continent,

---

[1] *The Vision of Pierce Plowman newlye imprinted after the authors olde copy... whereunto is also annexed the Crede of Pierce Plowman, neuer imprinted with the booke before* (London, 1561), sig. A1v. Reprinted from *Pierce the Ploughman's Crede* (London, 1553), sig. A1v.

[2] Foxe, *A&M*, I. 3.

[3] Also, I do not here discuss another avenue of enquiry recently opened by other scholars, namely the indebtedness of Thomas Churchyard's work to Langland. For this see Warner, 'An Overlooked *Piers Plowman* Excerpt', and especially Scase, '*Dauy Dycars Dreame*'.

in the early 1560s, *Piers Plowman* appeared again in print.[4] Owen Rogers' 1561 edition of the poem, a reprint of Crowley's editions a decade earlier, also appended a copy of *Pierce Plowman's Crede* to the text, cementing the interconnections between Langland, Lollardy and Protestantism that had been constructed in the mid-century. Moreover, it reproduced the prefacing poem printed by Reynor Wolfe in his 1553 edition of the *Crede*.[5] With its claim to plain 'Antiquitie' and its Chaucerian topoi – 'Loo, that is all I requier' – these seemingly innocuous few lines signalled the transmission of the Edwardian craze for medieval reformism, the time when, as Thomas Wilson put it, 'the fine courtier will talk nothing but Chaucer', into the tumultuous cultural milieu that produced the long feted 'golden' literature of the later sixteenth century.[6]

Both Wolfe's poem and Foxe's prose draw a significant line between what pertains to serious edifying reading – 'Antiquitie' – and what constitutes a popular demand for facile amusement and pleasure: 'news'. What is apparent is that by the Elizabethan period the medieval chronicles and polemical literature published by people like Foxe, Crowley and Wolfe were a central and serious part of Protestant discourse. Foxe's 1570 edition of *Acts and Monuments*, it is worth noting, reprinted texts like *The Prayer and Complaint* and *Jack Upland*, essentially providing a kind of anthologized form of the polemical ploughman tradition for readers after 1570; an anthology which was required by law to be present in every cathedral church in England.[7] As Robert Crowley had claimed the 'antiquity' of *Piers Plowman* in his

---

[4]   J. N. King writes that Rogers' edition had the effect of 'marking the end of its sudden vogue; following this edition the poem remained out of print until the nineteenth century', *English Reformation Literature*, p. 326. Certainly, Langland's text did remain out of print until 1813, but the sense that 1561 marks the 'end' of its significance is, as my discussion of Nashe's *Pierce Penniless* demonstrates, incorrect. Whilst the 'vogue' for Langland's text can be seen to evaporate in terms of its printing history, the significance and influence on literary and political culture can still be felt in the 1590s and indeed much later.

[5]   For the importance of 'antiquity' to Edwardian Protestantism, see Chapter 3.

[6]   For Chaucer's use of the interjection, see for example 'loo, thys is my sentence', *House of Fame*, *Riverside Chaucer*, II. 776; and especially *Troilus and Criseyde*, V. 1849–52. The phrasing of Wolfe's poem is distinctly archaic. According to the *OED*, the interjection was still current into the nineteenth century, but the use of it as an accompaniment to sober, 'high' moral purpose is likely to have seemed archaic by 1553. See for comparison Edgar's somewhat less dignified 'alow, alow, loo, loo!' in Shakespeare's *King Lear*, ed. R. A. Foakes (London, 2000), IV. 3. 79. For the contemporary judgement of Edwardian Chaucerianism, see Thomas Wilson, *The Arte of Rhetorique*, ed. G. H. Mair (Oxford, 1909), p. 162. Wilson's comment is also cited and discussed in David Norbrook, *Poetry and Politics in the English Renaissance* (London, 1984), pp. 42–3. Wilson is discussed by King in *Reformation Literature*, pp. 105, 139, 304, 429; for the influence of Chaucer on Protestant style see also pp. 50–52, 229.

[7]   See Kelen, *Langland's Early Modern Identities*, pp. 54–5. On the status of Foxe's text see, for example, V. Norskov Olsen, *John Foxe and the Elizabethan Church* (Berkeley, 1973), p. 1.

attempt to reformulate the chronology of religious history, Protestant writers like Tyndale and Bale inherited the 'ancient' topoi of spiritualized simplicity to construct a deeply controversial tradition of Protestant identity. Moreover, the combined emphasis that reformism and humanism placed on the moral, social and political efficacy of reading had formed a powerful discourse about the nature and ethics of literature, its 'seriousness', which is manifest in these texts.[8] As David Norbrook has written, 'the Edwardian period established a conception of the function of poetry, and a canon of reforming poetry, which was to remain influential until the civil war'.[9] Yet this tradition of radical pastoral that subsumed Langland in the sixteenth century has been seen for a very long time as essentially old, outdated and dull. For all the many great studies of both medieval and renaissance literature that he produced, C. S. Lewis, and his *English Literature in the Sixteenth Century, Excluding Drama* (1954) in particular, has rather a lot to answer for here.

Lewis' aesthetic divisions of sixteenth-century literature are strict and temptingly simple: the 'late medieval' gives way to the 'drab', the 'drab' to the 'golden'. This new poetry, according to Lewis' hugely influential study, is 'innocent', free of intrusive ideological intent, long alliterative lines and 'popular' reference. For all Lewis' attempts to defend his terms as non-judgemental, there is a palpable sense of relief when the 'drab' is finally put to rest: 'Here is the Golden literature at last'.[10] 'Golden' literature is courtly and classical, metrically skilled and ideologically 'innocent': it is, in Lewis' eyes, Sidney and Spenser. The underlying narrative of progressive sophistication and 'literariness' that underpins Lewis' study is, of course, not to be dismissed out of hand. There is a world of difference between reading Crowley's apologetic preface to *The Philargyrie of Greate Britaine* and reading Sidney's *Defence of Poetry*. But Lewis' divisions between 'drab' and 'golden' have marked out a serious division of critical fields that has done little justice to either literature. What is described as 'drab', moralistic and old-fashioned inevitably becomes separated from the 'important' writing of the later sixteenth century. The native tradition of highly politicized poetry and its formal accompaniments suffers a comparatively desultory amount of critical

---

[8]   As Lorna Hutson describes, citing Richard Helgerson's *The Elizabethan Prodigals* (Berkeley, 1976), a number of writers of the 1580s including Sidney, Greene and Gascoigne had internalized a persistent sense of guilt about the act of writing, a suspicion of literature as a prodigal waste of time and talent, which owed a great deal to the influence of Protestantism on Tudor social and economic values. They frequently wrote in an apologetic 'posture of repentance', even as they defended the moral power of literature. See Lorna Hutson, *Thomas Nashe in Context* (Oxford, 1989), pp. 9–10.

[9]   Norbrook, *Poetry and Politics*, p. 47.

[10]   C. S. Lewis, *English Literature in the Sixteenth Century, Excluding Drama* (Oxford, 1954), pp. 317–18. More recent studies such as Blair Worden's *The Sound of Virtue: Philip Sidney's Arcadia and Elizabethan Politics* (New Haven, 1996) might lead us to question how ideologically 'innocent' either of these writers were.

attention. Simultaneously, the 'golden' writing becomes ever more separated from the literary culture that informed it.

The claims of Foxe's and Wolfe's writing to 'antiquitie', then, have been taken on board in modern critical formulations of literary history. But the positive ideological connotations of 'simple antiquitie' have been replaced with the pejorative associations of 'old' writing. As Sarah Kelen has noted, and as the previous chapters have argued, it was precisely the antiquity of these texts which made them politically and rhetorically potent.[11] Yet this synthesis of antiquarianism with polemical intent is something that has left this tradition standing in something of a blind-spot for many modern narratives of literary history. Constructions of literary history tend to harbour a kind of catch-22 when it comes to this literature. Radical pastoral constantly seems to shift between being 'old-hat', stylistically derivative and staid, and being too contemporary, its attachment to contemporary ideological controversy marking it off as too much 'of its time'. Yet the writing of the Elizabethan period was hugely indebted to its polemical past. The question asked of the ploughman tradition in the Elizabethan period should not be 'How is it old-fashioned?' but 'How is it made new?'.

John King has argued that Spenser's *Shepheardes Calendar* (1579), the text most frequently cited as the first example of a 'new', 'golden' Elizabethan literature, also 'encompassed native Protestant and biblical elements whose significance has long been over-shadowed by concern for the classical and Italianate origins of the text'.[12] Spenser's respect for Chaucer as a pseudo-Virgilian predecessor is open and fulsome. His debt to Langland is unacknowledged, but the figure 'Piers' who appears in the 'May' and 'October' eclogues is clearly reminiscent of the polemical Protestant tradition which had grown up around Langland's text. As King argues, Spenser's eclogues are 'rooted in pre-Reformation satire against clerical abuses' and can be read as a testament to the 'extraordinary power of the plowman conceit during this age of religious renewal and reform'.[13] In particular, the 'May' eclogue which, according to 'E.K''s gloss pits a Protestant Piers against

---

[11]   As Kelen puts it, 'As documents from England's past, medieval texts could do ideological work different from that done by more recent writings; the very "obsolescence" of medieval literature therefore gave it a political currency'; Kelen, *Langland's Early Modern Identities*, p. 12.

[12]   John N. King, 'Spenser's *Shepheardes Calender* and Protestant Pastoral Satire' in *Renaissance Genres: Essays on Theory, History and Interpretation*, ed. Barbara K. Lewalski (London, 1986), pp. 369–98, 369. Moreover, it has been recognized that there are numerous connections between the 'ploughman tradition' and Spenser's poetry. See, for example, A. C. Hamilton, 'The Visions of *Piers Plowman* and *The Faerie Queene*' in *Form and Convention in the Poetry of Edmund Spenser*, ed. William Nelson (New York, 1961), pp. 1–34; Judith H. Anderson, *The Growth of a Personal Voice: Piers Plowman and The Faerie Queene* (New Haven, 1976); John N. King, *Spenser's Poetry and the Reformation Tradition* (Princeton, 1990), esp. pp. 14–46.

[13]   King, *Spenser's Poetry and the Reformation Tradition*, pp. 14, 22.

a Catholic Palinode, is packed with echoes of the radical pastoral tradition.[14] In the polemical attacks on the 'greedie gouernaunce' of prelates who 'match them selfe with mighty potentates / Louers of Lordship and troublers of states' ('May', ll. 121–3), Spenser encompasses the anticlericalism that links *The Plowman's Tale* and Fish's *Supplication*. The biblical texture of Piers' speech in lines such as 'what concord han light and dark ... / ... what peace has the lion with the lamb' (ll. 168–9) is deeply reminiscent of Crowley or Latimer. As King argues, it is quite clear that Spenser has been reading *The Plowman's Tale*, and is re-working this particular piece of Henrician medievalism for the Elizabethan era.[15] But regardless of whether we might talk of Spenser's direct knowledge of *Piers Plowman*, what is clear is that Spenser's astonishing range of possible sources for this kind of pastoral (Virgil; Marot; Petrarch; Mantuan; Sannazzaro) must have included the English, medieval, polemical pastoral with which this book has been concerned.

In the same year, somewhat paradoxically given the general Protestant distaste for 'news' texts, a work appeared containing the 'greate clark' and 'good ensample', Piers Plowman. *News from the North* (1579) has not been the subject of a great deal of critical attention, and unfortunately there is little space here to do it justice, but its appearance warrants at least brief recognition. The text is a kind of almanac, a combination of dialogue and a series of 'questions' reminiscent of Erasmus' *Adagia*. It is part of a continued tradition of 'Mirror for Magistrates' texts that proliferated in the early Elizabethan period, a tradition that updated the schema of, for example, Hoccleve's *Regiment of Princes* for the Tudor period.[16] Its sequence of fulsome dedicatory epistles and poems, one of them by Anthony Munday, directs the text's profitable content to the eyes of a real magistrate: Sir Henry Sidney, Lord Deputy Governor of Ireland, father of Philip Sidney, the dedicatee of Spenser's *Shepheardes Calender*.[17] Here, in the coterie surrounding Sidney and Spenser, the Areopagus of 'golden poetry', there was a keen interest in what Piers Plowman still had to say.[18]

---

[14]　See the 'argument' of the May eclogue: 'under the persons of two shepheards Piers and Palinode, be represented two formes of pastoures or Ministers, or the protestant and the Catholique'; Richard A. McCabe, ed, *Edmund Spenser: The Shorter Poems* (London, 1999), p. 72. All references to the text are to this edition, incorporated in the text. As McCabe notes, the Protestants here are 'represented by Piers, spiritual kinsman of Langland's Piers Plowman' (p. 534).

[15]　King, *Spenser's Poetry and the Reformation Tradition*, pp. 21–2.

[16]　The text was reasonably popular; it was reprinted twice: first in 1585, and again in 1603. The third edition appeared under the name of *News from Malta* (1603) STC 17215, but after a few pages on Malta, the text is a full reprint of *News from the North*.

[17]　*News from the North, Otherwise called the conference between Simon Certain and Pierce Plowman* (London, 1579). The dedicatory epistle to Sidney is on sig. A2r. For Henry Sidney's career see Katherine Duncan-Jones, *Sir Philip Sidney: Courtier Poet* (Oxford, 1991), pp. 46, 54.

[18]　Some doubt has been cast over the closeness of the connection between Sidney and Spenser. Katherine Duncan-Jones suggests that the image of a coterie of experimental 'new poets' might have been constructed by Gabriel Harvey as a way to emphasize his inclusion

Even if the poetics of the 1570s and 1580s were significantly different from those that characterized the Edwardian period, the associations of the ploughman tradition had not changed. Piers had become a radical Protestant by 1550, and his appearance in and around the Sidney–Spenser circle had similar connotations. When Piers appeared in the *Shepheardes Calender*, he appeared in a text whose title page advertised not the name of the author, but the name of the printer, Hugh Singleton, who only a few months earlier had printed John Stubbs' *The Discoverie of a Gaping Gulf Wherinto England is Like to be Swallowed* (1579).[19] Stubbs notoriously lost his right hand for writing a text that identified the threatening 'gaping gulf' as a potential marriage between Elizabeth and a French Catholic, the Duke of Alençon, a match which could potentially shatter England's status as a Protestant power. At the same time Spenser associated his text with the more fervent Protestant voices of the period, Sidney wrote a lengthy letter to Elizabeth arguing against the same match and, less than a decade later, died near Zutphen commanding English troops sent to support the Dutch Protestant provinces that had revolted against Spanish rule.[20] Sarah Kelen has argued that the Piers figure of *News from the North*, who is clearly a less central figure of reformist conviction than we have previously seen, is a sign that the 'literary role of Piers Plowman as social critic [had] begun to dissipate'.[21] But the network of connections surrounding Spenser, the Sidneys, The *Shepheardes Calender* and *News from the North* seem to me to suggest that, whilst the polemical ploughman found himself in more rarefied company in 1579, the conversation still centred on Protestant reformism. Indeed, when we move forward to the last decade of the sixteenth century, it is religious controversy – albeit of a rather distinctive new form – which still haunts Piers' steps. Moreover, the general sense of 'dissipation' which Kelen invokes – seconded by a number of scholars – needs, I think, to be looked at again.

The 1590s are frequently, and not mistakenly, seen to be a distinctively new era in the writing of satire. Native influences are seen to wane in influence as neoclassical models of satire become more dominant, particularly in the work

---

in an artistic and aristocratic community which could enhance his reputation. See Katherine Duncan-Jones, *Sir Philip Sidney*, pp. 191–2. However, at the very least, Spenser dedicated the *Shepheardes Calender* to Sidney, and Sidney complimented the text, barring its archaic language, in his *Defence of Poetry*.

[19]   For Singleton as printer of both texts, and the notoriety of Stubbs as a 'strident Puritan', see Louis Montrose, '"The perfect paterne of a poete": The Poetics of Courtship in *The Shepheardes Calender*' in *Edmund Spenser*, ed. A. Hadfield (London, 1996), pp. 30–63, 57; and also Paul E. McLane, *Spenser's Shepheardes Calender: A Study in Elizabethan Allegory* (Notre Dame, IN, 1961), esp. pp. 13–26.

[20]   See Duncan-Jones, *Sir Philip Sidney*, p. 162, 296; McCabe, ed., *Edmund Spenser: The Shorter Poems*, 'introduction', p. xiii.

[21]   Kelen, *Langland's Early Modern Identities*, p. 72.

of writers such as Donne, Marston and Jonson.[22] David Norbrook's excellent chapter on the 'prophetic' tradition of polemical poetry in *Poetry and Politics in the English Renaissance* (1984) observes that an older tradition of writing was preserved particularly amongst Elizabethan Puritans, even whilst 'The old "ploughman" tradition became overshadowed in the Elizabethan period by more courtly poetic modes'.[23] John N. King in his account of Spenser's poetry describes similarly both the power of the ploughman figure and, simultaneously, its waning influence: the feeling that 'the "honest" peasant is just about to disappear totally from popular religious propaganda'.[24] Most recently, Sarah Kelen has written that: 'when literary theory began to emphasise continental rather than native models, this long familiar figure [Piers] began to fade from the literary record'.[25] Even in the most recent account of Langlandian influences and afterlives, the picture is familiar: overshadowed, fading, and finally disappearing all together. While the broader mechanics of literary history that influence these narratives may not need to be completely overhauled, this pervasive sense of diminishing force needs, I think, to be revised a little.

As I have argued over the course of the last chapter, the ploughman figure underwent a particularly powerful process of appropriation in the period 1530–1550, in which its possible connotations narrowed into those of a polemical Protestant spokesman: Piers became an icon of early Reformation writing in England. But, strikingly, Piers reappeared in a number of texts in the years 1588–1594, and reappeared in remarkably diverse and contentious ways. These texts number two quite different polemical works which were closely associated with the cause of Presbyterian Church government, a prose satire by Thomas Nashe, and a play in the repertory of Lord Strange's Men: the playing company which we most readily associate with the first performances of plays by Kyd, Marlowe and Shakespeare. In the centre of this network of texts, connecting them all, lies the Marprelate controversy, a controversy that – just as much as neoclassicism – has been seen to play a central, catalytic role in the development of distinctly new forms of writing, both in terms of satire, and the theatre of the London stage.[26] What is perhaps most arresting about these uses of Piers Plowman is their diversity. At the beginning of the 1590s, at a time when Piers is so often seen to

---

[22] This is the narrative, for example, of John Peter's *Complaint and Satire in Early English Literature* (Oxford, 1956), esp. pp. 132–56. More recent scholars generally concur. See, for example, King, *Spenser's Poetry and the Reformation Tradition*, pp. 27–8.

[23] Norbrook, *Poetry and Politics in the English Renaissance*, p. 47.

[24] King, *Spenser's Poetry and the Reformation Tradition*, pp. 27–8.

[25] Kelen, *Langland's Early Modern Identities*, p. 74.

[26] On the pervasive influence of Martinist and Anti-Martinist writing, see Joseph L. Black, ed., *The Martin Marprelate Tracts: A Modernized and Annotated Edition* (Cambridge, 2008), pp. lxxiv–lxxv. Black notes influences in both broad generic terms (Elizabethan prose and theatre) and on individual writers such as Nashe, Greene, Middleton, Dekker and Shakespeare.

be fading from view, we can in fact see a fluidity, or more accurately a kind of fractious tension, returning to the figure of the ploughman and his place in the writing of religious controversy. Piers becomes again a figure that can be wrested one way and another into apparently opposing camps, providing a broader and more lively impression of how 'Playn Piers' could be appropriated in the later Elizabethan period than we might expect.

'Piers Marprelate'

> Contention is a coale, the more it is blowne by dysputation, the more it kindleth: I must spit in theyr faces to put it out.[27]

The Marprelate controversy is distinguished for a number of reasons, the most obvious being that it is perhaps the only time in literary and cultural history when the words 'puritanism' and 'fun' can be used in the same sentence. Between October 1588 and September 1589, a sequence of seven texts were produced on a secret and much sought-after printing press which travelled the country in order to evade censorship, and worse, by the authorities of both Church and state. These texts introduced a scandalous, and often very funny, manner to the writing of religious controversy, resulting in the remarkable sentence above, written by, possibly, Thomas Nashe: one of a number of writers (probably Lyly, Greene and Munday as well) to weigh into the controversy at the behest of an Elizabethan Church of England which could not, ultimately, shut them up again when the press was found.[28] Martin's writing, and the anti-Martinist writing that answered it, consisted not of carefully worded and researched arguments about the biblical and historical precedents for different forms of Church government – such texts had been produced throughout the 1580s when Presbyterianism had reached an abortive apex in the form of lobbying parliament about the nature and fate of the episcopacy – but was instead full of *ad hominem* attacks, scandalous gossip, conversational style and lucid comic diatribes about 'bouncing priests' and 'apish'

---

[27]   *The First Parte of Pasquils Apologie* (1590) in *The Works of Thomas Nashe*, ed. Ronald B McKerrow, 5 vols (Oxford, 1958), I. 110. McKerrow in fact doubted the attribution of the text, and other anti-Martinist texts, to Nashe. The identity of the writer, like that of 'Martin Marprelate' himself, and the author(s) of *A Knack to Know a Knave* are likely to remain un-provable. That Nashe appears as a kind of shadowy presence around all these texts is, however, interesting in itself. I turn to Nashe later in the chapter.

[28]   The brief account of the controversy given here is deeply indebted to Joseph L. Black's excellent recent edition of the tracts, and to that of McKerrow in *The Works of Thomas Nashe*, V. 34–65. All references to the Marprelate tracts are to Black's edition, by text and page number. It is strikingly ironic that Nashe, a writer siding with the established church in the controversy – if not perhaps in its actual employ – was later to find his works banned by Whitgift's proclamation in 1599.

Puritans.[29] It is therefore somewhat striking to find that amongst these texts we find a rather familiar one that begins 'I, Piers Plowman'.

In Chapter 3 I discussed a text named *I Plain Piers* (1550), which appeared in the mid-century as one of a number of polemical, antiquarian attempts to shape the figure Piers Ploughman into a prophetic spokesman of radical religious and economic reform. This text reappeared *c.* 1588–1589, but now as one of Martin's brethren, and, in fact, his 'Gransier' (see Figure 4.1).[30] There is something curiously appropriate about Piers becoming the 'Gransier of Martin mareprelitte', an antiquarian antecedent of Martin distinguished by his claims to be from a previous age ('O Read me for I am of great antiquitie'). Just as Langland's Piers Plowman, and in fact *Piers Plowman*, had been appropriated earlier in the sixteenth century to bolster the voice of a burgeoning Henrician and vociferous Edwardian reformism, now that mid-century figure of the polemical ploughman was appropriated in turn as a way to shape the identity of a more specific form of Protestantism – that of Presbyterianism (or 'Puritanism', if we can identify it as such) in the 1590s. Appropriations begin to form consecutive layers amongst themselves as Piers shifts now to a more complex religious context in which he must be more specifically the icon not of all Protestants but some forms of Protestantism amongst others.

It is also strikingly appropriate that Piers' entrance into the Marprelate controversy was something of a rushed job – being as it is a partial, unfinished reprint of an earlier text.[31] The sense of urgency and interruption that accompany such an unfinished text have led at least one scholar to suggest that the reprint was 'apparently suppressed' in the manner we imagine a Marprelate tract might be.[32] That the text is a reprint – and indeed it retains everything, including the rather idiosyncratic approach to marking prose and verse, that the 1550 edition had – makes the differences and additions more striking, for they give the impression that the text was surely from a Martinist press and perhaps was part of the earliest stages of the enterprise. As Joseph Black suggests, 'The prospective reprint might have

---

[29] On the growth of Elizabethan Puritanism see Patrick Collinson, *The Elizabethan Puritan Movement* (London, 1967). On the more specific background of Presbyterian thought on church government and its influence on the Marprelate tracts, see Black, *The Martin Marprelate Tracts*, pp. xviii–xxiv.

[30] *O Read me for I am of great Antiquitie* (?London, ?1589).

[31] In fact, the text comprises barely 20 per cent of the original 1550 print. Black notes that signatures B and C are corrected proofs, and that 'the failure to correct signature D suggests that printing was interrupted'. See Black, *The Martin Marprelate Tracts*, p. xcvii, note 44 and Percy Simpson, *Proof-Reading in the Sixteenth, Seventeenth and Eighteenth Centuries* (Oxford, 1935, repr. 1970), pp. 69–71.

[32] Joad Raymond, *Pamphlets and Pamphleteering in Early Modern Britain* (Cambridge, 2003), p. 31. The text is also discussed briefly in Kelen, *Langland's Early Modern Identities*, pp. 65–6.

been meant to play a role in the Marprelate project ... the title page and new preface both borrow (or anticipate?) words and phrases employed in Martin's *Epistle*'.[33]

What is conspicuously added to the title page is the heading emphasizing the antiquity of the text, but also the name – and more importantly the *manner* – of Martin Marprelate. The underlying point of the reprint – the polemical value of antiquity – is repeated in the title page's denial of having a 'greene' head, but rather a 'white or gray' one, but the point here descends into colloquial nonsense ('*bum fay*') and doggerel rhyme. The sudden turn of religious controversy into levity and nonsense is so characteristic of the Marprelate tracts as to be unmistakable. *The Epistle*, the first Marprelate tract, was to begin with the proclamation and explanation of its own nonsense by blaming its target – John Bridge's *A Defence of the Government Established in the Church of Englande for Ecclesiasticall Matters* (1587) – and invoking a playful, ironic and insulting idea of '*decorum personae*': 'Because I could not deal with his book commendably according to order, unless I should be sometimes tediously dunstical and absurd' (*Epistle*, p. 7). The absurdity frequently ends in derisive comedy. Martin describes Bridge's work as 'very briefly comprehended in a portable book, if your horse be not too weak' (*Epitome*, p. 56). After quoting a particularly long sentence from Bridge's text, Martin exclaims 'I was never so afraid in my life, that I should not come to an end till I had been windless. Do you not see how I pant?' (*Epitome*, p. 66). Frequently it ends in bursts of laughter: 'py hy hy hy. I cannot but laugh, py hy hy hy' (*Hay any Work for Cooper*, p. 103). Essentially, Martin's writing feels scandalously like the spoken word, and its target is as much the leaden, voluminous style of contemporary controversy as it is the episcopacy itself. As the title of *Hay any Work for Cooper* suggests (playing on the London street cry of coopers – barrel-makers – and Thomas Cooper, another of Martin's ecclesiastical opponents), Martin made the subject of religious controversy speak in the random and colloquial sounds of the street. As Peter Lake has written, what Martin introduced into the 'rather staidly academic' discourse of religious controversy was 'an unwonted note of levity ... the literary techniques and tone of the satirical and scurrilous pamphlet and the lewd interlude'.[34] It was precisely this note of levity that is added to 'Plain Piers' to make him simultaneously both instantly relevant and, one might say, somewhat more – and less – 'plain' than he was wont to be.

Just as the Marprelate tracts played with the paratextual commonplaces of printed title pages – the identification of the geographical location of the printer – so does this renewed version of *I Plain Piers*. *The Epistle* has advertised its origins in the following terms: 'Printed oversea, In Europe, within two furlongs of a Bouncing Priest' (*Epistle*, p. 5). The tracts consistently returned to the same joke: 'Printed on the other hand of some of the priests' (*Epitome*, p. 51); 'Printed in Europe, not far from some of the Bouncing Priests' (*Hay any Work for Cooper*,

---

[33]   Black, *The Martin Marprelate Tracts*, p. xxx.

[34]   Peter Lake with Michael Questier, *The Antichrist's Lewd Hat: Protestants, Papists and Players in Post-Reformation England* (New Haven, 2002), p. 505.

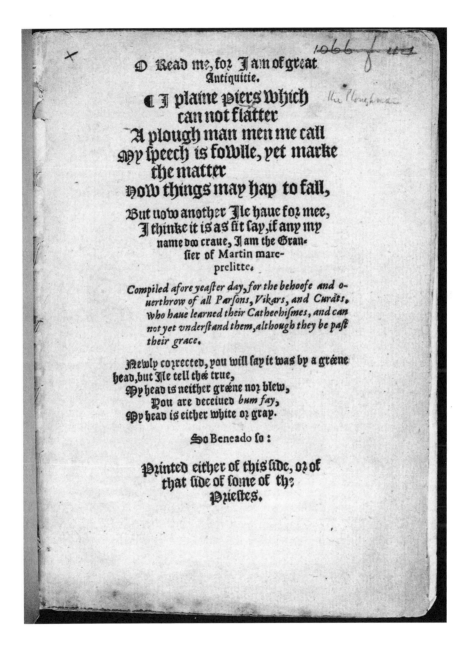

O Read me, for I am of great
Antiquitie.

¶ I plaine Piers which
can not flatter
A plough man men me call
My speech is fowlle, yet marke
the matter
How things may hap to fall,

But now another Ile haue for mee,
I thinke it is as fit say, if any my
name doo craue, I am the Gran-
fier of Martin mare-
prelitte.

Compiled afore yeaster day, for the behoofe and o-
uerthrow of all Parfons, Vikars, and Curàts,
who haue learned their Cathechifmes, and can
not yet vnderftand them, although they be paft
their grace.

Newly corrected, you will fay it was by a gréene
head, but Ile tell thée true,
My head is neither gréene nor blew,
You are deceiued bum fay,
My head is either white or gray.

So Beneado fo :

Printed either of this fide, or of
that fide of fome of the
Prieftes.

Figure 4.1   Title page of *O Read me ... the Gransier of Martin Mareprelitte*
(?1588). © The British Library Board.

p. 99). The reprint of *I Plain Piers* is identified as being 'Compiled afore yeaster day' and 'Printed either of this side, or of that side of some of the priests'.

The addition of an ironic dedicatory epistle added to the impression, both cementing the relationship between Piers and Martin and shifting the text – along with its polemical anticlericalism – into the mode of Martinist irony. The dedicatory epistle is addressed 'To the puissant paltrypolitanes, bouncing Lord Bishops, Popish Parsons, fickers, and Currats, with all that romish rable, Piers, Grandsier of Martin Marprelate, wisheth you better then I thinke you wishe your selues' (sig. A2r). The writer of the dedication recommends the text directly to the clergy 'bicause olde PIERS goeth soundly to worke, & vseth no flatterie, and hee sayth nothing but he bringeth good proofes for it' (sig. A2r). The vocal support for 'olde PIERS' – complete with full capitalization for the name – is accompanied by two stylistic habits characteristic of Martin's other tracts: a mischievously direct form of address and an equally impish threat of proliferation. The epistle is directed towards the clergy in mock-respectful terms: 'Ryght riuiued sirs, may it please your worships fulnesse to accept and reade ouer this worthy worke' (sig. A2r). The direct address turns into an ironic request for patronage: 'taking you for my Patrons … for I knowe that you can keepe mee harmelesse if you please' (sig. A2r) and ending with the comic signature: 'hoping of your accustomed clemencie and approoued protectorshippe of this booke, I cease to trouble you. Surpliced Sirs farewell, I can tell, my name full well' (sig. A2v). The deliberate flirtation with identifying an author only to simultaneously deny the identification is almost, in itself, a *nom de plume* for Martin, whose texts have been subjected more than any other to what Patrick Collinson has called 'the academic parlour game of hunt the disguised author'.[35] But the mock-polite stance came also with a threat: the text was only the product of the writer's 'first labours, which I pray you accept, but in time when I shall bee more able, you shall then here oftner from mee' (sig. A2v). Black's question-marked query over the place of *I Plain Piers* in the Marprelate sequence '(or anticipate?)' seems worth recalling. If – and it does have to be an 'if' – we are to take the promise of more anticlerical material in the phrase 'you shall here oftner from mee' as referring to the Marprelate tracts themselves, we can view *I Plain Piers* as not just a symbolic 'Gransier' of Martin, but literally as the progenitor; the originary text of Martinism. Regardless, the direct threat was to become one of Martin's motifs, for example in *The Epistle*: 'I'll kindle such a fire in the holes of these foxes, as shall never be quenched as long as there is a lord bishop in England' (*Epistle*, p. 19). The 'coale' of 'contention', as *Pasquill's Apology* had it, was something promised in deliberately fiery terms from the start

---

[35]   Patrick Collinson, 'Ecclesiastical Vitriol: Religious Satire in the 1590s and the Invention of Puritanism' in *The Reign of Elizabeth I: Court and Culture in the Last Decade*, ed. John Guy (Cambridge, 1995), pp. 150–70, 157. On the tracts' uses of anonymity see also Marcy L. North, *The Anonymous Renaissance: Cultures of Discretion in Tudor-Stuart England* (Chicago, 2003), pp. 139–58.

of the controversy in *The Epistle*, but the kindling for that threat was there too in the dedicatory epistle of a distinctly Martinist Piers.

There are also, of course, wider connections to be drawn between 'Playn Piers' and Martin Marprelate. Marcy L. North has argued that 'like the satirical Piers Plowman before him, Martin ... replaced the historical author as the figure most responsible for the text'.[36] Black lists Tyndale, Bale, Crowley and Fish as possible influences on Martinist style.[37] Annabel Patterson sees an echo of Wycliffite usages of coded terms like 'knowen men' in Martinist prose.[38] Moreover, Martin's 'naming and shaming' of Episcopal immorality frequently intersected with a persecutory narrative of Puritan identity which exactly echoed that of early- and mid-Tudor Protestantism. Just as the original writer of *I Plain Piers* lamented that 'the poore Prynter also whiche laboreth but for his lyuynge, is cast into prison and loseth all he hath' (sig. C2r), Martin focuses on the poor, persecuted state of his own printer:

> Robert Waldegrave dares not show his face for the bloodthirsty desire you have for his life, only for printing of books which toucheth the bishops' mitres. You know that Waldegrave's printing press and letters were taken away: his press being timber, was sawn and hewed to pieces, the iron work battered and made unserviceable, his letters melted ... and he himself utterly deprived for ever printing again, having a wife and six small children. (*Epistle*, p. 23)[39]

Here the images of persecutory violence are, in fact, centred on the printing press itself, as much as the person of the printer. The 'sawing', 'hewing' and 'melting' of the press becomes a curious form of torture, substituting the wood and metal of the press for the limbs of one of Foxe's Marian heroes. Cyndia Susan Clegg has argued that the degree of censorship and opposition between Puritan printers and the establishment – both in the form of the government and the Stationers' Company – has been overstated, 'particularly by Martin Marprelate'.[40] But it is precisely the rhetorical power – rather than the historical veracity – of such representations of persecution and censorship which is most important for Martin. The Martinists themselves become part of the history of persecuted reformers from Wycliffe, through Tyndale, to the Marian martyrs – a new chapter to the Foxean narrative of religious history. Similarly, Martin consistently plays on the rhetorical expectations brought about by the tradition of synthesizing reformist polemic with idealized 'simplicity'. Just as Piers is 'playn', Martin describes himself as 'such a simple ingram man' (*Epistle*, p. 18), playing on the dialectic version of 'ignorant'

---

[36] North, *The Anonymous Renaissance*, p. 152.

[37] Black, *The Martin Marprelate Tracts*, p. xxx.

[38] Annabel Patterson, *Reading between the Lines* (London, 1992), pp. 71–2.

[39] Waldegrave himself printed the first four Marprelate texts. See Black, *The Martin Marprelate Tracts*, pp. xlix–l.

[40] Clegg, *Press Censorship in Elizabethan England* (Cambridge, 1997), pp. 170–97, 175.

repeatedly, but turning it into a characteristically anti-Episcopalian joke: 'You must then bear with my ingramness. I am plain, I must needs call a spade a spade, a pope a pope' (*Epitome*, p. 53).[41] The play, the joke, is precisely what makes Martin Marprelate rather different to 'Plain Piers' as he had appeared in 1550, but the appropriative use of Piers as the 'Gransier' of Martin remains arresting. Martin's infamous threat to 'place a Martin in every diocese … I will place a Martin in every parish … every one of them able to mar a prelate' (*Epistle*, p. 35) brings with it the assertion that one of those 'Martins' would be, and indeed had been, a rather wizened-looking man with grey hair named 'olde PIERS', who clearly had some polemical energy left in his legs.

At the latter chronological edge of the Marprelate controversy, when various people associated with the project were either in exile, in prison, or dead; and the 'anti-Martinists' – Nashe amongst them – seem to have 'won' the argument, another text appeared which further strengthened the relationship between Piers, the earlier reformation tradition that had created the 'polemical ploughman' figure, and Martinism. This text was, most likely, penned by the man whom many scholars now consider to be Martin (or at least a substantial part of him): Job Throkmorton.[42] *A Petition directed to her most excellent Maiestie* (Middleburg, 1592) is well known as the text which, through the printed reactions of Matthew Sutcliffe, seems to provide some of the firmer ground in the quagmire of authorship debates about the Marprelate controversy.[43] But it is also a text in which Piers, and Protestant medievalism more generally, comes to the fore. What is striking about Throkmorton's *Petition* though, is not so much that it contains citations of

---

[41]   The stance of simplicity is, like everything else in Martin's texts, subject to irony. As Ritchie Kendall puts it: 'Exaggerated postures of rustic simple-mindedness warn the reader that Martin's rude mask is only partly genuine', Kendall, *The Drama of Dissent*, p. 185. For a less nuanced description of Martin's simplicity, see Kelen, *Langland's Early Modern Identities*, p. 66: 'Martin follows his predecessor, Piers Plowman (as he appears in all of the plowman texts), who constructs his ethos through the same combination of uneducated speech, nonmetropolitan location, and low social status'.

[42]   Throkmorton is the current front runner in the authorship race of Martinism, largely because of the work of Leland H. Carlson in *Martin Marprelate, Gentleman: Master Job Throkmorton Laid Open in his Colors* (San Marino, 1981). Previously, the finger had been pointed repeatedly at John Penry, the Welsh Presbyterian executed in 1593, who was still, clearly, a major presence in the project. See Black, *The Martin Marprelate Tracts*, pp. xxxvii–xxxviii. Black is convinced that Throkmorton was 'almost certainly' Martin (p. xxxv) and Patrick Collinson, while noting dryly that 'I doubt whether we have heard the last of this conundrum', suggests that Carlson's work may have brought 'this fascinating but in itself rather sterile exercise to a satisfactory conclusion'; Collinson, 'Ecclesiastical Vitriol', p. 157. Peter Lake also describes Throkmorton as 'the most plausible candidate'; see *The Antichrist's Lewd Hat*, p. 509, note 55.

[43]   See Black, *The Martin Marprelate Tracts*, p. xliv. On Throkmorton's authorship of *A Petition directed to her most excellent Maiestie*, see also Carlson, *Martin Marprelate, Gentleman*, pp. 117–20.

Piers Plowman and *The Plowman's Tale*; we have seen this kind of appropriation already in the *I Plain Piers* reprint; but that this antiquarianism is simultaneously Martinist yet keeps all the stylistic and comic pyrotechnics of Martinism at arms length. Just as we have seen Piers appearing as a kind of originary ancestor of Martin – 'Piers Marprelate' as I term him in the title of this chapter – we here see another productive twist on the appropriation of antiquity in the Marprelate controversy. Piers is used here, in line with the wider purposes of the text, as a figure definitely not printed anywhere near any bouncing priests, but a figure of reformist respectability, an antique voice not of slander but of rational deliberation that could be turned to in order to escape what had become the stigmatized mania of Martinism.

For Martin's voice was silent by 1592, but the voice had become increasingly problematic well before then. Francis Bacon was to comment simply that 'it is more than time that there was an end and surseance made of this immodest and deformed manner of writing'.[44] Richard Harvey's criticism of Martin as 'a ridiculous mad fellowe, that handleth so serious matters and persons so ridiculously' in *The Lamb of God* registered the same distaste, even as it sparked Nashe's temper.[45] Even while the controversy was in full flow, Martin had self-consciously described the problem of not only persecution, but opposition from his own party: 'I know I am disliked of many which are your enemies, that is, of many which you call puritans … There be many that greatly dislike of my doings' (*Hay any Work for Cooper*, pp. 119, 115). The 'coale' of 'contention' which caused writers to spit in each others' faces, the fire that Martin promised to kindle 'in the holes of these foxs' had run out of fuel as a viable tool of Puritan persuasion, even while it caught like wildfire in the theatre and satirical writing of Elizabethan London. Necessarily, Martin stepped away from the entertaining drive to 'prove them popes once more for recreation's sake' (*Epistle*, p. 12).

Throkmorton's purpose in the *Petition* is instead to try a different tack, one characterized by an ostentatious even-handedness – essentially the opposite of the swaggering comic self-confidence of Martin Marprelate. He begins:

> Crauing vppon my knees pardon for my boldness, I beseech your most excellent Maiestie, to heare me a little. All your Highnes subiects that loue the religion, honour your Maiestie, and desire the good of the Realme, doe hartily bewayle the bitter contention about the questions of reforming the Church … I doe not nowe write eyther to pull downe Bishoprickes, or erect presbyteries. With whom

---

[44]   Bacon, *An Advertisement Touching the Controversies of the Church of England* (*c.* 1589–1590), cited in Black, *The Martin Marprelate Tracts*, p. lxii. The text remained in manuscript until its publication, much later, in 1641. On the currency of the work in manuscript in the 1590s, see Black, *The Martin Marprelate Tracts*, p. cvii, note 212.

[45]   McKerrow, ed., *The Works of Thomas Nashe*, V. 177. Harvey saw Nashe as 'in civill learning, as Martin doth in religion' (V. 180). This was the origin of the very lengthy Harvey–Nashe quarrel; see McKerrow, ed., *The Works of Thomas Nashe*, V. 65–110.

the trueth is, I will not determine. For I knowe not … Writing of books in such manner as is nowe vsed, is endless: wearinesse to the fleshe: matter of further contention, by reason of impertinent and personall discourses.[46]

The brazen, combative irony of the dedicatory epistle to *I Plain Piers* could not be further away. Instead we have a respectably deferent writer – though Sutcliffe wouldn't see it as such – who takes on the voice of a lamenting public who have tired of the seemingly interminable struggle over Church government. The bald modesty topos ('I knowe not') is followed by a deliberate self-distancing from the Marprelate tracts – surely what is aimed at in the mention of 'impertinent and personall discourses', a description of the controversy's *ad hominem* style which could have come from Bacon's pen.

But the open-handed gesture of fairness, and the disclaimer that the writer harbours no particular Puritan bias is, while radically different to the various stances of Martin Marprelate, ultimately part of a new representational mode for old Presbyterian arguments – and this is, perhaps, the point of it. Throkmorton's ostentatious objectivity is a rhetorical and political point in itself, even while the text works to destabilize the sense of objectivity. Against the standard (and long-lived) accusation that ecclesiastical reformism must equate to sedition – a point stretching back to the earliest points of the English Reformation and before – Throkmorton asserts that 'the Seekers of Reformation … only seeke to haue (as they thinke) the corruption of the time redressed, as the Prophets & the holy men of God haue done heretofore, without intending anie dishonour to good Princes, such as hir Maiestie is' (pp. 18–19). The clear support, and indeed the passage becomes a sequence of biblical precedents for these modern-day 'Prophets', shows the writer to be a Presbyterian apologist. At the same time, the parentheses – '(as they thinke)' – does the rhetorical work of distancing the writer from what he clearly defends. In the history of sophisticated sixteenth-century parenthetical moments this does not quite challenge Thomas More's outrageously ambivalent '(in the popular view)' towards the end of *Utopia*, but it is nonetheless pointed and not to be taken as a facile, 'tokenistic' gesture towards objectivity. Throkmorton's rhetorical tightrope-walking may seem to allow him to have his controversial cake and eat it too, but more importantly it allows the Puritan cause a particular kind of voice – one deeply entwined in the respectable reformism of the Elizabethan Church's past, and one absolutely differentiated from the extemporary spoken diatribes of the arch-arsonist Martin Marprelate.

This placatory, 'respectable', Puritanism constantly attempts to build bridges, rather than burn them. Arguing that 'more curtesie should bee shewed to Seekers of Reformation', Throkmorton's proof is that:

---

[46]   *A Petition directed to her most excellent Maiestie* (Middleburg, 1592), sig. A2r. The text is paginated from p. 4 onwards. I follow the pagination when it begins, rather than the signatures.

> Verely all the Protestants in the world would wonder to heare that among
> Protestantes vnder a Protestant Prince and gouuernement, any protestant should
> haue his bloud shed for maintaining a doctrine of the Protestants, imbraced by
> Christian Churches, and confederate Princes round about. (p. 32)

Five repetitions of the word 'Protestant' in one sentence might be seen as overkill,
but it has a striking rhetorical effect. Throkmorton's prose here works as an inverted
form of a consistently useful topos in the writing of religious controversy. The chaos
of linguistic diversity is persistently returned to by writers attacking heterodoxy,
and defending it: Skelton throws 'Jovenyans heresy', 'Wycliffes flesshe flyes' and
'Luthers lute' into the same pot; Bale manages a full 20 lines of jostling Catholic
orders in *King Johan*.[47] Thomas Nashe, in a moment I return to below, gleefully
conflates 'Puritans' with 'anabaptists' and 'villians'. Throkmorton's sentence
essentially works in a diametrically opposite way, reducing all parties in 1590s
England, and Europe, to the homogeneity of one word. The plurality of 'Churches'
is not rendered as divisive, but all-encompassing: England is 'imbraced' in
Protestant fraternity.

This rhetorical effort to shore up the divides between Protestant and Puritan,
between established Church and 'Seekers of Reformation', does not – of course
– efface the need to promulgate a particular agenda. Throkmorton's text is still
polemical, it still demonstrates the appropriative antiquarianism that we have seen
in action throughout the sixteenth century. But the *Petition* is, in a different way to
the *I Plain Piers* reprint, preoccupied with ideas of precedent. The past becomes
a resource to be tapped in arguing for the licit, respectable and acceptable nature
of Presbyterian anti-Episcopalian writing. It is here that *Piers Plowman* appears,
along with Chaucer, Latimer, Cranmer, and a whole tradition of established and
reputable anticlerical figures. Following something that looks a great deal like
Crowley's preface to *Piers Plowman*: a list of reformers including Wycliffe,
Langland and Chaucer, Throkmorton shows a detailed and scholarly knowledge
of Langland's text:

> *Piers Plowman* likewise wrote against the state of Bishops, and prophecied their
> fall in these words:
>
> *If Knighthood and Kindwite and Comone by conscience*
> *Together loue Lelly, leueth it well ye Bishopes*
> *The Lordship of Landes for euer shall ye lese,*
> *And liue as Leuitici as our Lord ye teacheth*
> *Deut. 8. Numb. 5.* per primitias & decimas, &c. (p. 34)

---

47 Skelton, 'A Replycacion Agaynst Certayne Yong Scolers Abjured of Late', ll. 163,
166, 167, in *John Skelton: The Complete English Poems*; John Bale, *King Johan* in *The
Complete Plays of John Bale*, I. 440–60.

Scholarly marginal annotations surround the passage: 'Piers Plowman'; 'A prophecy of the fall of Bh.', and, perhaps most strikingly, 'Passus 15'. Langland's text still has that prophetic power that Puttenham identified and Crowley so anxiously tries to negotiate, but Throkmorton's knowledge of it is arrestingly detailed and accurate. The passage is indeed 'Passus 15', lines 552–5a. Whichever copy of *Piers Plowman* Throkmorton was reading (and he had a choice of three Crowley editions, the 1561 Rogers edition, plus a number of manuscripts), he was clearly able both to identify the passage accurately, and to modernize the spelling, consistently altering 'y' for 'i' and perhaps 'Knighthode' (the spelling in all the printed editions) to 'Knighthood'. This is also a passage which Crowley annotated with the comment 'An admonicion to the cleargy' (sig. Y1v), but the appropriation here is more specific, picking up on B.15.553's 'Bishopes' to make Langland not just anticlerical but anti-Episcopalian.

Throkmorton continues his list of 'licit anticlericalism' with a quotation from 'Chaucer's' *Plowman's Tale* (lines 693–708) and the argument that:

> Thus wrote this famous Poet against the English Bishops, and yet was neuer accounted diffamer of the Kinge, though the Bb. In his time did holde their Lordships of the Kinge as they doe nowe in England. Sir *Geffrey Chaucers* his works were in K. Henry the eight his days authorized to bee printed by d Act of Parliament, to which that glorious king would neuer haue condescended, if hee had thought that the diffamation of the Bishops had bin a diffamation of him selfe. (p. 34)

Throkmorton's arguments here, his use of Langland and Chaucer to legitimize the writing of anti-Episcopalian satire, was something Matthew Sutcliffe would react to with indignation, noting that the Petition's writer had:

> drawne out certain rimes out of Pierce Plowman, & Chaucer, men farre excelling him in all modestie and humanitie. For albeit they rimed against wicked bishops, yet doc they speake more ciuilly of them, then he doth of godly and learned men, whome with rime dogrell, and dogged railing, and many slaunderous reports, and that in the presence of a prince, he goeth about malitiously to disgrace.[48]

Sutcliffe's moral indignation is followed by a more detailed argument which attempts to counter Throkmorton's defence of anti-Episcopalian writing on grounds of legal precedent:

> That these books pase with this approbation, Seene and allowed, it followeth not, that all things therein conteined are allowed: but that they are allowed to be printed, as hauing nothing in the opinion of him that allowed them contrarie to

---

[48]   Matthew Sutcliffe, *An Answere to a Certaine Libel* (London, 1592), p. 69. The prefaces have only signatures, but the main text has pagination which I have followed here.

state. And rather, because we should reape some profite by that which is good;
then loose the good for the bad: or allow that is euil because it is ioyned with
that which is good. (p. 69).

The argument here is over the legality and acceptability of certain kinds of writing.
Throkmorton's *Petition* works to appropriate both the respectable, iconic nature
of 'Pierce Plowman, & Chaucer', something Sutcliffe seems to readily agree with,
but to use them as historical proof for the licit nature of opposition to Anglican
Church government. Sutcliffe's more nuanced reaction – that licit writing can
contain illicit matter – attempts to disperse the rhetorical force of Throkmorton's
appropriative use of the reformist literary tradition.

It is striking too that Throkmorton utilizes both the texts themselves, but also
their place in a reformist tradition which looks very similar to the one I have
attempted to sketch in this book. Citing Langland and Chaucer leads naturally to
citing 'the renowmed professor of the Gospell Maister Tindall' (p. 69) and from
there to citing Hugh Latimer: 'Thus Puritan-like wrote Father Latimer, the famous
martyr, yet hee was neuer esteemed a trouble of the state, a Mar-prince, and a
diffamer of the Kinge, though in deede he was a *Mar-bishop and Mar-prelate*'
(pp. 37–8).[49] The *Petition*'s argument is clear enough: Piers, Chaucer, Tyndale,
Latimer – all Protestants, all '*Mar-prelate*'s, but none of them 'Mar-Princes'. This,
argues Throkmorton, is the respectable face of Puritanism.

In this way, Piers again appears as a strong link in an appropriative chain, but
the chain here is – in line with Throkmorton's purpose – simultaneously both the
ancient links of English Protestantism and the more specific ones of Puritanism.
Piers is variously 'Gransier', 'Father', elder statesman, of Presbyterian reform in
the 1590s. The reformist antiquarianism, its appropriative methods and rhetorical
power, are all familiar; but here we find the phenomenon re-formed once again.
Piers is now part of a complex polemical strategy in which the invocation of
reformist community goes hand-in-hand with a straight-faced alternative to
Martinism and a defence of a specific Presbyterian agenda. Matthew Sutcliffe
would argue that 'nothing is more absurd, then to handle matters of controuersie by
way of supplication. Seeing he disputeth, he should rather haue come in schools,
then in court; and before lawyers, then courtiers' (sig. B3r), but in writing his
Petition, Throkmorton was self-consciously writing in precisely the 'supplication'
genre which has been associated with reformism since Fish's *Supplication for the*

---

[49]   It is striking also that Throkmorton foregrounds Latimer as 'the famous martyr' rather
than the man who held the bishopric of Worcester until 1539 (when his opposition to the Act of
Six Articles led to his arrest). Throkmorton's 'Father Latimer' is an appropriately Presbyterian
figure. This appropriative history was also a part of some of the Marprelate material 'proper',
see for example *Theses Martinianae*, pp. 152–3, in which Tyndale, Frith, Barnes and Foxe are
used in a similar manner. What is different about the *Petition*, as I have been arguing, is its
self-conscious distancing of itself from the manner of the Marprelate tracts.

Beggars (1529), and using the kind of reformist literary history that consistently found ways to make Piers Plowman and his associates relevant and vital.

From 'Piers Marprelate' to *Pierce Penniless*

But Martin was not the only writer to benefit from appropriating the 'plain Piers' image. The prose of one writer, perhaps the best known of Elizabethan prose satirists, and also now perhaps the highest-profile – if most shadowy – anti-Martinist writer, was marked indelibly with the stamp of both Martin and Piers. The Marprelate controversy has been described, in fact, as 'an enterprise which deeply influenced his whole literary career'.[50] Thomas Nashe has been rightly described as 'the greatest of the Elizabethan pamphleteers … the perfect literary showman'.[51] His reputation was formed by *Pierce Penniless his Supplication to the Devil* (1592), a text which depended on the form of the ploughman invective to create its 'flamboyantly structureless' shape, and the polemical moralism of its predecessors to produce its anarchic comedy.[52] The text was by far Nashe's most popular work, going through three editions in 1592, another the following year, and a fifth edition in 1595. Over a decade later, writers like Middleton and Dekker were still trying to wring some sales out of an association with Nashe's text.[53] The notoriety of the work was such that 'Pierce Penniless' became 'Nashe's nickname … his public image'.[54] *Pierce Penniless* is both a parody of, and a testament to, the success of the radical pastoral tradition, even as its ostentatious performative energy was so clearly formed by Nashe's hostile contact with Martin Marprelate.[55]

The text's title prompts the reader to associate Nashe's 'Pierce Penniless' with the 'Piers Plowman/Plain Piers' persona which had become synonymous

---

[50]   Charles Nichol, *A Cup of News: The Life of Thomas Nashe* (London, 1984), p. 62. On Nashe's likely part in the Marprelate controversy, see pp. 62–79.

[51]   Lewis, *English Literature*, p. 410.

[52]   Peter Holbrook, *Literature and Degree in Renaissance England: Nashe, Bourgeois Tragedy and Shakespeare* (Newark, 1994), p. 58.

[53]   Nichol, *A Cup of News*, p. 99. The texts in question are Middleton's *Blacke Booke* (1604) and Dekker's *Newes from Hell* (1606). Almost as soon as Nashe's text was printed he was forced into an early version of a copyright dispute, stating in no uncertain terms that any works professing to be a sequel to *Pierce Penniless* were 'a most ridiculous rogery'; McKerrow, ed., *The Works of Thomas Nashe*, I. 154. All references to Nashe are to McKerrow's edition, by volume and page number.

[54]   Nichol, *A Cup of News*, p. 99. Indeed, Nashe was so well known as 'Pierce' that when Gabriel Harvey replied to Nashe's attacks, it was with a lengthy piece titled *Pierces Supererogation, or A New Prayse of the Old Asse* (1593).

[55]   On the debt of Nashe's prose to Martin's, see also Neil Rhodes, *Elizabethan Grotesque* (London, 1980); Jonathan V. Crewe, *Unredeemed Rhetoric: Thomas Nashe and the Scandal of Authorship* (Baltimore, 1982), pp. 34–5, and Stephen S. Hilliard, *The Singularity of Thomas Nashe* (Lincoln, 1986), pp. 34–48.

with Protestantism. The 'supplication' title similarly suggests a relation to the tradition begun by Simon Fish's *Supplication of the Beggars*.[56] Indeed, Nashe attacks the tradition of supplications later in the text, criticizing the writers of such texts as greedy complainants who 'had rather (with the serving man) put up a supplication to the Parliament House that they might have a yard of pudding for a penny, than desire (with the baker) there might be three ounces of bread sold for a halfpenny' (I. 202). Nashe's puns on 'piscator' and his refusal to 'English the text for the edification of the temporality' suggest that this is a barely veiled and characteristically coarse attack on Fish as instigator of the supplication genre and its Protestant and popularist associations. Nashe's point, made in the language of civic regulation of the victualling trades, a common accompaniment of the ploughman polemic, is that the supplications which are apparently meant to appear as corrective protests are in fact written by an uneducated and greedy laity for their own benefit.

The fact that the supplication is no longer to the monarch, the parliament, or a patron, but to the devil, is a hallmark of the parodic inversion of readers' expectations which made the text so popular. As Lorna Hutson has argued, it is the novelty and shock value of this inversion which is vital to the text, and which is enabled by a knowledge of the preceding reformist tradition. *Pierce Penniless* is a text 'masquerading as the conventional probing of moral abuses for the reform of the commonwealth except, of course, that it claimed this moral and economic authority from a diabolic buffoon'.[57] As Hutson notes, the peculiar publishing history of the text may well have increased its shocking novelty. The text was originally to be published by Abell Jeffes without any prefaces or dedications. The manuscript ended up in the hands of Richard Jones after Jeffes was arrested for printing a number of ballads censored by the High Commission. Jones printed the text with an apologetic epistle to the reader, and a title that attempted to emphasize the traditional moral benefits of reading the text: 'Describing the over-spreading of vice and the suppression of virtue. Pleasantly interlaced with variable delights, and pathetically intermixed with conceited reproofs' (I. 149). Nashe's epistle to the reader at the opening of the second edition, printed by Jeffes on his release, attempted to distance himself from the 'long-tailed title' that misconstrued his work (I. 153). However bizarre the adverb 'pleasantly' sounds when applied to Nashe's work, the effect of Jones' modification could well have been to further encourage the first readers of *Pierce Penniless* to identify the text with the profitable reformist reading of previous 'plain piers' texts.[58]

But the reader of *Pierce Penniless* was in for a shock – unless, perhaps, he had read Martin's own version of 'olde PIERS'. This 'Pierce' was not that of Crowley's imagination, nor that of Spenser's. Instead of the figure of the poor, spiritualized ploughman, Nashe gives us an impoverished scholar as a narrator,

---

56   Fish's text is explored at length in Chapter 2.
57   Hutson, *Thomas Nashe in Context*, p. 174.
58   Hutson, *Thomas Nashe in Context*, pp. 176–80.

one who reacts to ill-fortune with anything but humility or reformist ambitions: 'in a malcontent humour, I accused my fortune, railed on my patrons, bit my pen, rent my papers, and raged in all points like a madman' (I. 157). After scribbling some poetry 'abruptly', 'I tossed my imaginations a thousand ways to see if I could find any means to relieve my estate; but all my thoughts consorted to this conclusion, that the world was uncharitable, and I ordained to be miserable' (I. 158). Nashe's parody is raucously funny. Taking the stern Protestant figure and turning him into an embittered, bad-tempered wit disdainful of just about everything and everybody was a manifesto of a new kind of writing – even whilst it was clearly indebted in many points to the anarchic energy of Marprelate. Whilst the Protestant 'Pierce' was linguistically 'plain', Nashe's persona is the product of a scandalous linguistic virtuosity without any stable moral intentions. The assault on what Nashe refers to critically as 'this moralising age' (I. 154) was to show itself in parodic inversions of conventional form which litter the text: a hearty dedication with all the appearance of a 'serious' dedication to a patron which is redirected to Satan; an epistle to the reader that appears at the end of the work, after the critique of the Seven Deadly Sins has given way to prolonged discourse on demonology. Hutson's parallel between Nashe and the great eighteenth-century anti-novel *Tristram Shandy* is extremely acute.[59] Whilst Puttenham had characterized Langland as a 'malcontent', Nashe's 'malcontent humour' was of a very different type.[60]

But Nashe's parody of the 'plain ploughman' genre was not simply an exercise in typographical experimentation or satiric virtuosity. The inversion of form was matched by a vitriolic attack on the ideological associations of that form. *Pierce Penniless* takes on the ostensible form of a Protestant ploughman text partly in order to launch a withering attack on the underlying cultural associations of reformism. Nashe's reputation as 'the scourge of puritans' had been formed originally in his role in the Marprelate controversy, and it is ostentatiously present here.[61] The characteristic values of 'plainness' and 'simplicity' that imbue Protestant culture are reconfigured by Nashe as the signs of miserly thrift and hypocrisy. When Nashe attacks 'a number of hypocritical hotspurs, that have God always in their mouths, will give nothing for God's sake' (I. 161), Friar Daw's attacks on Jack Upland's 'seeming' religion spring back into life.

The economic emphasis is significant. Texts such as *Pyers Plowmans Exhortation* (1550) concerned themselves persistently with the need for plainness in real economic terms, their emphasis on thrift, labour and economic self-sufficiency was unmistakable.[62] One answer to the perceived problem of idleness,

---

[59]   Hutson, *Thomas Nashe in Context*, pp. 172–96.

[60]   George Puttenham, *The Arte of English Poesie*, eds G. D. Willcock and A. Walker (Cambridge, 1936, repr. 1970), p. 62.

[61]   Nichol, *A Cup of News*, p. 4. For Nashe's anti-Marprelate writing, see esp. pp. 76–7.

[62]   The following discussion is indebted to Lorna Hutson's excellent thesis on the intersection between Tudor economic policy and Nashe's work in *Thomas Nashe in Context*. For a more detailed discussion of the *Exhortation*, see Chapter 3.

wrote the author of the *Exhortation*, was that all the goods that were currently 'brought from the parties of beyonde the seas' should be 'made wroughte or had within thys realme' (sig. B1v). Foreign luxury goods were not only a temptation to pride and over-consumption, but a threat to the well-being of the commonwealth. The plain English ploughman was a Protestant icon who made his own clothes and worked every moment when he wasn't reading the Bible. Protestantism's controversial self-fashioning made it clear that economic simplicity and spiritual value were correlative. The problem was that by the 1590s, the rhetoric of Protestant 'simplicity' and the imperative of the 'commonwealth' had become as malleable as the persona of simplicity regularly threatened to be. As Hutson puts it, 'what was persistently represented as a moral crusade in the interests of reforming the commonwealth, was increasingly becoming in practice a major source of income for the magistrates and noblemen who implemented it'.[63] If the persona of plainness propounded in places of high social status seemed like something of a rhetorical stance in the 1530s when Thomas Wyatt complimented the rustic pleasures of 'Kent and Christendom' over the luxury and deception of the court, by the 1590s we find Nashe asking rather more indignantly how seriously reformist 'simplicity' should be taken.[64]

The correlation between plainness in material terms and spiritual integrity that Protestant sensibility constructed was precisely the edifice that Nashe attempts to demolish. Nashe's portrait of 'Dame Niggardize' is a potent example of the controversial purpose behind his parody of reformist ploughman literature. We are introduced to Dame Niggardize, significantly the wife of 'Greediness', as she 'sat barrelling up the droppings of her nose, instead of oil, to saim wool withal' (I. 167). But for the characteristic grotesqueness of the description, one might take this to be analogous to the descriptions of the 'poor ploughman' that proliferated in Lollard and Protestant writing, such as that in *Pierce Plowman's Crede*. The Dame is apparently so poor that she uses mucus instead of oil to grease wool. Yet the 'house (or rather hell)' that she lives in is 'vast, large, strong built, and well furnished, all save the kitchen' (I. 167).[65] Dame Niggardize is miserly rather than 'plain'. Notably, the kitchen, where the household's communal stock of food is prepared, a place associated with the nourishing of others, is tiny. Niggardize is an example of those that 'will give nothing for God's sake'.

---

[63] Hutson, *Thomas Nashe in Context*, p. 182.

[64] Wyatt, 'My own John Poyntz', l. 100, in *The Complete Poems*, ed. R. A. Rebholz (London, 1978).

[65] The image has remarkable similarities to earlier satirical images of hoarding and greed, such as that of the fourteenth-century 'Winner' whose multiple houses are depicted stuffed with sacks of wool, and their ceilings bending under the weight of stored bacon; see Warren Ginsberg, ed., *Wynnere and Wastoure and The Parlement of the Thre Ages* (Kalamazoo, 1992, repr. 1997), ll. 250–251. Nashe's image emphasizes miserliness beyond Winner's, who at least hoards useful materials.

After a comic digression on the 'misery the rats and mice endured in this hard world', Nashe gets to the centre of the issue. Whilst Niggardize provides so little either for herself or others that the rats who live there resort to eating Greediness' codpiece, 'unfortunate gold, a predestinate slave to drudges and fools, lives in endless bondage there among them' (I. 168). Thrift and simplicity is here motivated by greed, not charity. Nashe refigures plainness as an avaricious hoarding, and ostentatious ascetic simplicity as a dynamic of greed. Time and time again, Nashe comes back to this plainness as hypocrisy, repeatedly his targets are those who are identified with 'Puritanism ... all underhand cloaking of bad actions with commonwealth pretences' (I. 220).

The devout simplicity that Protestantism saw as a reflection of its self-hood was persistently the butt of Nashe's satire. The success of Protestantism's self-fashioning as 'poor' and 'simple' by the 1590s was so complete that Nashe could simply use it as a kind of shorthand insult. As far as Nashe was concerned, if the radical Protestant wanted to be seen as poor and uneducated, then he could be reviled in exactly those terms. Those who, according to Nashe's anti-Reformation fable, 'did much harm under the habit of simplicity' (I. 224) are a combination of peasant and 'drudge', 'dull-headed divines' who 'preach pure Calvin' (I. 192). There was no more frequent recipient of Nashe's waspish pen than the poor Protestant, who like 'the cobbler of Norwich ... stept up into the pulpit very devoutly, and made me a good thrifty exhortation in the praise of plain dealing'.[66] Plainness, dullness and hypocrisy are constant companions in Nashe's attacks on the Puritans. They are either genuinely stupid or pretending to be 'plain' in order to line their own pockets.

Nashe's satire, so apparently novel in its energy and flamboyancy, persistently reminds the reader of an older kind of controversial writing which, rather than being surpassed or outrun, is reformulated. Nashe's savage animosity towards radical Protestantism is nowhere more apparent than in his gloating over the mangled corpses of Müntzer's Anabaptists in *The Unfortunate Traveller*: 'So ordinary at every footstep was the imbrument of iron in blood, that one could hardly discern heads from bullets, or clotted hair from mangled flesh hung with gore ... Hear what it is to be Anabaptists, to be Puritans, to be villains'.[67] But the antipathy towards the religious culture which produced the very synthesis of Martin and Piers that enabled Nashe's text went all the way back to *The Anatomie of Absurditie* (1588), in which he castigated those that think 'they are the Church millitant here vpon earth, when as they rather seeme a company of Malecontents, vnworthy to breath on the earth'.[68] The same hostile energy is omnipresent in *Pierce Penniless*. 'Like Herod's soldiers' writes Nashe, 'we divide Christ's garments amongst us in so many

---

[66]   *The Works of Thomas Nashe*, III. 351. The reference is to *An Almond for a Parrot*, an anti-Martinist text only doubtfully attributed to Nashe. The sneering dismissal of the 'very devout' cobbler seems, however, rather characteristic.

[67]   *The Works of Thomas Nashe*, II. 241.

[68]   *The Works of Thomas Nashe*, I. 22.

pieces, and of the vesture of salvation make some of us ... with the Martinists, a hood with two faces, to hide their hypocrisy' (I. 172). The image of casting lots for Christ's clothes, from John 19:23–4, appears again in *The Unfortunate Traveller*, when Nashe figures 'cynical reformed foreign churches' who are 'confiscating and casting lots for Church livings, as the soldiers cast lots for Christ's garments' (II. 237–8). This is an image with a long history. In 1389, John Trefaunt, Bishop of Hereford, wrote of Lollards 'molientes ... scindere tunicam Domini inconsutilem', 'endeavouring to cut asunder the Lord's unsowed coat'.[69] Nashe's *Summer's Last Will and Testament*, performed at Archbishop Whitgift's house in 1592, can be seen as another shot at 'Plain Piers'.[70] An eccentric ludic entertainment devised for the target of much of Martin's writing, Nashe's 'play' is presided over by one of Nashe's many 'ghosts': Will Summers.[71] Summer's persona can, like so much in Nashe's work, be traced back to the self-consciously 'dunstical and absurd' performance of Martin. His self-identification conjures up echoes of Martin's first experiments in '*decorum Personae*': 'I, fool by nature and by art, do speak to you in the person of the idiot our playmaker ... I'll sit as a chorus and flout the actors and him at the end of every scene' (III. 233, 236). But once again it is plainness, rendered as miserliness, that Nashe returns to repeatedly. Christmas is a 'snudge' (III. 287) who proclaims that the 'god of hospitality' has 'grown out of fashion' (III. 284); Harvest is accused of being:

> an engrosser of the common store:
> A carl, thou hast no conscience, nor remorse,
> But dost impoverish the fruitful earth,
> To make thy garners rise up to the heavens.
> To whom givest thou? (III. 259)

Martinists, Anabaptists, Puritans: all blur into one body who have 'God always in their mouths, [but] will give nothing for God's sake'. Nashe's satirical and theatrical anti-Puritanism, coupled with the inversion of plainness into miserliness, is the hallmark of the aftermath of the Marprelate controversy, when Piers became

---

[69] W. Capes, ed., *Registrum Johannis Trefnant episcopi Herefordensis* (London, 1916), p. 232. The accusations were to become better known when John Foxe translated them as part of his *Acts and Monuments* (1570). The translation used is Foxe's.

[70] On the likelihood of Whitgift's house at Croydon, and the dating of the performance to 1592, see Nichol, *A Cup of News*, pp. 135–7.

[71] While the supernatural in general can be seen to play on Nashe's mind – *The Terrors of the Night*, the demonology of *Pierce Penniless* – a striking number of Nashe's texts are dedicated to 'ghosts', particularly those occupying the stage. See, for example, the dedicatory epistle of *An Almond for a Parrot* (1589–1590): 'to the Ghost of Dicke Tarlton', and *Pierce Penniless*'s dedication to the ghosts of 'Macheuill, of Tully, of Ouid, of Roscius, of Pace the Duke of Norfols Iester; and lastly, to the Ghost of Robert Greene'; *The Works of Thomas Nashe*, III. 341; I. 153.

'penniless' again, but in order to attack those who had always figured themselves as poor, 'ingram', and therefore more godly. It may be that by 1592, the figure of Piers was 'familiar (and perhaps stale) enough to be available for parody', but Nashe's parody is, in a sense, a testament to the fact that the figure and his renewed associations with reformism were still powerful enough to provoke such a response. However, 1592 marked not only the appearance of Piers in Throkmorton's *Petition*, and his parody in Nashe's *Pierce Penniless*, it was also a year which saw him on the stage.

It is perhaps worth pausing at this intersection to re-establish the network of connections between the Marprelate controversy, Nashe, and the London stage in order to recognize quite how, and why, Piers Plowman was worth 'performing' as a theatrical character in 1592. We have seen how Piers played a role in the Marprelate tracts, and how 'Piers Marprelate' can be seen to enable the politicized parody of Nashe's prose. It is also worth noting that the London stage seems to have been the other central outlet (apart from prose satire) for anti-Martinist controversial culture. The anti-Martinist texts are rife with references to what seem to have been a minor craze for a theatrical form which has – annoyingly – left no textual traces but hearsay. *An Almond for a Parrot* (1589–1590) reported gleefully that Martin 'was attired like an Ape on the stage' and addressed Martin with the words 'Welcome, Mayster Martin, from the dead, and much good ioy may you haue of your stage-like resurrection'.[72] *Martin's Months Minde* (1589) stated that: 'everie stage Plaier made a just of him, and put him cleane out of countenance'.[73] *A Countercuffe given to Martin Junior* (1589) similarly gloated about the 'Anotamie latelie taken of him, the blood and the humors that were taken from him, by launcing and worming him at *London* vpon the common stage'.[74] John Lyly went so far in *Pappe with a Hatchett* (1589) to suggest that anti-Martinist theatre could play a significant part in Martin's identification: 'would those Comedies might be allowed to be plaid that are pend, and then I am sure he would be decyphered, and so perhaps discouraged'.[75] Martin clearly had the theatre, and one particular actor, in mind when he listed William Kempe among those associated with anti-Martinist attacks and lambasted:

> The stage-players, poor silly hunger-starved wretches, they have not so much as an honest calling to live in the commonwealth: and they, poor varlets, are so base minded, as at the pleasure of the veriest rogue in England, for one poor penny, they will be glad on open stage to play the ignominious fools for an hour or two together. And therefore, poor rogues (save only for their liveries), they in the

---

[72] *The Works of Thomas Nashe*, III. 354, 344.

[73] Cited in Black, *The Martin Marprelate Tracts*, p. lxv.

[74] *The Works of Thomas Nashe*, I. 59.

[75] Lyly, *Pappe with a Hatchett*, in *The Complete Works of John Lyly*, ed. R. Warwick Bond, 3 vols (Oxford, 1902), III. 408.

action of dealing against Master Martin, have gotten them many thousand eye witnesses of their witless and pitiful conceits. (*Theses Martinianae*, p. 162)

It would seem that the London stage was freely acknowledged by both sides of the controversy to be a hotbed of satirical theatre aimed at Martin Marprelate.[76]

At the same time, we find Nashe loitering – half in view – around the theatre almost constantly. Obviously, Nashe made his own attempts at dramatic writing. *Summer's Last Will and Testament* (1592) is one example; *Dido, Queene of Carthage* (1594), usually taken to be Marlowe's, is, if we take the title page at face value, likely to have been a collaboration with Nashe.[77] The *Isle of Dogs* affair, which got Ben Jonson – Nashe's collaborator – locked up in Marshalsea Prison, points to a more focused commitment to dramatic writing than we might expect.[78] But it is perhaps Nashe's open admiration for the theatre which is most striking. His praise for what appears to be Shakespeare's *1 Henry VI* in *Pierce Penniless* – 'brave Talbot ... newe embalmed with the teares of ten thousand spectators' (I. 212) – has rightly been seen as an effusive testimonial to 'the emotive impact of Elizabethan theatre.[79] But Nashe's enthusiasm for the stage was, in the early 1590s, not solely an emotional or aesthetic appreciation, but also a religious-political one. If we can take *An Almond for a Parrot* to be Nashe's, the dedicatory epistle to Will Kempe – 'Iestmonger and vice-gerent generall to the Ghost of Dicke Tarlton' – makes a great deal of sense.[80] The man attacked specifically by Martin as a 'prime mover' in anti-Martinist theatre was surely an appropriate ally for Nashe. But to make things more complicated, it is the theatre which by 1592 had come to be associated with anti-Martinist sentiment that is frequently seen to have enabled the writing of Martin. Patrick Collinson, for example, writes that:

Literary scholars have always known that Martin Marprelate would probably never have seen the light of day but for those areas of the Elizabethan popular

---

[76] A collection of references to anti-Martinist theatre can be found in E. K. Chambers, *The Elizabethan Stage* (Oxford, 1923), IV. 229–33. See also Andrew Gurr, *The Shakespearian Stage, 1574–1642* (Cambridge, 1970), pp. 33, 36, 118. The phenomenon is also discussed by Lake in *The Antichrist's Lewd Hat*, pp. 556–63, and by Kristen Poole in a remarkable essay on Shakespeare's Falstaff; 'Saints Alive! Falstaff, Martin Marprelate, and the Staging of Puritanism', *Shakespeare Quarterly*, 46 (1995), 47–75.

[77] On Nashe's authorship, see H. J. Oliver, ed., *Dido Queen of Carthage and The Massacre at Paris*, The Revels Plays (London, 1968), pp. xx–xxv; also Nichol, *A Cup of News*, p. 29.

[78] On the controversy surrounding this lost play, see Nichol, *A Cup of News*, pp. 242–56. Remarkably, the play is the subject of a sequence of modern, forged entries in Henslowe's diary. See R. A. Foakes and R. T. Rickert, eds, *Henslowe's Diary* (Cambridge, 1961), pp. 63, note 3, 67, note 3.

[79] Nichol, *A Cup of News*, p. 87.

[80] *The Works of Thomas Nashe*, III. 341–3.

theatre which operated, as it were, below the belt. Just behind Martin stands, or rather prances, that famous comedian, the Rabelaisian genius who was Dick Tarlton.[81]

Paradoxically, Will Kempe – the heir and 'vice-gerent generall' to Tarlton – seems to have become the arch-enemy of Martin, a movement which allowed the actors patronizingly scorned by Martin as 'poor silly hunger-starved wretches' to 'pose as the defenders of an order, orthodoxy and obedience now under threat from an insurgent puritan movement'.[82] The complexity and closeness of the cultural traffic between theatre, Martinism, Nashe, and prose satire more generally stands, for the most part, outside the scope of this study, but the brief outline sketched above is necessary, I think, to prepare us for the next appearance of Piers Plowman. For this appearance was conditioned by the shadow that the Marprelate controversy cast over the early 1590s. It was also an appearance in a play linked curiously to Nashe – through both its printer, and modern authorship debates – and to Will Kempe.

Piers Treads the Boards: Anti-Puritan Satire in the Strange's Men Reportory

A Knack to Know a Knave (1592, printed 1594) was printed, possibly in an attempt to make some money at a time when the playing company associated with it – Strange's Men – were undergoing decimation as its various members became parts of two other playing companies, by one Richard Jones – the same printer who had produced the first edition of Nashe's *Pierce Penniless*.[83] The printer's 'device' on the title page was identical to that on the title page of Nashe's text, and one used by Jones throughout 1592–1595.[84] The title page also marketed the text through its associations with particularly well-known members of the company: it states that the play 'hath sundrie tymes bene played by ED. ALLEN & his companie. With

---

[81] Collinson, 'Ecclesiastical Vitriol', pp. 158–9.

[82] Lake, *The Antichrist's Lewd Hat*, pp. 558–9.

[83] On the transformation of Strange's Men into Derby's Men, and its subsequent 'decapitation', which led to the enhancement of the Admiral's and Chamberlain's companies, see Andrew Gurr, *The Shakespearian Playing Companies* (Oxford, 1996), p. 265. In a brief note, Paul E. Bennett suggests that the extant text of *A Knack to Know a Knave* was a memorial reconstruction of the 1592 performances by Strange's/Derby's Men in 1593. See Paul E. Bennett, 'The Word "Goths" in *A Knack to Know a Knave*', *Notes & Queries*, 200 (1955), 462–3.

[84] Anon. *A Knack to Know a Knave 1594*, ed. G. R. Proudfoot (Oxford, 1963), p. v. All references to the play are to this edition, by line number. Compare the device re-printed by McKerrow, ed., *The Works of Thomas Nashe*, I. 149.

KEMPS applauded Merriments' (see Figure 4.2).[85] Edward Alleyn, the name most associated with Marlowe's 'mighty line' in the roles of Tamburlaine and Doctor Faustus, played with Strange's company from 1591 onwards, but retained the livery of the Lord Admiral's men at the same time.[86] Nashe commits one section of a related sequence on the theatre entirely to Allen, asking which of 'those admired tragedians that have lived ever since before Christ was born, could ever perform more in action than famous Ned Allen' (I. 215). Kempe, as we have seen already, was both the *bête noire* of Martin Marprelate, and the object of anti-Martinist adulation which was probably Nashe's too. And both were members of a company patronized by Fernando Stanley, Lord Strange, for whom Nashe is likely to have composed the proto-Rochesterian light pornography of *A Choice of Valentines*.[87]

The play, hardly a household name anymore, was something of a money-spinner for Strange's Men in the 1592 season, when it was performed at the Rose theatre six times between 10 June 1592 and 24 January 1593.[88] The company's repertory included Kyd's *Spanish Tragedy*; Marlowe's *Jew of Malta*; Shakespeare's *1 Henry VI*; and, possibly, *Sir Thomas More*.[89] *Knack* took, on its opening performance, £3 12s; substantially more than either the performance of Kyd's *Spanish Tragedy* the previous day (28s) or Marlowe's *Jew of Malta* four days later (38s). For all its obvious popularity and financial success, it has received little critical attention.

It is usually referred to briefly as an example of a brief phase for 'morality comedies' in the early 1590s, or as an example of transitions between 'estates' drama – with strong attachments to earlier morality drama – and the more sophisticated later theatre.[90] The same 'academic parlour game' that attends the Marprelate tracts is also present here, but while definite proof seems hard to come

---

[85] *A Knack to Know a Knave*, sig. A1r. All references are to this edition, by line reference.

[86] Gurr, *Shakespearian Playing Companies*, p. 259.

[87] Indeed, the patronage of Strange is hinted at at the close of *Pierce Penniless* in Nashe's praise of 'Amyntas'. Compare Spenser's eulogy for Strange in *Colin Clout*: 'Amyntas quite is gone and les full low' (l. 434), *Spenser: The Shorter Poems*, and Nichol, *A Cup of News*, p. 89. On the dedication of *A Choice of Valentines* to 'Lord S', see Nichol, *A Cup of News*, pp. 90–93.

[88] R. A. Foakes and R. T. Rickert, eds, *Henslowe's Diary*, pp. 19–20.

[89] See Gurr, *Shakespearian Playing Companies*, p. 263. A discussion of the company's history can be found at pp. 258–77.

[90] See particularly Martin Wiggins, *Shakespeare and the Drama of his Time* (Oxford, 2000), pp. 75–6; Alan C. Dessen, 'The "Estates" Morality Play', *Studies in Philology*, 62 (1965), 121–36, 130; G. K. Hunter, *The Oxford History of English Literature: English Drama 1586–1642, The Age of Shakespeare* (Oxford, 1997), pp. 367–9. A couple of critics find some interest in the play's representation of the fawning courtier 'Perin'; see Curtis Perry, *Literature and Favoritism in Early Modern England* (Cambridge, 2006), pp. 137–46; and Meredith Anne Skura, *Shakespeare the Actor and the Purposes of Playing* (Chicago, 1993), pp. 172–3. Both connect Perin to the tradition epitomized by Marlowe's Gaveston in *Edward II*.

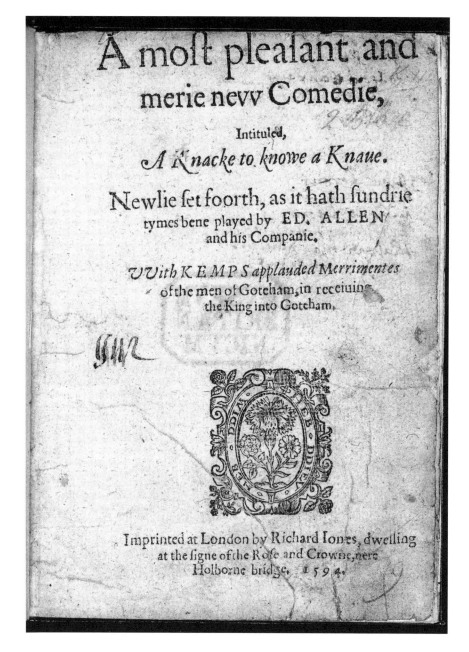

Figure 4.2   Title page of *A Knack to Know a Knave* (London: Richard Jones, 1594). © The British Library Board.

by it is not entirely surprising to see Nashe being mentioned.[91] Indeed, strikingly, the performance dates recorded in Henslowe's diary make the play almost exactly contemporary with Nashe's *Pierce Penniless*. Nashe's text was registered by Richard Jones on 8 August 1592, and there were two more editions on sale by the end of 1592. *Knack*'s performances began in June of the same year and continued until January 1593.[92] One could, perhaps, have read Nashe's *Pierce Penniless* (and Throkmorton's *Petition*) and watched a performance of *A Knack to Know a Knave* on the same day. What is even more surprising, then, given the general critical consensus about the 'staid' and 'fading' impact of the Piers figure, is the diversity of ways in which Piers would be appropriated in 1592. For Piers Plowman's role in *Knack* is both part of a long Tudor tradition of such appropriations, and one with specific resonances for the early 1590s.

The scene is worth quoting at some length:

> *Enter Honestie and Piers Plowman.*
>
> *Honesty.* What newes; where hast thou bene so long?
>
> *Honest.* A my Lord, I haue bene searching for a priuie knaue
> One (my Lord) that feeds upon the poore commons,
> And makes poore *Piers ploughman* weare a thread bare coate,
> It is a farmer (my Lord) which buys up all the corn in the market,
> And sends it away beyond seas, & thereby feeds the enemie.
>
> *Kin.* Alas, poore *piers plowman*, what ailest thou? Why doest
> Thou weep, peace man, if any haue offended thee,
> Thou shalt be made amends unto the most.
>
> *Piers plow.* I beseech your Grace to pitie my distresse,
> There is an vnknowne theefe that robs the common wealth,
> And makes me and my poore wife and children beg for maintenance,
> The tyme hath bene (my Lord) *in diebus illis*,
> That the Plowmans coat was of good homespun russet cloth,
> Whereof neither I nor my seruents had no want,
> Though now both they and I want,
> And all by this vuknown farmer:
> For there cannot be an aker of ground to be sold,

---

[91] See particularly Hanspeter Born, *The Rare Wit and the Rude Groom: the Authorship of A Knack to Know a Knave in Relation to Greene, Nashe and Shakespeare* (Bern, 1971). But see also H. Douglas Sykes, 'The Authorship of *A Knack to Know a Knave*', *Notes & Queries*, 146 (1924), pp. 389–91, 410–12. Sykes sees George Peele as the main author, though he also notes the occasional bit of plagiarism from Robert Greene's prose in the play.

[92] See Nichol, *A Cup of News*, p. 99. On the dating of the editions, see also McKerrow, ed., *The Works of Thomas Nashe*, I. 137–48; III. 33; IV. 77–9. A mention of 'purse pennilesse' on 14 June 1592 is worth noting too, suggesting that something of Nashe's text was known within four days of *Knack*'s first performance. See Nichol, *A Cup of News*, p. 295, note 1.

> But he will find money to buy it: nay my Lord, he hath money
> To buy whole Lordships, and yet but a farmer,
> I haue kept a poore house where I dwel this four score yeare,
> Yet was I neuer driuen to want till now:
>   I beseech your Grace, as you haue still bene iust,
>   To seek redresse for this oppression.
>   I beseech your Grace reade my humble petition.

Kin. Let me see the humble petition, of poor piers plowman,
>   Alasse poore piers, I haue heard my father say,
> That piers plowman was one of the best members in a commonwealth
> For his table was neuer emptie of bread, beefe, and beere,
>   As a help to all distressed traueilers.

(*A Knack to Know a Knave*, ll. 1219–49).

The Piers of texts like *Pyers Plowmans Exhortation* (1550), the spokesman of economic complaint, returns, almost at the same moment Nashe's parody appeared. Just as we found Throkmorton appropriating both Langland's text, and the mid-Tudor complaint tradition that had accumulated around it, we find the London stage offering another striking moment of Elizabethan medievalism. There is more afoot here than the skewed historicity that has Piers Plowman sharing the stage with King Edgar (959–975) and Archbishop Dunstan.[93] For one thing, there is the enigmatic use of Latin in Piers's speech: '*in diebus illis*'. There is no other Latin in the entire play, barring Dunstan's '*Veni Asmoroth*' (l. 1582), an eye-catching echo of Marlowe's 'Come Mephastophilis: / *Veni veni Mephastophile*'.[94] Why does Piers Plowman, of all the characters, speak Latin? One possible answer, I think, is that the nostalgia which circulates around Piers in the play also circulated around the sapiential image not only of medieval labourers but of medieval poets. Robert Greene's *Greenes Vision* (1592) contains a remarkable description of a dream-vision of two other 'ancient' figures: Chaucer and Gower, with '*In diebus illis*, hung vpon their garments'.[95] The phrase might well have conjured up a sense of general nostalgia, but it also perhaps conjured up a certain 1590s craze for medieval poetic figures – the same craze that led shortly to Speght's 1598 edition of Chaucer which, it should be remembered, still contained *The Plowman's Tale*.

---

[93] The key historical sources for the play's representations of Anglo-Saxon history were of course Foxe and Holinshed, though the idea of Dunstan's power over devils is something found in, for example, Caxton's *Golden Legend* (1483), which Protestant historians including Foxe and Matthew Parker tended to dismiss. See John D. Cox, *The Devil and the Sacred in English Drama, 1350–1642* (Cambridge, 2000), pp. 132–3.

[94] Christopher Marlowe, *Dr Faustus*, ed. Roma Gill, New Mermaids (London, 1989), Scene 5, ll. 28–9; and Cox, *The Devil and the Sacred*, p. 133.

[95] Alexander B. Grosart, ed., *The Life and Complete Works in Prose and Verse of Robert Greene*, 15 vols (New York, 1964), XII. 209.

The central act of Piers's role in *Knack* is also arresting. While the text does not contain a stage direction to make it explicit, the act of petitioning, the physical offering and acceptance of a document describing social abuses, seems to take place here. The extremely formal language throughout the scene – the deferential repetition of '(my Lord)' by Honesty and Piers – is picked up in the ceremonial repetition of: 'I beseech your Grace reade my humble petition. / *Kin.* Let me see the humble petition'. That Piers is so associated with petitioning is interesting. Throkmorton, we have seen, used *Piers Plowman* in his own *Petition*, setting up an association with the history of reformist texts that went back to Fish's *Supplication for the Beggars* (1529), the generic tradition which Sutcliffe found so inappropriate, and which Wendy Scase has recently described in detail. Moreover, the topics of Piers' complaints take us straight back to the mid-century 'commonwealth's men' like Crowley. Rent-racking, engrossing, manipulation of the market for 'necessary things', the preferment of personal profit over the interests of the 'commonwealth': all these hark back to the Henrician and Edwardian reformism that, as I argue in Chapter 1, found polemical inspiration in the pages of Langland's own anti-urban satire.

But there are wider continuities to be drawn as well. *Knack* is actually a play which is patterned with preoccupations about ruralism and the dangers of the urban market which are familiar. Indeed, the polemical interests of the play are a clear testament to the enduring force of some of the central concerns of the radical pastoral tradition, even as they are re-formed for the economic – and, as we shall see, religious – circumstances of the 1590s. Piers is not the only icon of rural ethics and complaint in the play, in fact the play splits different 'versions of pastoral' between different characters. Honesty, the character who has the 'knack to know a knave', is introduced in opposition to Perin, a courtier who assumes Honesty's 'knack' must be the product of esoteric court sciences – 'you are some Uissitian, or skild in Uisognomy, or in palmistry … Astronomie' (ll. 74–5). But those who know what knaves are, says Honesty, can be 'But a plaine man of the country, lyke me' (l. 79). Edgar's first reaction to this allegorical figure is equally telling. Honesty's role as truth-teller is established in the first scene by his breaking into a rather sycophantic and self-aggrandizing dialogue between Edgar and his advisor, Dunstan, with a testing criticism of the king himself, for which he receives the curt response: 'base Peasant, wilful as thou art, / I tell thee troth, thou hast displeased the king' (ll. 59–60). But Edgar's patronizing pronouns quickly reform into an enthusiasm for this blunt 'plain man of the country' who is able:

> To stifle such catterpillers as corrupt the common welth:
> For manie tymes such simple men as he,
> Bewray much matter in simplicitie. (ll. 118–20)

In fact, the language of agriculture begins to seep into many aspects of the play. In a trial of a Conicatcher, Dunstan suddenly appears disguised as a farmer who proclaims that he 'was no farmer that inricht my selfe: / By raysing markets and oppressing poore' (ll. 866–7), and laments that 'such loathsome weeds must needs infect the corne, / Such Cankers perish both the root and branch' (ll. 888–9). Edgar catches the reformist mood, and style, to state 'Ile be the husbandman to mowe such tares' (l. 891). Political governance, self-governance, and reform; all are inherently connected in *A Knack to Know a Knave*, and begin to take on Honesty's, and Piers Plowman's, language. Just as the idealized, polemical pastoralism of the Edwardian reign is found in the language of reform, the play cycles back to the idea of the poor as a key piece of political rhetoric. Walter's 'confession' repeats the phrases found in Piers Plowman's petition: 'I haue raised the markets, and opprest the poore, / And made a thousand goe from dore to dore' (ll. 308–9).

The play's immersion in the agrarian language and imagery of economic reform also fits into its broader theme of generosity and its opposite – Nashe's favourite way to denigrate Puritans: miserliness. The downfall of hospitality, the idea that links Nashe's Dame Niggardize in *Pierce Penniless* with Christmas's lament for the 'god of hospitality' in *Summer's Last Will and Testament*, is a central part of *A Knack to Know a Knave*. All its economic complaint is attached to the ideal not – interestingly enough – of plainness, but of generosity. Edgar remembered Piers as the best member of a commonwealth because: 'his table was neuer emptie of bread, beefe, and beere, / As a help to all distressed traueilers' (ll. 1248–9). Just so, Dunstan in agricultural disguise proclaims that he has sold corn 'At better rate, than I could well afford, / And all to help my needie brethren' (ll. 869–70). Likewise, the play's representative figure of the knightly estate says 'my goods are lent me to no other end / But to releeue my needie brethren' (ll. 966–7). He is in conversation with Walter, Piers' enemy, who advises the knight – significantly – to 'leaue so great a traine of men … And those you keepe, let them be simple men / for they will be content with simple fare' (ll. 943–6). Walter's 'simplicity' is significant. The play renders some aspects of rural simplicity as ideals of a reformed commonwealth, but other uses of 'simplicity' are, like those in Nashe's satires, glossed as a destructive and self-absorbed corruption, an opposite to everything suggested by the word commonwealth. Just as Nashe had turned 'plain piers' on his head partly, at least, in order to attack those 'puritans, Anabaptists, villains' – like Throkmorton we might say – who had laid such a close claim on 'plainness', *A Knack to Know a Knave* does something similar. While still utilizing the style of mid-Tudor economic complaint, the play turns 'plainness' in two different directions, and one of those directions led straight back to radical Protestantism.

For *A Knack to Know a Knave* is perhaps best known as an anti-Puritan play, even the first anti-Puritan play: the progenitor of figures like Jonson's brilliantly-named 'Zeal-of-the-Land Busy' in *Bartholomew Fair* (1614, printed 1631).[96] The play's moral and satirical ire is directed towards a familial group: the Bailiff of

---

[96]   The anti-Puritanism of the play was first described in Mary G. M. Adkins, 'The Genesis of Dramatic Satire against the Puritan, as Illustrated in *A Knack to Know a Knave*', *Review of English Studies*, 22 (1946), 81–95; its status as the 'first anti-Puritan play' is

Hexham (carried off to hell by a one of the play's Faustus-like devils) and his four sons – Walter the farmer, Perin the courtier, a Conicatcher, and finally a priest. The sons are clearly designed to represent all the estates and, therefore, the ubiquity of corruption. But the priest is of a particular kind, and receives the following advice from his vice-like father:

> Thou must (my son) make shew of holinesse,
> And blinde the world with thy hipocrisie:
> And sometime giue a pennie to the poore,
> But let it be in the church or marketplace,
> That men may praise thy liberalitie
> Speak against usurie, yet forsake no pawnes,
> So thou maist gaine three shillings in the pound
> …
> So by this means thou shall be tearmed wise
> And with thy pureness blind the peoples eies. (ll. 283–93)

The advice, of course, focuses on those things held to be most ideal in the play: 'Honesty' and generosity. In a sharp way, the 'pureness' of the priest is attached to hypocrisy and self-enrichment. The connection between Puritan identity and the priest is cemented by the terms of his own 'confession': 'Thus doe we blind the world with holinesse, / And so by that are tearmed pure Precisians' (ll. 343–4). 'Precisians', which we can perhaps see as an early prototype of the modern 'Puritanical', is clearly here a term for precisely the people who Nashe viewed as having 'God always in their mouths', while giving 'nothing for God's sake'. While we can hardly see this play as an example of the anti-Martinist theatre to which both sides of the controversy refer, it surely – as Katrin Poole puts it – 'emanates from the Marprelate controversy'.[97] When Will Kempe stepped onto the stage and the audience heard the terms 'pureness' and 'Precisians', Martin and his many opponents surely sprang to life. Moreover, whilst the explicit self-definition of characters as Puritans is important, they are part of a wider attack which is, again, closely entwined with the issue of hospitality, generosity and miserliness. The priest's extortion of a beggar is introduced to the audience with the Puritan-priest's plotting:

> He is my neere kinsman, I confesse, and a Clergie man,
> But fiftie shillings is money, & though I might trust him
> Simply with it for a tweluemoneth, where hee craues it but for a
> Moneth, yet simply I will not be so simple. (ll. 1603–6)

---

restated in, for example, David Bevington, *Tudor Drama and Politics: A Critical Approach to Topical Meaning* (Cambridge, MA, 1968), pp. 227–9.

[97]   Poole, 'Saints Alive! Falstaff, Martin Marprelate, and the Staging of Puritanism', p. 60, note 43.

The word 'simply' is very heavily loaded here, the repetition extremely pointed. Simplicity, one of the play's favourite terms, is the thing which is subject to the most distortion by this particular 'precisian'. Likewise, the Puritan-priest's refusal to give anything to a beggar without a substantial amount of interest is couched in sharply satirical terms which parody both Puritan theology and linguistic style. Asked to 'for God's sake, giue one pennie to the poore ... good maister giue something' (ll. 1619–20) he replys 'Read the blessed saying of S. Paul ... looke in the blessed Prouerb of Salomon, which is, good deeds do not iustify a man, therefore I count it sinne to giue thee any thing' (ll. 1622, 1633–5). His speech peters out into a breathless – and overtly hypocritical – rant against usurie: 'Fie upon usurie ... fie upon it, fie ... fie on it, tis ungodlie' (ll. 1652–6). The audience has 'Honesty' to tell them quite plainly what to think of the Puritan-priest's Biblicism: 'See how he can turne and wind the Scripture to his owne use?' (ll. 1636–7). In fact, Honesty's counter-reading of scriptural passages about charity – 'but he remembers not where Christ saith' (ll. 1625, 1637) – is a familiar literary trope of religious controversy which goes back through Bale's *Temptation of our Lord* to the 'glosing' friars populating the Piers Plowman Tradition poems and *Piers Plowman* itself.

So while Piers may, from one perspective, seem to be 'fading' as a presence in the writing of religious controversy, the figure and all the controversial connotations that had accumulated over the two centuries since Langland wrote *Piers Plowman* can be clearly seen to be powerfully relevant in the arena of religious disputes of the 1590s. Just as Lollard 'plainness' had been the subject of a literary-polemical argument, 'the entity of Puritanism itself was subject to constant polemical construction and construal, from both sides of the puritan / conformist argument', and Piers still had an important role to play in those constructions.[98] In some ways, we can even see Piers freed, at least briefly, from the narrowing connotations of mid-Tudor Protestantism, and see his return to a more contested role. Piers became, in the shadow of the Marprelate controversy, a figure who almost embodies religious controversy itself: a powerful icon for political and religious idealism and identity-formation which is necessarily combative and oppositional, and can be used with equal freedom and ingenuity by opposing sides of the same debate.

Repeatedly, literary history has told us that Nashe's era, indeed his text itself, was a breaking point between 'drab' and 'golden' eras, that 'English poetry naturally moved farther and farther' from its medieval past, that by the 1590s 'there is very little of the plodding medieval' genre left.[99] Yet the self-fashioned rustic anti-authoritarianism of the genre is found proliferating amongst an increasingly powerful group. In 1641, Thomas Herbert published *News out of Islington*, the title page of which announced that the text was a dialogue 'betwixt a knavish Projector, and honest Clod the Ploughman'. The subject of the ploughman's attack on 'knavish'

---

[98]   Lake, *The Antichrist's Lewd Hat*, p. 520.

[99]   Peter, *Complaint and Satire in Early English Literature*, p. 110; Alvin Kernan, *The Cankered Muse: Satire of the English Renaissance* (New Haven, 1959), p. 50.

courtiers was now the possibility of open war between a parliamentarian cause and England's monarch. Milton lines the medieval ploughman up in a sequence of ancient authorities from Dante and Petrarch to Chaucer, who all become opponents of episcopacy. William Prynne, one of the most prolific Puritan writers of the 1630s and 1640s, cites 'Pierce Plowman, an ancient English poet' as evidence for an anti-Episcopal revolution in Church government, and lists Langland's ploughman amongst a tradition of anti-tyrannical figures who reinforce his critical assessment, made in December 1648, of 'the satisfactoriness of the kings answers' regarding 'the feared regal invasions and encroachments'.[100] Radical pastoral was still alive and well less than two months before Charles I's execution, and the establishment of a Protestant republic, in January 1649.

---

[100] William Prynne, *The Antipathy of the English Lordly Prelacy* (London, 1641), p. 336; *The Substance of a Speech made in the House of Commons by William Prynne...on Monday the fourth of December, 1648* (London, 1648), p. 70.

Bibliography

Primary Sources

A godly dialogue and dysputacyon between Pyers plowman and a popish preest. London?: 1550?

A Knack to Know a Knave. Oxford: Malone Society Reprints, 1964.

A Lyttle Geste how the plowman lerned his Paternoster. London: Wynken de Worde, 1510.

A Proper Dyaloge between a Gentillman and a Husbandman eche complaynyng to other their miserable calamite through the ambicion of the clergye. London?: William Barlowe?, 1530.

Augustine. *Confessions*, trans. R. S. Pine-Coffin. London: Penguin, 1961.

Axton, Richard, ed. *Three Rastell Plays: Four Elements, Calisto and Melebea, Gentleness and Nobility.* Cambridge: D. S. Brewer, 1979.

Bale, John. *The Vocacyon of Johan Bale*, eds P. Happé and John N. King. New York: Renaissance English Text Society, 1990.

————. *The Complete Plays of John Bale.* 2 vols, eds P. Happé. Cambridge: D. S. Brewer, 1985.

————. *The Plays of John Bale*, ed. T. Blatt. Copenhagen: Gad, 1968.

————. *Index Britanniae Scriptorum*, eds C. Brett and J. Carley. Cambridge: D. S. Brewer, 1990.

Barr, Helen, ed. *The Piers Plowman Tradition: a Critical Edition of Pierce the Ploughman's crede, Richard the redeless, Mum and the sothsegger and The crowned king.* London: Dent, 1993.

Black, Joseph L., ed. *The Martin Marprelate Tracts: A Modernized and Annotated Edition.* Cambridge: Cambridge University Press, 2008.

Bond, Warwick, ed. *The Complete Works of John Lyly.* Oxford: Clarendon Press, 1902.

Brinklow, Henry. *Henry Brinklow's Complaint of Roderyck Mors*, ed. J. Meadows Cowper. EETS e.s. 22. London: Kegan Paul, 1874.

British Library MS Harley 207.

Brown, X., ed. *London 1066–1914: Literary Sources and Documents*, 2 vols. Mountfield: Helm Information, 1997.

Capes, W., ed. *Registrum Johannis Trefnant episcopi Herefordensis.* London: Canterbury and York series, vol. 20, 1916.

Chandos, John, ed. *In God's Name: Examples of Preaching in England from the Act of Supremacy to the Act of Uniformity, 1534–1662.* London: Hutchinson, 1971.

Chaucer, Geoffrey. *The Riverside Chaucer*, ed. L. D. Benson. Oxford: Oxford University Press, 1987.

Clairvaux, B. *The Letters of Bernard of Clairvaux*, trans. B. S. James. Stroud: Sutton Publishing, 1953, repr. 1998.

Clare, John. *John Clare*, ed. E. Powell and E. Robinson. Oxford: Oxford University Press, 1984.

Crowley, Robert. *The Select Works of Robert Crowley*, ed. J. M. Cowper. EETS e.s. 15. London: Kegan Paul, 1872.

————. 'Philargyrie of Greate Britayne by Robert Crowley', ed. John N. King. *English Literary Renaissance*, 10 (1980), 46–75.

Davis, R. T., ed. *Medieval English Lyrics: A Critical Anthology*. London: Faber and Faber, 1963.

Dean, J., ed. *Six Ecclesiastical Satires*. Kalamazoo: Michigan University Press, 1991.

————. *Medieval English Political Writings*. Kalamazoo: Michigan University Press, 1996.

Dieulacres Chronicle, eds M. V. Clark and V. H. Galbraith. *Bulletin of the John Rylands Library*, 14 (1930), 164–81.

Dobson, R. B., ed. *The Peasants' Revolt of 1381*. London: Macmillan, 1970.

Elyot, Thomas. *The Boke Named The Governour*. London: Dent, 1907.

Erasmus, D. *Christian Humanism and the Reformation: Desiderius Erasmus, Selected Writings*, ed. J. C. Olin. New York: Harper, 1965.

Fish, Simon. *A Supplication for the Beggers*, ed. F. J. Furnivall. EETS e.s. 13. London: Kegan Paul, 1871.

Foakes, R. A. and Rickert R. T., eds. *Henslowe's Diary*. Cambridge: Cambridge University Press, 1961.

Foxe, John. *The Acts and Monuments of John Foxe*, 8 vols, ed. J. Pratt. London: Religious Tract Society, 1877.

————. *Acts and Monuments*. London: John Day, 1583.

Fraser, R., ed. *The Court of Venus*. Cambridge: Cambridge University Press, 1955.

Furnivall, F. J. and Meadows Cowper, J., eds. *Four Supplications, 1529–1553*. EETS e.s. 13. London: Kegan Paul, 1871.

Ginsberg, W., ed. *Wynnere and Wastoure and The Parlement of the Thre Ages*. Kalamazoo: Medieval Institute Publications, 1992.

Gower, John. *The Complete Works of John Gower*, 4 vols, ed. G. C. Macaulay. Oxford: Clarendon Press, 1902, repr. 1968.

Greene, Robert. *A Quip for an Upstart Courtier*. London: ?, 1592. *STC* 2nd edn 12301a.3.

Grosart, Alexander B., ed. *The Life and Complete Works in Prose and Verse of Robert Greene*, 15 vols. New York: Russell and Russell, 1964.

Habig, M., ed. *St. Francis of Assisi: Writings and Early Biographies*. Chicago: Franciscan Herald Press, 1973.

Hake, E. *News out of Paul's Churchyard*. London: John Charlewood and Richard Jones, 1579. *STC* 2nd edn 12606.

Harris, M. D., ed. *The Coventry Leet Book*. 4 vols in 2 EETS o.s. 134, 135, vol. 1; 138, 146, vol. 2. London: Kegan Paul, 1907–1913.

Herrtage, S. J., ed. *England in the Reign of King Henry the Eighth*. EETS e.s. 32. London: N. Trübner & Co, 1871–1878.

Heyworth P. L., ed. *Jack Upland, Friar Daw's Reply and Upland's Rejoinder*. Oxford: Oxford University Press, 1968.

Hoccleve, Thomas. *The Regement of Princes*, ed. F. J. Furnivall. EETS e.s. 72. London: Kegan Paul, 1897.

———. *Hoccleve's Regiment of Princes*, ed. Charles R. Blyth. Kalamazoo: University of Michigan Press, 1999.

Holinshed, Raphael. *Chronicles of England, Scotland and Ireland*, 6 vols. London: J. Johnson, 1807–1808.

Horace, *Satires, Epistles and Ars Poetica*, trans., H. Rushton Fairclough. London: Loeb Classical Library, 1926, repr. 1961.

I Playn Piers. London: ?, 1550?

I Playne Piers which cannot flatter. London?, 1550.

Jerome, *Select Letters*, ed., and trans. F. A. Wright. Cambridge: Harvard University Press, 1933, repr. 1999.

Juvenal. *Satires*, trans. C. G. Ramsey. London: Loeb, 1940.

Knighton, H. *Chronicon*, ed. J. R. Lumby. *RS* 1889–1895.

Lambert, J. and Bale, J. *A Treatise Made by John Lambert unto King Henry the viii*. Wesel: B. van der Straten, 1548?

Langland, William. *The Vision of Piers Plowman*, ed. R. Crowley. London: Robert Crowley, 1550. *STC* 2nd edn 19906–19907a.

———. *The Vision of Pierce Plowman newlye imprinted after the authors olde copy…whereunto is also annexed the Crede of Pierce Plowman, neuer imprinted with the booke before*. London: Owen Rogers, 1561, *STC* 2nd edn 19908.

———. *The Vision of Will, regarding Piers Plowman*, ed. W. W. Skeat, 2 vols. Oxford: Oxford University Press, 1886.

———. *Piers Plowman: The Prologue and Passus I–VII of the B-Text*, ed. J. A. W. Bennett. Oxford: Clarendon Press, 1972.

———. *Piers Plowman: The C-Text*, ed. D. Pearsall. Exeter: Exeter Medieval Press, 1978.

———. *Piers Plowman: A Parallel-Text Edition of the A, B, C, and Z Versions*, ed. A. V. C. Schmidt. London: Longman, 1995.

———. *The Vision of Piers Plowman*, ed. A. V. C. Schmidt. London: J. M. Dent, 1973, repr. 1995.

Leland, J. and Bale, J. *The Laboryous Journey and Serche of Johan Leylande, for Englandes Antiquities*. London: S. Mierdman, 1549.

McCarl, M. R., ed. *The Plowman's Tale: The c. 1532 and 1606 Editions of a Spurious Canterbury Tale*. London: Garland, 1997.

Macherey, P. *A Theory of Literary Production*, trans. Geoffrey Wall. London: Routledge, 1978.

Marlowe, Christopher. *Dr Faustus*, ed. Roma Gill, New Mermaids. London: A & C. Black, 1989.

———. H. J. Oliver, ed. *Dido Queen of Carthage and The Massacre at Paris*. The Revels Plays. London: Methuen, 1968.

Marx, K. *Capital. A Critical Analysis of Capitalist Production*, 2 vols, trans. S. Moore and E. Aveling. New York: Lawrence and Wishart, 2003.

Matarasso, P., ed. *The Cistercian World: Monastic Writings of the Twelfth Century*. London: Penguin, 1993.

Matthew, F. D., ed. *The English Works of Wyclif Hitherto Unprinted*. EETS o.s. 74. London: Kegan Paul, 1880.

Milton, J. *The Works of John Milton*, 18 vols, general ed. F. A. Patterson. New York: Columbia University Press, 1931–1938.

———. *The Complete Shorter Poems*, ed. J. Carey. London: Longman, 1968, repr. 1997.

———. *Paradise Lost*, ed. A. Fowler. London: Longman, 1968.

Monmouth, Geoffrey. *The History of the Kings of England*, trans. L. Thorpe. London: Penguin, 1966.

More, Thomas. *The Complete Works of St. Thomas More*, 15 vols, ed. J. B. Trapp. New Haven: Yale University Press, 1963–1997.

———. *Utopia*, ed. and trans. R. Adams. London: Norton, 1992.

Nashe, Thomas. *The Works of Thomas Nashe*, 5 vols, ed. R. B. McKerrow. Oxford: Blackwell, 1958.

News from the North, Otherwise called the conference between Simon Certain and Pierce Plowman. London: John Allde, 1579.

Of Gentylnes and Nobylyte. London: John Rastell, 1525.

O Read me for I am of great Antiquitie. London?, 1589?

Oxford, Bodleian Library, MS Digby 41.

Parker, Douglas H., ed. *The praier and complaynte of the ploweman vnto Christe*. Toronto: University of Toronto Press, 1997.

Pierce the Plowmans Crede. London: Reynor Wolfe, 1553.

Prynne, W. *The Antipathy of the English Lordly Prelacy*. London, 1641.

———. *The Substance of a Speech made in the House of Commons by William Prynne ... on Monday the fourth of December, 1648*. London, 1648.

Puttenham, G. *The Art of English Poesie*, ed. G. D. Willcock and A. Walker. Cambridge: Cambridge University Press, 1970.

Pyers Plowmans exhortation unto the lords, knights and burgoysses of the parlyamenthouse. London: ?, 1550.

Riley, H. T., ed. and trans. *Liber Albus: The White Book of The City of London*. London: Richard Griffin, 1861.

———. *Memorials of London and London Life in the Thirteenth, Fourteenth and Fifteenth Centuries*. London: Longman, 1868.

Robbins, R. H., ed. *Historical Poems of the XIVth and XVth Centuries*. New York: Columbia University Press, 1959.

Shakespeare, William. *Troilus and Cressida*, ed. D. Bevington. London: Arden, 1998.

————. *Love's Labours Lost*, ed. H. R. Woudhuysen. London: Arden, 1998.

————. *King Lear*, ed. R. A. Foakes. London: Arden, 2000.

————. *Hamlet*, ed. Anne Thompson and Neil Taylor. London: Arden, 2006.

Sidney, Philip. *A Defence of Poetry*, ed. J. van Dorsten. Oxford: Oxford University Press, 1966.

————. *The Countess of Pembroke's Arcadia*, ed. Maurice Evans. London: Penguin, 1977.

Skelton, John. *John Skelton: The Complete English Poems*, ed. J. Scattergood. London: Penguin, 1983.

Spenser, Edmund. *Edmund Spenser: The Shorter Poems*, ed. Richard McCabe. London: Penguin, 1999.

Sutcliffe, Matthew. *An Answere to a Certaine Libel*. London: Christopher Barker, 1592.

Swinburn, L. M., ed. *The Lanterne of Lighte*. EETS o.s. 151. London: Kegan Paul, 1917.

The Courte of Venus. London: T. Gibson, *c.* 1538, *STC* 2nd edn 24650.5.

The Lanterne of Light. London, Robert Redman, ?

The Prayer and Complaynt of the Ploweman unto Christ: written nat longe after the yere of our Lorde. M and thre hundred. London, *c.* 1532.

The Statutes of the Realm, 11 vols. London: Dawson, 1810, repr. 1963.

Throckmorton, Job(?). *A Petition directed to her most excellent Maiestie*. Middleburg, 1592.

Thynne, F. *Animadversions upon the Annotations and Corrections of some Imperfections of Impressions of Chaucer's Works*, eds G. Kingsley and F. Furnivall. EETS o.s. 9. London: Truebner, 1865.

Tyndale, W. *The Obedience of a Christian Man*, ed. D. Daniell. London: Penguin, 2000.

————. *The Work of William Tyndale*, ed. G. E. Duffield. London: Sutton Courtenay Press, 1964.

Virgil, *Eclogues, Georgics, Aeneid 1–6*, ed. and trans. H. Rushton Fairclough. London: Loeb Classical Library, 1916, repr. 1978.

Walsingham, Thomas. *Historia Anglicana*, ed. H. T. Riley. *RS* 1864.

Wilson, Thomas. *The Arte of Rhetorique*, ed. G. H. Mair. Oxford, Oxford University Press, 1909.

Wright, T. *Political Poems and Songs Relating to English History Composed During the Period from the Accession of Edward III to that of Richard III*. London: Camden Society, 1861.

Wyatt, Thomas. *The Complete Poems*, ed. T. R. A. Rebholz. London: Penguin, 1978.

Secondary Sources

Adkins, Mary G. M. 'The Genesis of Dramatic Satire against the Puritan, as Illustrated in *A Knack to Know a Knave*', *Review of English Studies*, 22 (1946), 81–95.

Aers, David. *Chaucer, Langland and the Creative Imagination*. London: Routledge, 1980.

————. 'Altars of Power', *Literature & History*, 3:2 (1994), 90–105.

————. 'The Humanity of Christ: Representations in Wycliffite Texts and *Piers Plowman*' in *The Powers of the Holy: Religion, Politics and Gender in Late Medieval English Culture*, ed. D. Aers and L. Staley. Philadelphia: University of Pennsylvania Press, 1996, pp. 43–76.

Aers, David and Staley, L., eds. *The Powers of the Holy: Religion, Politics and Gender in Late Medieval English Culture*. Philadelphia: University of Pennsylvania Press, 1996.

Alford, John, ed. *A Companion to Piers Plowman*. Berkeley: University of California Press, 1988.

————. 'Langland's Learning', *YLS*, 9 (1995), 1–17.

Alpers, Dear *the Invention of the Human*. New York: Riverhead Books, 1998.

Bolgar, R. R. *The Classical Heritage and its Beneficiaries*. Cambridge: Cambridge University Press, 1958.

Bolton, J. L. *The Medieval English Economy, 1150–1500*. London: Dent, 1980.

Born, H. *The Rare Wit and the Rude Groom: the Authorship of A Knack to Know a Knave in Relation to Greene, Nashe and Shakespeare*. Bern: Francke Verlag, 1971.

Borsay, P. 'Early Modern Urban Landscapes, 1540–1800' in *The English Urban Landscape*, ed. P. Waller. Oxford: Oxford University Press, 2000, pp. 99–124.

Bowers, John M. '*Piers Plowman* and the Police: Notes toward a History of the Wycliffite Langland', *YLS*, 6 (1992), 1–50.

————. *Chaucer and Langland: The Antagonistic Tradition*. Notre Dame, IN: University of Notre Dame Press, 2007.

Brewer, Charlotte. *Editing Piers Plowman: The Evolution of the Text*. Cambridge: Cambridge University Press, 1996.

Brigden, Susan. *London and the Reformation*. Oxford: Clarendon Press, 1989.

Britnell, R. H. *The Commercialisation of English Society, 1000–1500*. Cambridge: Cambridge University Press, 1993.

Brown, Peter, ed. *A Companion to Chaucer*. Blackwell: Oxford, 2000.

Burrow, J. 'The Action of Langland's Second Vision', *Essays in Criticism*, 15 (1965), 247–68, repr. in *Style and Symbolism in Piers Plowman*, ed. Robert J. Blanche. Knoxville: University of Tennessee Press, 1969, pp. 209–27.

Burton, J. B. *Theocritus' Urban Mimes: Mobility, Gender, Patronage*. Berkeley: University of California Press, 1995.

Cameron, K. W. *The Authorship and Sources of 'Gentleness and Nobility': A Study in Early Tudor Drama*. Raleigh, NC: Thistle Press, 1941.

Camille, Michael. '"When Adam Delved": Labouring on the Land in English Medieval Art' in *Agriculture in the Middle Ages, Technologies, Practise and Representation*, ed. D. Sweeny. Philadelphia: University of Pennsylvania Press, 1995, pp. 247–76.

Carlson, Leland H. *Martin Marprelate, Gentleman: Master Job Throkmorton Laid Open in his Colors*. San Marino: Huntingdon Library, 1981.

Carrel, H. 'Food, Drink and Public Order in the London *Liber Albus*', *Urban History*, 33:2 (2006), 176–94.

Carter Hailey, R. '"Geuyng light to the Reader": Robert Crowley's Editions of *Piers Plowman* (1550)', *Publications of the Bibliographic Society of America*, 95:4 (2001), 483–502.

––––––. 'Robert Crowley and the Editing of Piers Plowman (1550)', *YLS*, 21 (2007), 143–70.

Chadwick, David. *Social Life in the Days of Piers Plowman* Cambridge: Cambridge University Press, 1922.

Chadwick, Henry. *The Early Church*. London: Penguin, 1967.

Chambers, E. K. *The Elizabethan Stage*. Oxford: Clarendon Press, 1923.

Cirino, A. and Raischl, J., eds. *Franciscan Solitude*. New York: Franciscan Institute, 1995.

Clarke, P., Smith, A. and Tyacke, N., eds. *The English Commonwealth, 1547–1640: Essays on Politics and Society Presented to Joel Hurstfield*. Leicester: Leicester University Press, 1979.

Clebsch, W. A. *England's Earliest Protestants, 1520–1535*. New Haven: Yale University Press, 1964.

Clegg, Cyndia Susan. *Press Censorship in Elizabethan England*. Cambridge: Cambridge University Press, 1997.

Clopper, Lawrence M. 'Need Men and Women Labor? Langland's Wanderer and the Labor Ordinances' in *Chaucer's England: Literature in Historical Context*, ed. Barbara Hanawalt. Minneapolis: University of Minnesota Press, 1992.

––––––. *Songes of Rechlesnesse: Langland and the Franciscans*. Ann Arbor: University of Michigan Press, 1997.

––––––. 'Franciscans, Lollards, and Reform' in *Lollards and their Influence*, ed. Somerset et al. Woodbridge: Boydell Press, 2003, pp. 177–96.

Coetzee, J. M. *White Writing: On the Culture of Letters in South* Africa. New Haven: Yale University Press, 1988.

Coghill, N. K. 'The Pardon of Piers Plowman', *Preceedings of the British Academy*, 30 (1944), 303–57.

Cole, Andrew. 'William Langland and the Invention of Lollardy' in *Lollards and Their Influence in Late Medieval England*, ed. F. Somerset et al. Woodbridge: Boydell Press, 2003, pp. 37–58.

––––––. *Literature and Heresy in the Age of Chaucer*. Cambridge: Cambridge University Press, 2008.

Collette, Carolyn. 'Afterlife' in *A Companion to Chaucer*, ed. Peter Brown. Oxford: Blackwell, 2000, pp. 8–22.

Collinson, Patrick. *The Elizabethan Puritan Movement*. London: Cape, 1967.

————. 'Ecclesiastical Vitriol: Religious Satire in the 1590s and the Invention of Puritanism' in *The Reign of Elizabeth I: Court and Culture in the Last Decade*, ed. John Guy. Cambridge: Cambridge University Press, 1995, pp. 150–70.

————. 'English Reformations' in *A Companion to English Renaissance Literature and Culture*, ed. M. Hattaway. Blackwell: Oxford, 2000, pp. 27–43.

Contamine, P. *War in the Middle Ages*, trans. Michael Jones. Oxford: Blackwell, 1984.

Cooper, Helen. *Pastoral: Mediaeval to Renaissance*. Cambridge: D. S. Brewer, 1977.

————. 'Langland's and Chaucer's Prologues', *YLS*, 1 (1987), 71–81.

————. *The English Romance in Time: Transforming Motifs from Geoffrey of Monmouth to Shakespeare*. Oxford: Oxford University Press, 2004.

Coote, L. A. *Prophecy and Public Affairs in Later Medieval England*. York: York Medieval Press, 2000.

Cox, John D. *The Devil and the Sacred in English Drama, 1350–1642*. Cambridge: Cambridge University Press, 2000.

Crane, M. T. 'Early Tudor Humanism' in *A Companion to English Renaissance Literature and Culture*, ed. Michael Hattaway. Oxford: Blackwell, 2000, pp. 13–26.

Crewe, Jonathan V. *Unredeemed Rhetoric: Thomas Nashe and the Scandal of Authorship*. Baltimore: Johns Hopkins University Press, 1982.

Cummings, Brian. *The Literary Culture of the Reformation: Grammar and Grace*. Oxford: Oxford University Press, 2002.

Curtius, E. R. *European Literature and the Latin Middle Ages*, trans. W. R. Trask. Princeton: Princeton University Press, 1953.

Daniell, David. *William Tyndale: A Biography*. New Haven: Yale University Press, 1994.

Davies, Charlotte. *A Religion of the Word: The Defence of the Reformation in the Reign of Edward VI*. Manchester: Manchester University Press, 2002.

Davis, Isabel. *Writing Masculinity in the Later Middle Ages*. Cambridge: Cambridge University Press, 2007.

Dessen, Alan C. 'The "Estates" Morality Play', *Studies in Philology*, 62 (1965), 121–36.

Dickens, A. G. 'The Shape of Anti-clericalism and the English Reformation' in *Politics and Society in Reformation Europe: Essays for Sir Geoffrey Elton*, ed. E. Kouin and T. Scott. New York: St. Martin's Press, 1987, pp. 379–410.

Dimmick, J., Simpson, J. and Zeeman, N., eds. *Images, Idolatry, and Iconoclasm in Late Medieval England. Textuality and the Visual Image*. Oxford: Oxford University Press, 2002.

Dobin, H. *Merlin's Disciples: Prophecy, Poetry and Power in Renaissance England*. Stanford: Stanford University Press, 1990.

Dollimore, Jonathan. *Radical Tragedy: Religion, Ideology and Power in the Drama of Shakespeare and his Contemporaries*. London: Harvester Wheatsheaf, 1989.

Donaldson, E. T. *Piers Plowman: The C-Text and Its Poet*. New Haven: Yale University Press, 1949.

Du Boulay, F. R. *The England of Piers Plowman: William Langland and his Vision of the Fourteenth Century*. Cambridge: D. S. Brewer, 1991.

Duffy, Eamon. *The Stripping of the Altars: Traditional Religion in England 1400– 1580*. New Haven: Yale University Press, 1992.

Duncan-Jones, Katherine. *Sir Philip Sidney: Courtier Poet*. Oxford: Oxford University Press, 1991.

Dyer, Christopher. *Standards of Living in the later Middle Ages, Social Change in England c. 1200–1520*. Cambridge: Cambridge University Press, 1989.

———. 'Piers Plowman and Plowmen: A Historical Perspective', *YLS*, 8 (1994), 155–76.

———. *Making a Living in the Middle Ages: The People of Britain, 850–1520*. New Haven: Yale University Press, 2002.

Ellis, Steve. *Chaucer: An Oxford Guide*. Oxford: Oxford University Press, 2005.

Elton, G. R. 'Reform and the "Commonwealths-men" of Edward VI's Reign' in *The English Commonwealth, 1547–1640: Essays on Politics and Society Presented to Joel Hurstfield*, eds P. Clarke, A. Smith and N. Tyacke. Leicester: Leicester University Press, 1979, pp. 23–38.

Empson, William. *Some Versions of Pastoral*. London: Chatto and Windus, 1935, repr. Penguin, 1995.

Ferster, Judith. *Fictions of Advice: The Literature and Politics of Counsel in Late Medieval England*. Philadelphia: University of Pennsylvania Press, 1996.

Fox, Alistair. *Thomas More: History and Providence*. Oxford: Blackwell, 1982.

———. 'Prophecies and Politics in the Reign of Henry VIII' in *Reassessing the Henrician Age: Humanism, Politics and Reform, 1500–1550*, eds A. Fox and J. Guy. Oxford: Blackwell, 1986, pp. 77–94.

———. *Politics and Literature in the Reigns of Henry VII and Henry VIII*. Oxford: Blackwell, 1989.

Fox, Alistair and Guy, John, eds. *Reassessing the Henrician Age: Humanism, Politics and Reform, 1500–1550*. Oxford: Blackwell, 1986.

Frank, R. W. 'The Pardon Scene in *Piers Plowman*', *Speculum*, 26 (1951), 317– 31.

Freedman, Paul. *Images of the Medieval Peasant*. Stanford: Stanford University Press, 1999.

Friedrichs, C. R. *The Early Modern City, 1450–1750*. London: Longman, 1995.

Galloway, Andy. *The Penn Commentary on Piers Plowman*, vol. 1. Philadelphia: University of Pennsylvania Press, 2006.

Geremek, B. *Poverty: A History*, trans. A. Kolakowska. Oxford: Blackwell, 1994.

Gersh, S. and Roest, B., eds. *Medieval and Renaissance Humanism: Rhetoric, Representation and Reform*. Leiden: Brill, 2003.

Ghosh, Kantik. *The Wycliffite Heresy: Authority and the Interpretation of Texts*. Cambridge: Cambridge University Press, 2002.

————. 'Bishop Reginald Pecock and the Idea of "Lollardy"' in *Text and Controversy from Wyclif to Bale: Essays in Honour of Anne Hudson*, eds H. Barr and Anne Hutchison. Turnhout: Brepolis, 2005, pp. 251–65.

Gibbon, E. *The Decline and Fall of the Roman Empire*, 3 vols. New York: Modern Library, 1932.

Gillespie, Alexandra. *Print Culture and the Medieval Author: Chaucer, Lydgate and their Books, 1473–1557*. Oxford: Oxford University Press, 2006.

Gilmont, J. *The Reformation and the Book*, trans. K. Maag. Aldershot: Ashgate, 1990.

Gleason, J. B. *John Colet*. Berkeley: University of California Press, 1989.

Godden, Malcolm. *The Making of Piers Plowman*. London: Longman, 1990.

Goehring, J. 'The Dark Side of Landscape: Ideology and Power in the Christian Myth of the Desert', *Journal of Medieval and Modern Studies*, 33 (2003), 437–51.

Gordon, B. 'The Changing Face of Protestant History and Identity in the Sixteenth Century' in *Protestant History and Identity in Sixteenth Century Europe*, ed. B. Gordon. Aldershot: Aldershot, 1996, vol. 1: *The Medieval Inheritance*, 1–22.

Gordon, Bruce, ed. *Protestant History and Identity in Sixteenth Century Europe*, 2 vols. Aldershot: Aldershot, 1996.

Gradon, Pamala. 'Langland and the Ideology of Dissent', *Proceedings of the British Academy*, 66 (1980), 179–209.

Gray, D. and Stanley, E. G. *Middle English Studies*. Oxford: Clarendon Press, 1983.

Green, Ian. *Print and Protestantism in Early Modern England*. Oxford: Oxford University Press, 2000.

Green, R. F. 'John Ball's Letters: Literary History and Historical Literature' in *Chaucer's England: Literature in Historical Context*, ed. B. Hanawalt. Minneapolis: University of Minnesota Press, 1992, pp. 176–200.

Greenblatt, Stephen. *Renaissance Self-Fashioning: from More to Shakespeare*. London: University of Chicago Press, 1980.

————. *Hamlet in Purgatory*. Princeton: Princeton University Press, 2001.

Gurr, Andrew. *The Shakespearian Stage, 1574–1642*. Cambridge: Cambridge University Press, 1970.

————. *The Shakespearian Playing Companies*. Oxford: Clarendon Press, 1996.

Guy, John, ed. *The Reign of Elizabeth I: Court and Culture in the Last Decade*. Cambridge: Cambridge University Press, 1995.

Hadfield, Andrew, ed. *Edmund Spenser*. London: Longman, 1996.

Haigh, Christopher. *The English Reformation Revised*. Cambridge: Cambridge University Press, 1987.

Hamilton, A. C. 'The Visions of *Piers Plowman* and *The Faerie Queene*' in *Form and Convention in the Poetry of Edmund Spenser*, ed. William Nelson. New York: Columbia University Press, 1961, pp. 1–34.

Hanawalt, Barbara, ed., *Chaucer's England: Literature in Historical Context*. Minneapolis: University of Minnesota Press, 1992.

Hanna III, R. 'Will's Work' in *Written Work: Langland, Labour and Authorship*, eds S. Justice and K. Kerby-Fulton. Philadelphia: University of Pennsylvania Press, 1997, pp. 23–66.

Hanrahan, Michael. 'Speaking of Sodomy: Gower's Advice to Princes in the *Confessio Amantis*', *Exemplaria*, 14 (2002), 423–46.

Hardwick, Paul. '"Biddeth Peres Ploughman Go to his werk": Appropriations of *Piers Plowman* in the Nineteenth and Twentieth Centuries', *Studies in Medievalism*, 12 (2002), 171–95.

Hattaway, Michael. *A Companion to English Renaissance Literature and Culture*. Oxford: Blackwell, 2000.

Havely, N. R. 'Feeding the Flock with Wind: Protestant uses of a Dantean Trope, from Foxe to Milton' in *John Foxe at Home and Abroad*, ed. D. Loades. Aldershot: Ashgate, 2004, pp. 91–104.

————. *Dante and the Franciscans: Poverty and the Papacy in the Commedia*. Cambridge: University of Cambridge Press, 2005.

Havens, Jill C., Pitard, Derrick G. and Somerset, Fiona, eds. *Lollardy and Its Influence in Late Medieval England*. Woodbridge: Boydell, 2003.

Heffernan, Thomas. 'Aspects of the Chaucerian Apocrypha: Animadversions on William Thynne's Edition of the *Plowman's Tale*' in *Chaucer Traditions: Studies in Honour of Derek Brewer*, eds R. Morse and B. Windeatt. Cambridge: Cambridge University Press, 1990, pp. 155–67.

Helgerson, Richard. *The Elizabethan Prodigals*. Berkeley: University of California Press, 1976.

Hellinga, L. and Trapp, J. B. 'Introduction' in *The Cambridge History of the Book in Britain*, vol. 3, eds L. Hellinga and J. B. Trapp. Cambridge: Cambridge University Press, 1999.

————. *The Cambridge History of the Book in Britain*, vol. 3. Cambridge: Cambridge University Press, 1999.

Hewett-Smith, K. M., ed. *William Langland's Piers Plowman: A Book of Essays*. London: Routledge, 2001.

Heyworth, P. L. 'The Earlist Black-letter Editions of *Jack Upland*', *Huntingdon Library Quarterly*, 30 (1967), 307–14.

Hill, Christopher. 'From Lollards to Levellers' in *Religion and Rural Rebellion*, eds J. Bak and G. Benecke. Manchester: Manchester University Press, 1984, pp. 86–103.

Hilliard, Stephen S. *The Singularity of Thomas Nashe*. Lincoln: University of Nebraska Press, 1986.

Holbrook, P. *Literature and Degree in Renaissance England: Nashe, Bourgeois Tragedy and Shakespeare*. Newark: University of Deleware Press, 1994.

Horobin, Simon and Mooney, L. R. 'A *Piers Plowman* Manuscript by the Hengwrt/ Ellesmere Scribe and Its Implications for London Standard English', *Studies in the Age of Chaucer*, 26 (2004), 65–112.

Hoskins, W. G. *The Age of Plunder: The England of Henry VIII, 1500–1547*. London: Longman, 1976.

Hudson, Anne. '"No newe thyng": The Printing of Medieval Texts in the Early Reformation Period' in *Middle English Studies*, eds D. Gray and E. G. Stanley. Oxford: Clarendon Press, 1983, pp. 153–74.

————. *Lollards and Their Books*. London: Hambledon Press, 1985.

————. *The Premature Reformation*. Oxford: Oxford University Press, 1988.

————. 'Epilogue: The Legacy of *Piers Plowman*' in *A Companion to Piers Plowman*, ed. John Alford. Berkeley: University of California Press, 1988, pp. 251–66

————. '*Piers Plowman* and the Peasants' Revolt: A Problem Revisited', *YLS*, 8 (1994), 85–106.

————. 'Laicus Litteratus: the Paradox of Lollardy' in *Heresy and Literacy, 1000–1530*, eds P. Biller and A. Hudson. Cambridge: Cambridge University Press, 1994.

Hunt, A. *Governance of the Consuming Passions: A History of Sumptuary Law*. London: Macmillan, 1996.

Hunter, G. K. *The Oxford History of English Literature: English Drama 1586– 1642, The Age of Shakespeare*. Oxford: Clarendon Press, 1997.

Hussey, S. S., ed. *Piers Plowman: Critical Approaches*. London: Methuen, 1969.

Hutson, Lorna. *Thomas Nashe in Context*. Oxford: Clarendon Press, 1989.

Jansen, Sharon. L. *Political Protest and Prophecy under Henry VIII*. Woodbridge: Boydell Press, 1991.

Johnston, Michael. 'From Edward III to Edward VI: *The Vision of Piers Plowman* and Early Modern England', *Reformation*, 11 (2006), 47–78.

Jones, Eric. 'Langland and Hermits', *YLS*, 11 (1997), 67–86.

Justice, Steven. *Writing and Rebellion: England in 1381*. Berkeley: University of California Press, 1994.

Justice, Steven and Kerby-Fulton, Kathryn, eds. *Written Work: Langland, Labor and Authorship*. Philadelphia: University of Pennsylvania Press, 1997.

————. 'Langlandian Reading Circles and the Civil Service in London and Dublin, 1380–1427', *New Medieval Literatures*, 1 (1997), 59–83.

Kaske, R. E. 'The Character Hunger in *Piers Plowman*' in *Medieval English Studies Presented to George Kane*, ed. E. D. Kennedy et al. Woodbridge: D. S. Brewer, 1988, pp. 187–97.

Keen, M. H. *English Society in the Later Middle Ages 1348–1500*. London: Penguin, 1990.

Kelen, Sarah A. 'Plowing the Past: "Piers Protestant" and the Authority of Medieval Literary History', *YLS*, 13 (1999), 101–36.

————. *Langland's Early Modern Identities*. London: Palgrave, 2007.

Kelly, R. L. 'Hugh Latimer as Piers Plowman', *Studies in English Literature*, 17 (1977), 13–26.

Kendall, Ritchie. *The Drama of Dissent: The Radical Poetics of Non-Conformity, 1380–1590*. Chapel Hill: University of North Carolina Press, 1986.

Kenney, E. J. 'The Age of Augustus' in *The Cambridge History of Classical Literature*, ed. E. J. Kenney, Cambridge: Cambridge University Press, 1982.

Kennedy, E. D., Waldron, R. and Witting, J. S., eds. *Medieval English Studies Presented to George Kane*. Woodbridge: D. S. Brewer, 1988.

Kerby-Fulton, Kathryn. 'Langland and the Bibliographic Ego' in *Written Work: Langland, Labor and Authorship*, eds S. Justice and K. Kerby-Fulton. Philadelphia: University of Pennsylvania Press, 1997, pp. 67–143.

Kernan, Alvin. *The Cankered Muse: Satire of the English Renaissance*. New Haven: Yale University Press, 1959.

Kerridge, E. *The Agricultural Revolution*. London: Allen and Unwin, 1967.

Kim, M. 'Hunger, Need and the Politics of Poverty in *Piers Plowman*', *YLS*, 16 (2002), 131–68.

King, John N. *Reformation Literature: the Tudor Origins of the Protestant Tradition*. Princeton: Princeton University Press, 1982.

————. 'Spenser's *Shepheardes Calender* and Protestant Pastoral Satire' in *Renaissance Genres: Essays on Theory, History and Interpretation*, ed. B. K. Lewalski. London: Harvard University Press, 1986.

————. *Tudor Royal Iconography: Literature and Art in the Age of Religious Crisis*. Princeton: Princeton University Press, 1989.

————. *Spenser's Poetry and the Reformation Tradition*. Princeton: Princeton University Press, 1990.

Kirk, Elizabeth D. 'Langland's Plowman and the Recreation of Fourteenth-Century Religious Metaphor', *YLS*, 2 (1988), 1–21.

Kouin, E. and Scott, T., eds. *Politics and Society in Reformation Europe: Essays for Sir Geoffrey Elton*. New York: St. Martin's Press, 1987.

Kuskin, William. 'Caxton's Worthies Series: The Production of Literary Culture', *English Literary History*, 66 (1999), 511–51.

Lake, Peter with Questier, Michael. *The Antichrist's Lewd Hat: Protestants, Papists and Players in Post-Reformation England*. New Haven: Yale University Press, 2002.

Lawrence, C. H. *Medieval Monasticism: Forms of Religious Life in Western Europe in the Middle Ages*. London: Longman, 1984.

Lawton, David. 'Lollardy and the Piers Plowman Tradition', *Modern Language Review*, 76 (1981), 780–793.

————. 'Dullness in the Fifteenth-Century', *English Literary History*, 54 (1987), 761–90.

Leff, G. *Heresy in the Later Middle Ages: the Relation of Heterodoxy to Dissent, 1250–1450*. Manchester: Manchester University Press, 1967.

Lewalski, Barbara K., ed. *Renaissance Genres: Essays on Theory, History and Interpretation*. London: Harvard University Press, 1986.

Lewis, C. S. *English Literature in the Sixteenth Century, Excluding Drama.* Oxford: Clarendon Press, 1954.

Lewis, R. E., Kurath, H., Kuhn, S. A. and Reidy, J., eds. *The Middle English Dictionary*, 24 vols. Ann Arbor: University of Michigan Press, 1952–2002.

Lindenbaum, S. 'London Texts and Literary Practice' in *Cambridge History of Medieval English Literature*, ed. D. Wallace. Cambridge: Cambridge University Press, 1999, pp. 284–309.

Little, Lester. K. *Religious Poverty and the Profit Economy in Medieval Europe.* Ithaca: Cornell University Press, 1978.

Loades, David. 'Books and the English Reformation prior to 1558' in *The Reformation and the Book*, ed. Jean-Francois Gilmont, trans. K. Maag. Aldershot: Ashgate, 1990, pp. 264–91.

————, ed., *John Foxe at Home and Abroad.* Aldershot: Ashgate, 2004.

Lock, J. 'Plantagenets against the Papacy: Protestant England's Search for Royal Heroes' in *Protestant History and Identity*, ed. B. Gordon, 2 vols. Aldershot: Ashgate, 1996, I. pp. 153–73.

MacCulloch, Diarmaid. *Tudor Church Militant: Edward VI and the Protestant Reformation.* London: Penguin, 1999.

————. *Reformation: Europe's House Divided, 1490–1700.* London: Penguin, 2003.

MacCulloch, Diarmaid and Fletcher, A. *Tudor Rebellions.* London: Longman, 1997.

McGinnis, M. E. *Piers the Plowman in England, 1362–1625, A Study in Popularity and Influence.* Unpublished PhD Thesis, Yale, 1970.

McKerrow, Ronald B. *Printers' & Publishers' Devices in England & Scotland, 1485–1640.* London: Bibliographical Society, 1913.

McLane, P. E. *Spenser's Shepheardes Calender: A Study in Elizabethan Allegory.* Notre Dame, IN: University of Notre Dame Press, 1961.

McMullan, Gordon and Matthews, David, eds. *Reading the Medieval in Early Modern England.* Cambridge: Cambridge University Press, 2007.

McRae, Andrew. *God Spede the Plough: The Representation of Agrarian England, 1500–1660.* Cambridge: Cambridge University Press, 1996.

McSheffrey, Shanon. *Gender and Heresy: Women and Men in Lollard Communities, 1410–1530.* Philadelphia: University of Pennsylvania Press, 1995.

Maddison, F., Pelling, M. and Webester, C., eds. *Essays on the Life and work of Thomas Linacre.* Oxford: Clarendon Press, 1977.

Manley, L. *Literature and Culture in Early Modern London.* Cambridge: Cambridge University Press, 1995.

Mann, Jill. *Chaucer and Medieval Estates Satire.* Cambridge: Cambridge University Press, 1973.

Marshall, Peter. *Religious Identities in Henry VIII's England.* Aldershot: Ashgate, 2006.

Marshall, Peter and Ryrie, Alec, eds. *The Beginnings of English Protestantism.* Cambridge: Cambridge University Press, 2002.

Matthews, David. 'The Medieval Invasion of Early-Modern England', *New Medieval Literatures*, 10 (2008), 223–44.

Meyer-Lee, Robert. *Poets and Power from Chaucer to Wyatt*. Cambridge: Cambridge University Press, 2007.

Middleton, Ann. 'The Idea of Public Poetry in the Reign of Richard II', *Speculum*, 53 (1978), 94–114.

Mollat, M. *The Poor in the Middle Ages: An Essay in Social History*, trans. A. Goldhammer. New Haven: Yale University Press, 1986.

Montrose, Louis. '"The perfect paterne of a poete": The Poetics of Courtship in *The Shepheardes Calender*' in *Edmund Spenser*, ed. A. Hadfield. London: Longman, 1996, pp. 30–63.

Morgan, C. *Godly Learning: Puritan Attitudes Towards Reason, Learning and Education, 1560–1640*. Cambridge: Cambridge University Press, 1986.

Morse, R. and Windeatt, B., eds. *Chaucer Traditions: Studies in Honour of Derek Brewer*. Cambridge: Cambridge University Press, 1990.

Mueller, Janel. 'Literature and the Church' in *The Cambridge History of Early Modern English Literature*, ed. Janel Mueller and David Lowenstein. Cambridge: Cambridge University Press, 2002, pp. 257–309.

Mueller, Janel and Lowenstein, David, eds. *The Cambridge History of Early Modern English Literature*. Cambridge: Cambridge University Press, 2002.

Nelson, W. ed. *Form and Convention in the Poetry of Edmund Spenser*. New York: Columbia University Press, 1961.

Neville-Sington, P. 'Press, Politics and Religion' in *The Cambridge History of the Book in Britain*, vol. 3, eds L. Hellinga and J. B. Trapp. Cambridge: Cambridge University Press, 1999.

Nichol, Charles. *A Cup of News: The Life of Thomas Nashe*. London: Routledge and Kegan Paul, 1984.

Nightingale, Pamala. 'Capitalists, Crafts and Constitutional Change in Late Fourteenth-Century London', *Past and Present*, 124 (1989), 3–35.

Norbrook, David. *Poetry and Politics in the English Renaissance*. London: Routledge, 1984.

Norskov Olsen, V. *John Foxe and the Elizabethan Church*. Berkeley: University of California Press, 1973.

North, Marcy L. *The Anonymous Renaissance: Cultures of Discretion in Tudor-Stuart England*. Chicago: University of Chicago Press, 2003.

Owst, G. R. *Literature and Pulpit: A Neglected Chapter in the History of English Letters and of the English People*. Oxford: Blackwell, 1961.

Palliser, D., ed. *The Cambridge Urban History of Britain*, 3 vols. Cambridge: Cambridge University Press, 2000.

Patterson, Annabel. *Pastoral and Ideology: Virgil to Valéry*. Oxford: Oxford University Press, 1988.

————. *Reading between the Lines*. London: Routledge, 1992.

Patterson, Lee, ed. *Literary Practise and Social Change in Britain, 1380–1530*. Berkeley: University of California Press, 1990.

Paxson, J. J. *The Poetics of Personification*. Cambridge: Cambridge University Press, 1994.

Pearsall, Derek. 'Langland's London' in *Written Work: Langland, Labor and Authorship*, eds S. Justice and K. Kerby-Fulton. Philadelphia: University of Pennsylvania Press, 1997, pp. 185–207.

Pearsall, Derek and Salter, Elizabeth. *Landscapes and Seasons in the Medieval World*. London: Paul Elek, 1973.

————. 'The Apotheosis of John Lydgate', *Journal of Medieval and Early Modern Studies*, 35:1 (2005), 25–38.

Peikola, M. *Congregation of the Elect: Patterns of Self-Fashioning in English Lollard Writings*. Turku: University of Turku Press, 2000.

Perkins, Nicolas. *Hoccleve's Regiment of Princes: Counsel and Constraint*. Cambridge: D. S. Brewer, 2001.

Perry, Curtis. *Literature and Favoritism in Early Modern England*. Cambridge: Cambridge University Press, 2006.

Peter, John. *Complaint and Satire in Early English Literature*. Oxford: Clarendon Press, 1956.

Plumb, Derek. 'The Social and Economic Status of the Later Lollards' in *The World of Rural Dissenters, 1520–1725*, ed. M. Spufford. Cambridge: Cambridge University Press, 1995, pp. 103–31.

————. 'A Gathered Church? Lollards and their Society' in *The World of Rural Dissenters, 1520–1725*, ed. M. Spufford. Cambridge: Cambridge University Press, 1995, pp. 132–63.

Poole, Kristen. 'Saints Alive! Falstaff, Martin Marprelate, and the Staging of Puritanism'. *Shakespeare Quarterly*, 46 (1995), 47–75.

Raymond, Joad. *Pamphlets and Pamphleteering in Early Modern Britain*. Cambridge: Cambridge University Press, 2003.

Rex, Richard. *The Lollards*. London: Palgrave, 2002.

————. 'The Friars in the English Reformation', in *The Beginnings of English Protestantism*, eds Peter Marshall and Alec Ryrie. Cambridge: Cambridge University Press, 2002, pp. 38–59.

Rhodes, Neil. *Elizabethan Grotesque*. London: Routledge & Kegan Paul, 1980.

Ronan, N. '1381: Writing in Revolt. Signs of Confederacy in the Chronicle Accounts of the English Rising', *Forum for Modern Language Studies*, 25 (1989), 301–14.

Rundle, David. 'Humanism before the Tudors: On Nobility and the Reception of the "Studia Humanitatis" in Fifteenth-Century England' in *Reassessing Tudor Humanism*, ed. J. Woolfson. Basingstoke: Palgrave, 2002, pp. 22–42.

Rydzeski, J. *Radical Nostalgia in the Age of Piers Plowman: Economics, Apocalypticism and Discontent*. New York: Peter Lang, 1999.

Ryrie, Alec. 'The Problem of Legitimacy and Precedent in English Protestantism, 1539–47' in *Protestant History and Identity*, ed. B. Gordon, 2 vols. Aldershot: Ashgate, 1996, I. pp. 78–92.

—————. *The Gospel and Henry VIII: Evangelicals in the Early English Reformation.* Cambridge: Cambridge University Press, 2003.

Salter, Elizabeth. *Fourteenth Century English Poetry: Contexts and Readings.* Oxford: Clarendon Press, 1983.

Saul, Nigel. *Richard II.* New Haven: Yale University Press, 1997.

Saward, J. *Perfect Fools: Folly for Christ's Sake in Catholic and Orthodox Spirituality.* Oxford: Oxford University Press, 1980.

Scanlon, Larry. 'Langland, Apocalypse and the Early Modern Editor' in *Reading the Medieval in Early Modern England*, eds Gordon McMullan and David Matthews. Cambridge: Cambridge University Press, 2007, pp. 51–73.

Scarisbrick, J. J. *The Reformation and the English People.* Oxford: Oxford University Press, 1984.

Scase, Wendy. *Piers Plowman and the New Anticlericalism.* Cambridge: Cambridge University Press, 1989.

—————. *Literature and Complaint in England, 1272–1553.* Oxford: Oxford University Press, 2007.

—————. '*Dauy Dycars Dreame* and Robert Crowley's Prints of *Piers Plowman*', *YLS*, 21 (2007), 171–98.

Scattergood, John. 'Misrepresenting the City: Genre, Intertextuality and William FitzStephen's Description of London' in *Reading the Past: Essays on Medieval and Renaissance Literature*. Dublin: Four Courts Press, 1996, pp. 15–36.

Schoff, Rebecca L. '*Piers Plowman* and Tudor Regulation of the Press', *YLS*, 20 (2006), 93–114.

Shepherd, S. H. A. 'Langland's Romances' in *William Langland's Piers Plowman: A Book of Essays*, ed. Kathleen M. Hewett-Smith. London: Routledge, 2001, pp. 69–81.

Shrank, Cathy. 'John Bale and Reconfiguring the "Medieval" in Reformation England', in *Reading the Medieval in Early Modern England*, eds Gordon McMullan and David Matthews. Cambridge: Cambridge University Press, 2007, pp. 179–92.

Simpson, James. 'Spirituality and Economics in Passus 1–7 of the B Text', *YLS*, 1 (1987), 83–103.

—————. *Piers Plowman: An Introduction to the B-Text.* London: Longman, 1990.

—————. 'Grace Abounding: Evangelical Centralisation and the End of *Piers Plowman*', *YLS*, 14 (2000), 49–73.

—————. *Reform and Cultural Revolution.* Oxford: Oxford University Press, 2002.

—————. *Burning to Read: English Fundamentalism and it Reformation Opponents.* Cambridge, MA: Belknap Press of Harvard University Press, 2007.

Simpson, Percy. *Proof-Reading in the Sixteenth Seventeenth and Eighteenth Centuries.* Oxford: Oxford University Press, 1935, repr. 1970.

Skura, Meredith Anne. *Shakespeare the Actor and the Purposes of Playing.* Chicago: University of Chicago Press, 1993.

Smith, A. *Traditional Imagery of Charity in Piers Plowman*. Paris: Mouton, 1966.

Somerset, Fiona. *Clerical Discourse and Lay Audience in Late Medieval England*. Cambridge: Cambridge University Press, 1998.

————. 'Wycliffite Spirituality' in *Text and Controversy from Wyclif to Bale*, eds Helen Barr and A. Hutchison. Turnhout: Brepolis, 2005, pp. 375–86.

Southern, R. W. *Western Society and the Church in the Middle Ages*. London: Penguin, 1970.

Sponsler, Claire. *Drama and Resistance: Bodies, Goods and Theatricality in Late Medieval England*. Minneapolis: University of Minnesota Press, 1997.

Spufford, M., ed. *The World of Rural Dissenters, 1520–1725*. Cambridge: Cambridge University Press, 1995.

Stanbury, Sarah. 'The Vivacity of Images: St. Katherine, Knighton's Lollards, and the Breaking of Idols' in *Images, Idolatry, and Iconoclasm in Late Medieval England: Textuality and the Visual Image*, ed. J. Dimmick, J. Simpson and N. Zeeman. Oxford: Oxford University Press, 2002, pp. 131–50.

Stearns, M. W. *Robert Henryson*. New York: Columbia University Press, 1949, repr. 1966.

Strohm, Paul. *Social Chaucer*. Cambridge: Harvard University Press, 1989.

————. 'Politics and Poetics: Usk and Chaucer in the 1380s' in *Literary Practise and Social Change in Britain, 1380–1530*, ed. L. Patterson. Berkeley: University of California Press, 1990, pp. 83–112.

Summit, Jennifer. *Lost Property: The Woman Writer and English Literary History, 1380–1589*. Chicago: University of Chicago Press, 2000.

Swanson, R. N. *Religion and Devotion in Europe, c. 1215 – c. 1515*. Cambridge: Cambridge University Press, 1995.

Sweeny, D., ed. *Agriculture in the Middle Ages, Technologies, Practise and Representation*. Philadelphia: University of Pennsylvania Press, 1995.

Sykes, H. Douglas. 'The Authorship of *A Knack to Know a Knave*', *Notes & Queries*, 146 (1924).

Szittya, P. R. *The Antifraternal Tradition in Medieval Literature*. Princeton: Princeton University Press, 1986.

Taithe, B. and Thornton, T., eds. *Prophecy: The Power of Inspired Language in History, 1300–2000*. Stroud: Sutton, 1997.

Tawney, R. H. *The Agrarian Problem in the Sixteenth Century*. London: Franklin, 1912.

————. *Religion and the Rise of Capitalism*. London: John Murray, 1929.

Thirsk, Joan. *The Agrarian History of England and Wales*, vol. 4, 1500–1640. Cambridge: Cambridge University Press, 1967.

Thompson, J. J. 'Reception: Fifteenth to Seventeenth Centuries' in *Chaucer: An Oxford Guide*, ed. Steve Ellis. Oxford: Oxford University Press, 2005, pp. 497–511.

Thorne, J. R. and Uhart, M. 'Robert Crowley's *Piers Plowman*', *Medium Aevum*, 55:2 (1986), 248–53.

Trapp, J. B. *Erasmus, Colet and More: The Early Tudor Humanists and their Books*. London: British Library Publications, 1991.

————. 'The Humanist Book' in *The Cambridge History of the Book in Britain*, vol. 3, 1400–1557, eds L. Hellinga and J. B. Trapp. Cambridge: Cambridge University Press, 1999, pp. 285–315.

Tribble, Evelyn. B. *Margins and Marginality: The Printed Page in Early Modern England*. Virginia: University of Virginia Press, 1993.

Turner, J. *The Politics of Landscape: Rural Scenery and Society in English Poetry, 1630–1660*. Cambridge, MA: Harvard University Press, 1979.

Turville-Petre, Thorlac. 'Sir Adrian Fortescue and his Copy of *Piers Plowman*', *YLS*, 14 (2000), 29–48.

Tyacke, Nicholas. *Aspects of English Protestantism c. 1530–1700*. Manchester: Manchester University Press, 2001.

Walker, Greg. *John Skelton and the Politics of the 1520s*. Cambridge: Cambridge University Press, 1988.

————. *Plays of Persuasion: Drama and Politics at the Court of Henry VIII*. Cambridge: Cambridge University Press, 1991.

————. *Writing under Tyranny: English Literature and the Henrician Reformation*. Oxford: Oxford University Press, 2007.

Wallace, David, ed. *Cambridge History of Medieval English Literature*. Cambridge: Cambridge University Press, 1999.

————. *Pre-modern Places: Calais to Surinam, Chaucer to Aphra Behn*. Oxford: Oxford University Press, 2004.

————. 'Afterword' in *Reading the Medieval in Early Modern England*, eds Gordon McMullan and David Matthews. Cambridge: Cambridge University Press, 2007, pp. 220–27.

Waller, P., ed. *The English Urban Landscape*. Oxford: Oxford University Press, 2000.

Warner, Lawrence. 'An Overlooked *Piers Plowman* Excerpt and the Oral Circulation of Non-Reformist Prophecy, *c.* 1520–55', *YLS*, 21 (2007), 119–42.

Watson, Nicholas. '*Piers Plowman*, Pastoral Theology, and Spiritual Perfectionism: Hawkyn's Cloak and Patience's Pater Noster', *YLS*, 21 (2007), 83–118.

Wawn, Andrew N. 'The Genesis of the *Plowman's Tale*', *Yearbook of English Studies*, 2 (1972), 21–40.

————. 'Chaucer, The *Plowman's Tale* and Reformation Propaganda: The Testimonies of Thomas Godfray and *I Playne Piers*', *Bulletin of the John Ryland's Library*, 56 (1973), 174–92.

White, Helen. C. *Social Criticism in Popular Religious Literature of the Sixteenth Century*. New York: Macmillan, 1944.

White, Paul W. *Theatre and Reformation: Protestantism, Patronage and Playing in Tudor England*. Cambridge: Cambridge University Press, 1993.

Wiggins, Martin. *Shakespeare and the Drama of his Time*. Oxford: Oxford University Press, 2000.

Wilcockson, C. '*Mum and the Sothsegger*, *Richard II*, and *Henry V*', *Review of English Studies*, 46 (1995), 219–24.

Williams, Raymond. *The Country and the City*. London: Chatto & Windus, 1973.

————. *Keywords: A Vocabulary of Culture and Society*. London: Fontana, 1976.

————. *Marxism and Literature*. Oxford: Oxford University Press, 1977.

Wood, Andy. *The 1549 Rebellions and the Making of Early Modern England*. Cambridge: Cambridge University Press, 2007.

Woolf, K. B. *The Poverty of Riches: St. Francis of Assisi Reconsidered*. Oxford: Oxford University Press, 2003.

Woolf, R. 'The Tearing of the Pardon' in *Piers Plowman: Critical Approaches*, ed. S. S. Hussey. London: Methuen, 1969, pp. 50–75.

Woolfson, J., ed. *Reassessing Tudor Humanism*. Basingstoke: Palgrave, 2002.

Worden, Blair. *The Sound of Virtue: Philip Sidney's Arcadia and Elizabethan Politics*. New Haven: Yale University Press, 1996.

Wrightson, Keith. *Earthly Necessities: Economic Lives in Early Modern England*. New Haven: Yale University Press, 2000.

Yeager, R. F., ed. *Fifteenth-Century Studies: Recent Essays*. Hamden: Archon Books, 1984.

Yunck, J. A. *The Lineage of Lady Meed: The Development of Mediaeval Veniality Satire*. Notre Dame, IN: University of Notre Dame Press, 1963.

Index